THE SKILFUL MIND

THE SKILFUL MIND

An Introduction to Cognitive Psychology

EDITED BY

Angus Gellatly

Open University Press
Milton Keynes · Philadelphia

Open University Press
Celtic Court
22 Ballmoor
Buckingham
MK18 1XW

and
1900 Frost Road, Suite 101
Bristol PA 19007, USA

First published 1986
Reprinted 1991

British Library Cataloguing in Publication Data
The skilful mind: an introduction to
    cognitive psychology.
    1. Cognition
    I. Gellatly, Angus
    155.4'13   BF311

    ISBN 0–335–15336–4
    ISBN 0–335–15335–6 Pbk

Library of Congress Cataloging in Publication Data
Main entry under title:
The skilful mind.
    Bibliography:p.
    Includes index.
    1. Cognition.   I. Gellatly, Angus.
    BF311.S5687   1986   153   86–8622
    ISBN 0–335–15336–4
    ISBN 0–335–15335–6 (pbk.)

Text design by Carlton Hill
Typeset by Marlborough Design, Oxford
Printed in Great Britain by St Edmundsbury Press Ltd,
Bury St Edmunds, Suffolk

For MJB and TAMG

CONTENTS

Section IV   Thought and Skill

PREFACE

'Man is the measure of all things', the Greek thinker Protagoras is reported to have said and, leaving aside the sexual politics of the terminology (see also below), his words ought to provide psychologists with food for thought. What Protagoras seems to have meant is that all understanding is ultimately in human terms, and this could scarcely be more so than in the case of psychology. Of course, it is true that we learn a great deal about human psychology from making cross-species comparisons, or by studying the properties of individual nerve cells or assemblies of cells, or by pursuing analogies between people and machines. All such enterprises contribute to the sum of our understanding of the ways in which human beings function. However, in the final analysis human abilities and achievements have to be comprehended in human terms alone. In this introduction to cognitive psychology there will be occasion to refer to animal studies, to findings from the neurosciences, and to the relevance of computers for an understanding of the mind, but these occasions will be relatively few. Our interest will be centred very much on humans and their abilities.

What is offered in this book is an analysis of human skills, their natures, the ways in which they are acquired, and the techniques by which they can be improved. For the most part the focus will be on common cognitive skills such as talking, remembering and reasoning; skills which, because they are taken for granted, may appear superficially unremarkable. It is important not to be misled in this regard. For example, literacy and marathon running afford dramatic examples of skills that were once thought to exceed the capabilities of all but a few individuals yet which are now mastered by many. The frequency with which a skill is displayed within a population is determined by factors other than the intrinsic difficulty of that skill, just as the limits on skilled performance are constantly being extended through the exercise of human ingenuity. Common skills can be quite as remarkable as uncommon ones and in the following chapters you will be invited to admire the complex performances of which you and other people are capable. Psychological research illuminates the details of these performances, and its findings can add to the legitimate pride in our achievements which all of us are entitled to enjoy.

The book comprises sixteen chapters specially written by members of the Psychology Department at the University of Keele. Each chapter can stand alone as an introduction to a particular topic and therefore the various chapters could, in theory at least, be read in any order. There are, however, various themes which are developed and elaborated upon throughout the book. These themes link the different chapters together and provide an overall unity and coherence. As a consequence of this organization it is best that at least the first three chapters are read in order before any other parts of the book are tackled.

Chapter 1 provides an introduction to the concepts of cognition and cognitive skills, to the methods by which they can be studied, and to the nature of the knowledge which constitutes cognitive psychology. Two major themes of the book are given especial prominence in this opening chapter. First, that cognition is a matter of skill and that cognitive skills are analogous in many respects to bodily skills. Second, that the cognitive psychologist has twin roles to play: that of *scientist* and that of *coach*.

In Chapters 2 and 3 ideas about skills in general, and about cognitive skills in particular, are taken up in greater detail. Characteristics of skill are identified and the manner in which skills are acquired is described. Notions about how we organize our behaviour in the pursuit of everyday goals are also introduced. Then, in Chapter 4, all these aspects of skill are examined and illustrated with respect to the case of reading. A variety of reading skills are identified, with differences in these being shown to distinguish 'good' from 'poor' readers; some suggestions for the improvement of reading are also made.

Chapters 5 to 8 are all concerned with memory. In each of these emphasis is given to another theme of the book, which is that skills have to be understood in their social context. First, the reader is given an introduction to the topic of memory and to the language and methods with which psychologists attempt to analyze it. Chapter 6 then describes how children, starting from the passive memory abilities that humans share with other animals, manage to develop the purposeful memorizing techniques that are practised in their own culture. In Chapter 7, exceptional expertise at a particular memory task is analyzed in some detail, and also memory expertise in general. Chapter 8 is then devoted to the issue of how what is known about memory can be used to improve the memory performances of normal people, the educable retarded, people with head injuries, and others.

Communication and comprehension provide a common topic linking Chapters 9, 10, 11, and 12. Chapter 9 describes the many levels of skill which the individual must master in order to be able to speak coherently and understandably. Speaking proves to be particularly well suited to an analysis in terms of skill. So, too, is listening, the subject of Chapter 10. The listener is shown to be an active not a passive recipient of information, and one who exercises skills complementary to those of the speaker.

Closely related to language skills of both kinds are social skills, which form the topic for Chapter 11. The unconscious signals that social actors are constantly transmitting and receiving are identified, and recently devised methods for improving social skills are described and evaluated. The enhancement of existing skills is also a major theme of Chapter 12. In this case it is study skills that are at issue. Research into the nature of the skills of studying and learning are described, followed again by an evaluation of methods for their improvement.

Chapters 13 to 16 all focus on thinking and problem solving skills of one sort or another. The first of these chapters examines some kinds of reasoning that people tend to find difficult, some that they usually do automatically, and the relationship between the two. Once again, the social embeddedness of cognitive skills is made apparent, what 'comes naturally' to a member of one culture being quite alien to someone from a different culture. In Chapter 14 the concern is with general problem solving, the features that are important to it, and the unconscious habits that can so easily thwart it. Once again the question is raised of whether cognitive skills of this kind can be successfully coached. The same issue comes up also in Chapter 15 in connection with creativity and problem solving. This chapter draws upon historical records as well as laboratory studies. Various aspects of creative thinking are examined with an eye to suggestions for their improvement. Finally, Chapter 16 concentrates on the analogy between computers and minds, and on the question of whether or not machines can, or ever could, be said to think. Although ideas drawn from computing inform much of the discussion and theorizing in earlier chapters, Chapter 16 provides the occasion to consider the analogy with mind at length. Yet even here an emphasis on the human dimension in cognition is upheld.

These, then, are the major themes of the book: that cognition is best understood in terms of skill; that skills have to be seen in their social context; that deliberate improvements in skill can be brought about through coaching; that it is the business of the cognitive psychologist both to investigate the nature of skills and to apply the knowledge gained to help those who wish to enhance their cognitive skills.

The politics of pronouns

English usage has bequeathed to us an awkward problem with respect to the use of pronouns referring to an individual whose gender is unspecified, and often immaterial to the matter in hand. In this book it has been left to the author of each chapter to adopt their own policy with regard to the use of 'he', 'she, or 'they'. The resultant non-uniformity may help to keep readers on their metaphorical toes.

Acknowledgements

I am extremely grateful to the many people who have assisted in the production of this book. In particular I would like to thank Mr E.M. Bestwick for information on chick-sexing, Jonathan Dancy for comments on Chapter 13, John Coleman who drew and produced the figures, Margaret Woodward and Dorothy Masters for hour upon hour of patient and painstaking typing, and, finally, all the contributors for their hard work, their long-suffering acceptance of ever more revisions, and their constant support.

SECTION I

THE NATURE OF SKILLS

CHAPTER 1

COGNITION AND PSYCHOLOGY

Angus Gellatly

Although in this book we are going to concentrate on cognitive and other skills familiar to all of us, it will be helpful to an initial understanding of the nature of skill in general to begin with two rather exotic examples. The first is of a relatively simple skill, but one which is confined to a very few members of the population. The second is of an extremely complex skill that has been developed in a culture different from our own, and which is again restricted to a relatively small number of practitioners.

Two Examples of Skill

Chick Sexing

Poultry farming is a competitive business and, for various reasons, it is economically advantageous that the sexual identities of the chicks are determined as soon after hatching as possible. Because young males and females are visually very similar, even in the appearance of their genitalia, it used to be believed in the West that chick sexing was possible only after the males began to 'make comb'. During the first quarter of the century, however, rumours reached western poultry breeders of the existence in Japan of skilled chick sexors who were able to discriminate males from females on the first day after hatching. These rumours were followed up in the 1930s. Expert Japanese sexors were invited to exhibit their skills in both North America and Europe, and subsequently to give instruction to their hosts. They demonstrated that by holding the chicks appropriately so as to better reveal the genital area, it was possible to learn to discriminate males from females. What was more, expert sexors were able to sort the chicks at high speed and with great accuracy.

As a consequence of this meeting of East and West, chick sexing schools were established in North America and Britain. Typically, students trained for from four to six weeks before obtaining a qualification entitling them to employment as professional chick sexors. At this stage, the new professional might be capable of sexing around 200 chicks in 25 minutes, with an accuracy of 95 per cent or better (Lunn, 1948). After years of additional experience, this could rise to 1000 or 1100 chicks an hour, or even to the 1400 per hour with 98 per cent accuracy reported of one expert. Chick sexing is a highly repetitive and attentionally demanding task but one that allows for the development of astonishingly high levels of skill.

In the first years following the establishment of training schools, in the late 1930s, graduating sexors were able to look forward to extensive employment at good rates of pay, with the additional prospect of even better earnings as they became increasingly adept at the work. In the fifties and sixties, however, the job market underwent a sharp contraction. This was largely due to the success of selective breeding techniques leading to the development of strains of chicken which exhibited sex linked colour differences. Male and female chicks were now readily distinguishable so that skilled, and expensive, sexors could be dispensed with. Recruitment into the training schools slumped as earnings and employment prospects suffered. It seemed that the history of skilled chick-sexing in the West was to be a brief one. Then, towards the end of the 1960s, there came an added twist to the story, resulting once again from the activities of the stock breeders. Further experiments with selective mating had produced chickens with lighter bones and which therefore required less feed to bring them to their full adult weight. These new strains proved popular with cost conscious mass breeders, who raise animals for consumption. But many of the new strains suffered from a particular failing. In the drive to develop animals with lighter bones, the linkage between the sex and colour of chicks had been broken. The chick sexors were back in business.

Some Features of Skill

Now it may seem strange to begin a book on the psychology of cognition with a thumbnail history of an obscure area of poultry farming. But, in fact, chick sexing is an excellent example of a relatively simple human skill. It exhibits many of the features common to all skills. One of these is the seeming impossibility, to the eyes of the uninitiated, of the task that has to be performed. In the circus the achievements of jugglers, acrobats, and trapezists appear astonishing, yet everyday life abounds with amazing feats of skill. Some of these, such as walking and talking, are so widespread as to attract little attention, while others, though confined to a relatively few practitioners, are exercised only out of the public eye, as in panel beating or precision lathe work. Still other skills, and this is true particularly of cognitive and perceptual skills as opposed to physical (motor) skills, pass unremarked because their performance has no public aspect. Thinking is the prime example of this, especially thinking that leads to neither speech nor action, as when one silently rehearses an argument or, indeed, a piece of music.

Another feature that chick sexing shares with other skills is its dependence on intensive practice. To learn how the task can be done requires practical experience. Even when considerable mastery has been achieved it may take years of further practice before the topmost levels of expertise are approached, especially in terms of speed of performance (Chapter 2).

Finally, for present purposes, the history of chick sexing illustrates a third, absolutely fundamental feature of human skill, and that is its dependence on social context. We have already noted that certain skills, such as walking and talking, are so widely represented as to be almost characteristic of human life itself. Yet in their specifics even these skills are socially determined. A language can become a dead tongue if the social requirement for people to speak it ceases; a style of marching can be deeply emblematic of a particular society or regime. In cases of less universal cognitive skills, their social embeddedness is even more apparent. Perceptual and cognitive demands vary dramatically between habitats. Tracking animals in the wild and negotiating the traffic system of a city are both skills shaped by their respective physical and social environments. In the case of chick sexing, the skill reached the West at all only as a result of the rapid growth of trading and cultural links with Japan in the early part of this century. The dissemination of the skill in Britain and North America was then dependent on the existence of an intensive poultry industry that had grown up to supply the needs of an increasingly urban society well served by transport and communication networks. Lastly, the changing fortunes of the chick sexors have been determined by the activities of another group within the same industry, the stock breeders. Human skills are elaborated in response to social conditions and they can fall into disuse and rapidly be lost when those conditions alter.

Chick sexing is a relatively simple skill of perceptual classification; it calls for what are in many ways less complex discriminations than those required of a tea-blender or a wine-taster. Our second example is of a very much more complex skill that can be described here only in brief outline.

The Skill of Navigation

The islanders of Puluwat are renowned for their ability to navigate without instruments. Their home lies in the Pacific about a thousand miles north north east of New Guinea, and seafaring plays the central role in Puluwat culture. Gladwin (1970) describes the importance placed upon the building and maintenance of outrigger canoes, the vital social functions of inter-island voyages, and the special respect accorded to the navigator-captains who have achieved expertise in their art. Everyone on Puluwat participates in voyages but only a few are able to navigate their way across two or three hundred miles of open sea; and do so in almost any weather, and even when less than fully sober. How is it done?

There are three preliminary facts to be noted from Gladwin's description of Puluwat navigation skills. First, it takes a very long time to become a proficient navigator, as much as two or three decades. Second, the skill is localized to the chain of islands to which Puluwat belongs, an area perhaps four hundred miles north to south and a thousand miles east to west. Third, the system of navigation is highly conservative. Gladwin (1970) emphasizes that the Puluwat do not take risks, navigators make use of many mutually reinforcing kinds of knowledge to ensure the accuracy of their dead-reckoning.

Knowledge is, in fact, the characteristic feature of Puluwat navigation. It is a deeply knowledge based skill. Navigators are, first of all, thoroughly versed as to the disposition of stars in the heavens, the positions at which they rise and the trajectories they follow. Being close to the equator the night sky over Puluwat changes little with the seasons, and the stars, when visible, offer reliable guides. Navigators, however, can also set courses during the day. Departing an island for any other island, they know which landmarks when lined up will give the course they require, a technique known as back-sighting. Even in the dark and with cloud cover, navigators can still guage direction by distinguishing between three kinds of wave, originating from the east, north, and south, respectively. A navigator steers by the feel of these waves under the canoe and by the characteristic intervals between them.

During their apprenticeships, navigators also learn the positions and outlines of all the major reefs in their area of ocean, some of them more than a hundred feet down. They learn to identify the effects a reef has on the water and thereby also on the motion of a canoe. Where a stranger would see only a featureless expanse of ocean, the Puluwat navigators see clear signposts marking the seaways. They are also familiar with the behaviour of seabirds, knowing which ones fly direct to land at the end of the day and using these to home in on sometimes very tiny destinations. Finally, the navigators also have mastery of a complex theory of navigation that allows them to calculate distance travelled when tacking against the wind. The theory makes use of reference islands, which will often be over the horizon, and it represents the canoe as stationary while ocean and islands move past it. The theory is the most purely cognitive, as opposed to perceptual, aspect of Puluwat seamanship.

What is Cognition?

The term 'cognitive' skill has been used several times in the preceding pages without explanation. But what is cognition?

An idea of the answer to this question can be gained by reflecting for a moment on some everyday words. We talk about *recognition* when someone or something is identified as previously known. Or, borrowing from the Italian, we describe a person as 'travelling *incognito*' when that person takes pains to hide his or her identity. As these examples help to illustrate, cognition refers to the activities of knowing, of gathering, organizing, and making use of knowledge. When an encounter with someone gives us a feeling of familiarity, we say that this is an act of re-cognition, or re-knowing; we cognize the individual afresh. But cognition includes many kinds of activity besides recognition of identity. Remembering that you have a dental appointment in the morning, calculating the discount on an article you are buying, finding the way home from work without getting lost, these are all matters of cognition. So too would be playing a game of chess, trying to diagnose why your car will not start, understanding what someone else is saying to you, or comprehending what else that person means in addition to what he or she puts into words. In fact, anything that involves either perception, memory, learning or thinking is a part of cognition, which means that just about everything anyone ever does has at least a cognitive component.

However, you should not be overly dismayed to learn that 'cognition' is such a broad term. First, you can safely assume that the coverage of topics in this text will be selective. Secondly, although the field of cognition is a broad one, there is a relatively small number of principles underlying it. Indeed, a central theme of this book is that cognition in all its manifestations is a matter of skill, and that therefore all cognitive accomplishments can be analysed in terms of certain principles involved in the acquisition of skill (see Chapters 2 and 3). Thirdly, since cognition enters into more or less everything we do, there are plenty of opportunities for putting those principles to good use, for improving our own cognitive abilities. For instance, people often remark that although they have a good memory for faces they have difficulty in remembering names to go with them. Yet, as we shall see, there are steps that can be taken to improve this cognitive skill (Chapter 5).

Studying Cognition

The Historical Background

How can we study cognition? An obvious answer might be that we can study cognition either directly by observing our own minds at work, that is by introspecting, or indirectly by asking other people about their observations of their minds at work, that is by collecting reports of their introspections. Certainly introspection is an important and frequently used method of studying the mind. A great deal of our commonsense knowledge about perception, thinking, and memory is based upon the introspective reports of reflective people from the ancient Greeks down to our own time. Moreover, when towards the end of the nineteenth century psychology was set up as an independent science of the mind, separate from philosophy or any other branch of enquiry, introspection was adopted as its natural method. However, it was not supposed that just anyone could become a psychologist by introspecting on their own cognitions. On the contrary, observations of conscious experience had to be made by individuals highly trained in specially developed introspective techniques, and they had to address significant theoretical issues. Understanding the operation of the mind was to be a serious business.

In fairness to these early psychologists, their ideas about technique and training were motivated not so much by the desire to mark out a territory and hedge it around with restrictive practices as by their belief that introspective observations could be worthwhile only within the framework of a specially constructed methodology. This belief was echoed some years later in the carefully worked out observational techniques of ethology, the discipline that studies animal (including human) behaviour in natural settings. By unravelling the secret of the honey bee's dance and by making sense of the behaviour of fish, geese, and many other species, ethologists demonstrated how much can be known through observation that an untutored observer may miss. But whereas the achievements of the ethologists were to be recognized in 1973 by the award of a Nobel prize, the introspectionist psychologists made little headway with their systematic observations of consciousness. (But see Chapter 9 for recent and brilliant analyses of the skills of speaking, these being largely based on observations of naturally occurring speech errors.)

Weaknesses and Strengths of Introspection

There are a number of reasons why introspection on its own is inadequate as a method for revealing the nature of cognition. Probably the most serious flaw is that introspecting upon your own consciousness is itself liable to alter the content of that consciousness. Rather than being aware of current cognitive activity, one becomes aware of the fact that one is introspecting! The problem becomes particularly acute when non-verbal cognitions have to be translated into words for an introspective report, for it may not be possible to capture their essential nature in verbal terms.

A second and related problem has been noted by Neisser (1976). He remarked that a psychology of any significance has to have something to say about what people actually do and think in real, culturally significant situations. However, those are likely to be just the situations in which people are too busy to introspect carefully. As a result, introspection can be applied in the main only to artificial tasks in laboratory settings. It was this sterility – the lack of what is often called 'ecological validity' – on which Neisser principally blamed the downfall of the introspective method. But additional flaws are not hard to spot. For example, it is a common observation, at least since Freud laid such emphasis upon the fact, that behaviour is frequently determined by unconscious motives. Sometimes a shrewd observer may have a better idea of the reasons for a person's actions than does that person herself. Although cognitive psychology is not much concerned with motives, it does have an important place for unconscious cognitions. The unconscious in this sense does not have the connotation of purposeful repression associated with Freud's notion of the unconscious. Rather it refers to the simple fact that we are unaware of many of the processes that support our bodily and mental functions. Regulation of the blood supply is one example of this and the processes involved in recognizing and understanding the words on this page would be another. As in the case of unconscious motives, the message is clear. What goes on outside consciousness cannot be revealed by introspection – no matter how carefully conducted.

Clearly, then, as a method introspection has many shortcomings. But having voiced a number of criticisms of it, we should also acknowledge that it possesses certain strengths. For it is inescapably true that introspective accounts of cognitive activity can be extremely useful and informative in appropriate circumstances. Some individuals are able to communicate their own techniques for tackling particular cognitive problems. The rest of us benefit from learning how they reason about ignition failures or the appropriate way to approach a mathematical problem, the steps they take to facilitate social interactions or enhance memory for important information, and the details they attend to when assessing the strength of a legal case or making a diagnosis on the basis of radiographs. We have learnt too much about the workings of the mind through introspection to want to dispense with it altogether. Although there is a continuing debate as to the exact status of various types of introspective report (Evans, 1982), cognitive psychologists continue to rely upon them. It should also be noted that 'expert knowledge systems', which represent one of the major achievements of artificial intelligence research, are all based upon the introspections of human specialists. The lesson to be drawn from the failure of early introspectionist psychology is not that the method is valueless but that it has to be seen as only one amongst many methods of investigating cognition.

The Contemporary Study of Cognition

Between the two world wars, *behaviourism* came to dominate psychology in the United States and, to a lesser extent, in Britain. Not only introspectionism but the whole study of cognition waned. The behaviourists rightly stressed the importance of objective data and carefully specified experimental methods. This led them to favour explanations in terms of observable stimuli and responses, and to deny any need to refer to intervening cognitive states. John Watson, the founding father of behaviourist psychology, proposed that thinking was nothing but sub-vocal speech, a case of talking to oneself. Sufficiently delicate measurement of the activity in the speech musculature was expected to confirm this fact, but behaviourism allowed few other means of investigating thinking and was especially silent on non-verbal thinking.

In continental Europe, however, a somewhat different picture was emerging. Introspectionism had been succeeded not by behaviourism but by Gestalt psychology, which was very much concerned with internal cognitive processes and with phenomena such as 'insight' (see Chapter 14). Additionally, it was in France and then in Switzerland that Jean Piaget initiated his profoundly influential studies of children's cognitive development. A basic theme of Piaget's theroy was to be that thinking develops as a result of *internalization*. Previously overt behaviour, both actions and speech, could become totally internalized, leaving no external manifestations. So at the very time that behaviourists were seeking to create a methodologically sound psychology of observable behaviour, Piaget was simultaneously emphasizing the continuity between behaviour and cognition.

Modern cognitive psychology combines the methodological rigour of the behaviourists with the Piagetian emphasis on internal processes that underpin overt behaviour. It also includes a third important strand.

The Computer Metaphor for Mind

Despite Piaget, the interest of mainstream psychologists in cognitive processes did not revive until the 1950s, when there was an explosive growth of research that has continued ever since. Undoubtedly the most important cause of this change was the rapid evolution and diffusion of the digital computer. A machine that performs complex operations without benefit of moving parts is immediately suggestive of the internal processes of mind. Unobservable operations are performed on the input to the machine, they can be precisely specified and they have demonstrable effects on the behaviour of the machine's output devices. To understand what the computer is up to you cannot rely solely on a knowledge of what goes in and what comes out. It is necessary to know what the programme is making the machine do, what transformations and manipulations of the coded input are being carried out, what goals the programme is intended to achieve (Chapter 16). But if such understanding is possible in the case of a computer, why not also for the human mind? Given the computer as a model, suddenly the cognitive processes of perception, thinking, and memory seemed more real, less ethereal. Just as moving-part machines have often yielded fertile metaphors for bodily functions (e.g. the heart as a pump), the new type of machine suggests a metaphor for mind.

During the last twenty-five years, cognitive psychologists have extensively explored the computer metaphor for mind and contemporary books on cognition are commonly written in the language of information processing. This frequently makes for difficult reading. It can also yield the impression that cognitive psychologists are concerned with the nature of computer programmes rather than with the nature of human cognition. Only those aspects of cognition that can be discussed plausibly in programming terminology receive attention; the points of disanalogy between computers and minds thereby being effaced from the reader's (and the author's) consciousness. For this reason a purposeful attempt is made in the present book to avoid the metaphor and its associated jargon. This in not easily done because the computer metaphor already pervades much of our thinking, especially in cognitive psychology. From time to time we will make use of the metaphor but it will only be taken up and examined explicitly in the final chapter.

Cognition and Behaviour

If we are not going to avail ourselves of the language and analogies of computing how, it may be asked, are we going to talk about cognition? How can unobservable mental processes be described? The answer has already been hinted at above in the reference to Piaget's emphasis on the continuity between behaviour and thought. Many cognitions can be considered as internal actions. They are actions which have become so practiced that we can 'carry them out in our heads' (e.g. counting on your fingers giving way to mental arithmetic); or, if they build upon previous knowledge and expertise, we may have learnt to do them in our heads in the first place. Action metaphors for thought, and more particularly manipulative metaphors, which refer to use of the hands, are common in ordinary langauge. When we talk of 'getting hold of an idea' or accuse someone else of 'stretching a point', the notion of internalized actions is implicitly brought into play. However, not all cognitions are akin to actions. Everyday langauge has a second major group of metaphors to describe cognitions; these are based on perception, especially visual perception. Jokes of the 'I see, said the blind man' variety trade on these metaphors, as do such expressions as 'that's a bright idea' or 'I saw it in a flash'. The prevalence of the two types of metaphor is not coincidental. In dealing with the world, an organism has to perceive what is happening nearby and take appropriate action, perhaps feeding, mating, or running away. In simple creatures, both perceptions and responses tend to be inbuilt, the former automatically activating the latter. However, for animals with more complex nervous systems an element of choice creeps in because in most circumstances more than one action may be possible. The nervous activity intervening between perception and response becomes elaborated, it evolves into what is called cognition. Through the medium of the two kinds of metaphor, ordinary language very sensibly recognizes that cognition shares features of both perception and action. Visual and manipulative metaphors predominate because for humans the eyes are the major channel for perceptual information and the hands offer the most flexible and delicate means of acting on the world.

Cognition and Skill

To follow up Piaget's insight concerning the relationship between cognition and behaviour is not in itself, therefore, to break new ground. Ordinary language has long recognized the relationship. Yet there is a further and important feature of it that needs to be stressed here. The psychologist Bartlett (1958) pointed out that thinking – or more generally cognition – is in many respects similar to *skilled* behaviour. Perceptual-motor skills such as playing tennis involve perceiving and interpreting some part of the world (e.g. the trajectory, speed, spin of the tennis ball) and performing some sort of motor action (e.g. striking the ball to an advantageous point in the opponent's court). Both perceiving and responding call for a high degree of skilfulness. In a similar way, many cognitive activities which we take for granted are skilful performances. Although our cognitions may on occasion be rather wild and uncoordinated they are for the most part impressively controlled, and as adults we are nearly all accomplished at perceiving, remembering, thinking, and understanding each other. It is these cognitive accomplishments that will be the focus of this book.

In fact, no firm boundary can be drawn between perceptual-motor and cognitive skills. Almost all motor behaviours are under cognitive control and many cognitions are for purposes of acting on the world. This interpenetration was well represented in a classic report on the acquisition of morse telegraphy by Bryan and Harter (1899), the first thorough analysis of skilled performance. Telegraphy involves acquisition both of new perceptual-cognitive skills for indentifying and interpreting patterns of dots and dashes and of new cognitive-motor skills for manipulating the sending key. Together with Bartlett, their successor, Bryan and Harter laid the foundations for a psychology of cognitive skill.

Psychological Knowledge

Theory and Practice

The sixteenth-century thinker Francis Bacon drew up a plan for a new method of obtaining knowledge in what were to become the natural sciences. Bacon was concerned with both theoretical and practical knowledge. As part of his method, he advocated that sound theoretical understanding of a subject must first be established and that practical applications could then be derived from it. In other words, science would lead to technology, or, in Bacon's terminology, after the 'light' would come the 'fruit'. Although the relationship of theory to practice is rarely quite as simple as Bacon implied, the undoubted success of science-based technologies in the last three hundred years has markedly affected our ideas about knowledge. It is hardly going too far to say that nowadays the validity of theoretical knowledge is assessed on the basis of what technologies it spawns. Theories without instrumental applications are scarcely considered to constitute knowledge at all.

One consequence of this development is that cognitive psychologists, like investigators in other disciplines, are under considerable pressure to demonstrate the practical implications of their work. The general public, students, and those who dispense research funds tend to be unimpressed by theoretical niceties. They want to know what is the use of cognitive psychology. Nor is the pressure all external. Psychologists themselves constantly exhort one another to make their discipline more socially significant and utilitarian. In the remainder of this chapter two possible ways of responding to this pressure for practical results will be examined.

The Cognitive Psychologist as Scientist

The two ways in which psychologists can respond to pressure involve the adoption of alternative roles. These roles need not be mutually exclusive. Psychologists can play one and then the other in sequence, or if they are clever both at the same time. The two roles are those of *scientist* and *coach*.

One response psychologists sometimes give to the demand for practical results from cognitive psychology is to represent themselves as still in the first of Bacon's two phases – that is, still establishing a theoretical understanding, still in need of just a little more time for pure research. The psychologist as scientist is presented as a specialist whose knowledge will shortly put him in a position of privileged expertise with regard to cognition. This, however, is not a realistic picture. Although cognition has to be studied scientifically, and even allowing for possible advances in artificial intelligence, there is no indication that scientific enquiry is about to – or ever will – lead to shattering innovations in the uses of our minds (see e.g. Joynson, 1974). The subject matter of psychology simply does not lend itself to a Baconian model of theory followed by practice. Unlike nuclear physics, for instance, where applications were impossible until precise theories had been established, psychology deals with a subject matter where practice long preceded explicit theories. Experts, whether nuclear physicists or television repairers, build and fix things that the rest of us do not expect to understand. Psychologists, by contrast, do not stand in an expert relationship to other people. Individuals consulting a psychologist already know a great deal about their own minds. The position is very different from if they wanted a television repaired. It is true that people do sometimes look to psychiatrists and psychologists to 'fix' their minds for them, but this is an unfortunate attitude for them to adopt. Drug treatments can sometimes serve to control psychotic thinking or mood disturbances, but they are not *cures*. Mental health specialists can do no more than assist people to sort out their minds and their behaviour for themselves.

This is not to claim that such assistance is unimportant. In many cases it may be vital. What we do mean is that the value of studying cognition scientifically is not to be found in new technologies. Rather, its value lies in the knowledge that is made available to the psychologist acting in a capacity other than that of scientific expert.

The Cognitive Psychologist as Coach

When it comes to applying knowledge, the role of coach or teacher offers an alternative to the role of technological expert. Neither athletics coaches nor piano teachers, for example, have formal theories from which to deduce their practice, but their ability to contribute to improvements in performance is scarcely in question. It is the contention of this book that cognitive psychologists have a similar ability to help others to improve their cognitive performances. Not in the fashion of the expert, but in the manner of the coach.

The role of athletics coach provides, in fact, a useful analogy that demonstrates how scientific knowledge can have a practical value that is not in any obvious sense technological. Athletics coaches turn increasingly to sports medicine for information, they take from physiology, anatomy and biochemistry, applying this scientific knowledge to the problems of raising levels of performance. These sciences do not enable us to make novel *uses* of our bodies but they do contribute to improvements in the efficiency with which the old uses – running, swimming, jumping, throwing – can be executed. In like manner, the scientific study of cognition is never going to reveal unsuspected cognitive abilities, but it does provide us with information that can serve to enhance the skill with which our long familiar capabilities are exercised.

There are several advantages to cognitive psychologists of presenting themselves as coaches. First and foremost, adopting the role of coach will bring them into line with many of their colleagues in counselling and clinical psychology where 'partnership' with a 'client' is frequently stressed. The psychologist can deal directly with people in a non-authoritarian but constructive manner, essentially providing a form of feedback on how the client is performing on the task of interest. A second advantage is that the role of coach makes it clear where the onus lies when it comes to achieving cognitive improvements. As in tennis, a coach can only assist those who are prepared to make an effort for themselves. Skill cannot be injected from outside. The third advantage of playing the role of coach is precisely that it saves cognitive psychologists from the label of expert. No longer do they need to fear those familiar taunts such as: 'So you study thinking/memory. Why isn't your thinking/memory a lot better than everyone else's?' After all, no one expects that the best tennis coaches need have been champions, nor that champions are bound to make good coaches.

The twin roles of the cognitive psychologist will be demonstrated in the remainder of this book. Where research is reported we will see the psychologist at work as a scientist, proposing and testing hypotheses, conducting experiments, analysing data and making observations of case studies. When it comes to formulating advice on how to improve cognitive performances, however, we will see the psychologist at work as a coach: advising, guiding, directing, making use of maxims, rules of thumb, and a few rather general principles of human skill.

Summary

This chapter has sketched out a number of topics and themes that will be elaborated throughout the rest of the book. The notion of cognitive skill was introduced by way of two examples, chick sexing and navigation without instruments. It was pointed out that cognitive skills may seem almost miraculous to the uninitiated, that their acquisition requires intensive practice, and that they are deeply embedded in their social context. Some account was given of the way in which psychologists have and do study cognition, and cognition was compared to both perception and motor behaviour. A preference was stated for analyzing cognitions in terms of a model of perceptual-motor skills, rather than in terms of the computer metaphor for mind, although the influence and value of the metaphor was recognized.

Finally, the nature of psychological knowledge was briefly considered. It was argued that cognitive psychologists have two roles to play: the role of scientist when thay are engaged in basic research; the role of coach when they are applying their knowledge to human problems.

FURTHER READING

NEISSER, U. (1976) *Cognition and Reality*. San Francisco: Freeman.
Provides a vivid introduction to the subject matter of cognitive psychology as viewed within a skills perspective, but with a heavy emphasis on perceptual skills.

CHAPTER 2

WHAT IS SKILL?

John Sloboda

There are two rooms in my house that have recently been repainted, one by a professional decorator, the other by me. The decorator was skilled at his job. I was not. By what marks might one detect the difference? Well, the end product certainly tells something. If you look closely at the walls that I painted you will find unevenness of texture; too much paint here, barely enough to cover there. You will find faint vertical streaks where the paint has run, and you will find small overshoots and undershoots at the edges. The walls painted by the professional are even in texture, and the edges are beautifully straight.

Notwithstanding these differences, I actually managed to cover my tracks quite well. Unless you gave my walls a very close examination you would not find any obvious faults. The most dramatic differences between myself and the professional would have been apparent had you actually stood and watched us at work.

To begin with, the professional finished the job in about half the time it took me. Not only were his individual strokes faster, but he stopped less often, I was stopping very regularly, not through laziness, but because I continually needed to assess what I had done, and decide what needed doing next. Other delays occurred too. For instance, I ran out of paint with only three quarters of the job done, and had to go to the shop for more.

Secondly, the professional made his job appear easy. The paint just seemed to flow onto the wall in a relaxed and coordinated sequence of movements. My own movement sequence was jerky and effortful. For instance, one brushful would have too much paint on it, the next too little; once I would start with an upstroke, next with a down; I would constantly be attending to minor 'bugs', such as spillages and drips.

Finally, the professional's sequencing was impeccable. He arranged things so that he was not constantly having to move apparatus around. He always ended up in the right place at the right time (e.g. returning to put on the second coat just at the time when the first coat was dry enough), and was completely systematic in the way each wall was tackled. I worked haphazardly, treating each wall in a different way, leaving odd patches unpainted when, for example, a ladder was not conveniently placed. I was constantly having to stop painting in order to get something I needed or to move obstacles out of the way.

The Characteristics of Skill

For a long time, psychologists have wanted to specify exactly what the characteristics of skilled activities are. My painting example informally includes many of the major characteristics, but I would like to deal with them in a more systematic way under five principal headings; Fluency, Rapidity, Automaticity, Simultaneity, and Knowledge. The first-letter mnemonic FRASK may be helpful in keeping these in mind. (See Chapter 5 for what a mnemonic is.)

Fluency

An activity is fluent if the components of it run together in an integrated and uninterrupted sequence. The term 'fluency' is usually applied to the microstructure of a task (elements occurring over a span of a few seconds) rather than to its long-term structure. Thus we speak of a fluent translator as one who can provide an appropriate translation with a minimum of pauses or hesitations. A fluent typist is one who can maintain a relatively even and continuous output of key presses.

It seems likely that fluency is brought about by two things. One is the overlapping in time of a sequence of movements. That is to say, preparatory movements for action B are begun whilst action A is still being completed. The other is the building of a set of actions into a single 'chunk', which can be controlled and run off as a single unit of behaviour.

The existence of chunking in skilled typists has been elegantly demonstrated by Shaffer (1976). In this study, typists saw a computer console on which was displayed a single line of text. The console was linked to a keyboard in such a way that every time a key was pressed the text moved one space to the left. This meant that the leftmost character (or space) 'fell off' the screen and a new character appeared on the right.

Shaffer was able to vary both the window size (i.e. length of line displayed) and also the amount of preview (i.e. how far from the right a letter had moved before the subject was required to type it). With no preview, a subject had to type a character as soon as it appeared on the right of the screen. With preview, the subject typed a character as it arrived at a preordained position towards the middle of the screen. Typists were given three different varieties of text to work on:
(a) normal English prose;
(b) jumbled prose in which English words were printed in random order;
(c) jumbled words, where letter order was randomized.
These three conditions are illustrated in Figure 2:1.

The vertical line indicates the position of the letter to be typed under
8–character preview

(a)   in Ayrshire. I told John about the meeting, |and also

(b)   meeting told. About, John also in the Ayrsh|ire I and

(c)   metegni ldto. Atoub, nJoh slao ni eht sirAeyha I dna
     |

Figure 2:1   Types of text used in Shaffer's typing study.

Shaffer found that typists required about eight characters of preview to obtain
their fastest speeds. Increasing preview beyond eight characters did not result in
further improvements in speed or accuracy. Fastest consistent speeds were
about 10 characters per second (100 words per minute) in conditions (a) and (b),
but were only two characters per second in condition (c). It seems that skilled
typists can deal with familiar English words much better than with strings of
nonsense letters. We can get a better insight into *why* words are typed faster
when we look at what happened when Shaffer reduced preview below eight
characters. In condition (c), reducing preview to zero had no effect whatsoever
on speed, which remained at two characters per second. However, such
reduction had a dramatic effect in the other two conditions which dropped right
down to two characters per second as well.

It seems that fluent typing depends on the typist being able to see the whole of
an average English word (six characters) before beginning to type it. Only then
can the full set of finger movements required to type the word be assembled into
a single performance unit. Such a unit can be 'rattled off' at speed. When there
is no preview, or when the letters do not make up familiar words, such chunking
is not possible, and the job must be done letter by letter.

The lack of difference between conditions (a) and (b) is also of interest. It
shows that these typists were not forming chunks bigger than individual words
(unlike speakers, see Chapter 9). If they had been then we would have expected
condition (a) to be even faster than condition (b). It looks as though in general
any given pair of adjacent words occurs too infrequently to be chunked in the
way that individual words are. It is, however, likely that word sequences such as
'Dear Sir' or 'Yours sincerely' could attain the status of chunks for some
secretaries.

There are, of course, two levels of chunking occuring in fluent typing. There
is what one might call *input* chunking – the perceptual act of grouping letters
into units such as words; and there is also *output* chunking – the assembling of
coordinated movement sequences. Perhaps the best way of appreciating the

nature of output fluency is to experience the loss of it. One effective way of disrupting fluency is to upset the sensory feedback we normally receive from motor behaviour. This interferes with the ability to dovetail separate move-ments with one another. For instance, suppose you were wearing a set of headphones and speaking into a microphone which fed into the headphones. Under these conditions it is possible to introduce a delay, so that instead of hearing your own voice as you speak you hear it a little while later. Delaying the auditory feedback from one's own voice by about 0.2 seconds usually causes severe speech disruption. It induces stuttering, repetition of sounds, and excessive pausing between words and syllables. Fluent behaviour is crucially dependent upon normal feedback arriving at the normal time. More commonly, loss of fluency is experienced when we are nervous. We trip over our feet and stumble on our words. Fluency is usually the last feature of skill to be acquired and its loss the first sign of disruption due to disease, intoxication, or fear.

Rapidity

Most skills involve the ability to make an appropriate response quickly. The skilled tennis player must not only get to the right place on the court and choose an appropriate stroke, she must do these things in an incredibly short time. It is the ability to make the right response almost immediately that is so characteristic of all skills.

One of the most widely quoted and influential studies which demonstrates the speed of skilled performance is a study of chess players carried out by Chase and Simon (1973). They took subjects at differing levels of expertise from novice up to grandmaster and showed them chessboards on which were placed some pieces copied from the middle of an actual game between experts. Subjects were allowed to view the board for five seconds. It was then removed and they were asked to reconstruct the positions of the pieces on a blank board. A novice was able, on average, to replace about four out of 20 pieces correctly. A master, in contrast, replaced about 18 out of 20 correctly.

Since the subjects viewed the board for the same period of time, these results show that a master is able to deal with the same amount of information much more rapidly than a novice. A second part of the study shed substantial light on the mechanisms involved. In this, the boards shown to subjects contained pieces placed on them at random, in a way that could not have occurred in any rational game. Faced with such boards, a novice performed exactly the same as in the first experiment, getting about four out of 20 pieces correct. The master, however, showed a dramatic drop in performance, from 18 down to four out of 20. On these random boards the master was no better than the novice.

This shows us that the master's skill does not rest simply on superior perception or memory, it is linked to the detection of familiar and game-relevant patterns in the stimulus. The master immediately 'understands' what he sees in meaningful terms so that, for instance, one group of four pieces becomes a 'castled king', another a 'knight fork' and so on. This view is confirmed by the way in which the master carries out the reconstruction task. He tends to put down linked groups of pieces together, with longer pauses between groups. The ability of the knowledgeable player to perceive meaningful patterns on the board is analogous to the ability of a knowledgeable football spectator to recognize carefully rehearsed moves amidst the frantic activity on the pitch.

Automaticity

One of the most universal characteristics of skill is the way in which it becomes 'easy' to its practitioners. We no longer experience any effort when carrying out some well-learned skill such as walking. It 'just happens' without us having to think about it. If this were not the case, our ability to act upon the world would be drastically limited. Our whole time would be spent attending to the simplest things.

The sight-reading of piano music is a complex skill. In a study of professional sight-readers, Wolf (1976) interviewed several practitioners and asked them what were the principal problems in sight-reading. One pianist answered: 'for me, personally, there are none'. This is not arrogance, but an honest answer about a highly automated skill. It is the kind of answer that most of us would have to give if asked about the problems we had in walking. Yet that is a skill of comparable complexity to piano sight-reading, and one that takes infants a long time to learn.

One of the ways of testing whether a skill is automatic is to see whether the practitioner can deal appropriately with a situation, even when not concentrating or expecting it. So, for instance, a skilled driver is able to brake rapidly at a potential hazard, even if her mind were on something else in the immediately preceding moments.

A clear experimental demonstration of this type of phenomenon was provided by LaBerge (1973). Subjects' primary task was to look at a visually displayed symbol. After a short while, this symbol would disappear, and would be replaced by another symbol. The two symbols could be either both familiar letters (e.g. a b p d) or both unfamiliar characters (e.g. ↑ ↓). A subject was asked to judge whether the two symbols were the same or different, and press one of two buttons to indicate her decision as quickly as possible after the presentation of the second symbol. The time between presentation of the second symbol and the response was measured. This time is commonly known as the *reaction time*, and it is a frequently used measure in the study of all kinds of skill. Figure 2:2 summarizes La Berge's results. On this task, he found no difference in reaction time between the familiar and the unfamiliar symbols. He argued that the first symbol cued the subject about what type of symbol to expect on the second presentation, so making it easy to decide whether the two were of the same form, regardless of their familiarity.

In some trials, however, LaBerge introduced an unexpected task. In place of the second symbol he presented a *pair* of symbols. Whenever this happened subjects were primed to ignore the earlier symbol and concentrate on the second pair. They were to judge whether the members of this pair were identical or not. In this unexpected task, LaBerge found a significant reaction-time difference between familiar pairs (e.g. bd) and unfamiliar pairs (e.g. ↑ ↓). Subjects were faster at responding to the familiar letters. LaBerge argues that this result shows that in experienced readers, skilled letter-recognition is automatic whilst recognition of the new unfamiliar symbols is not. When an unexpected task arises, only the letters can still be processed quickly. Unfamiliar symbols are associated with slower responses precisely because they cannot be recognized automatically.

	expected task		unexpected task	
	1.	2.	3.	4.
first stimulus	a	↑	a	a
second stimulus	a	↑	bb	↑↑
reaction speed	fast	fast	fast	slow

Figure 2:2   La Berge's tasks and findings.

Another characteristic of automatic skills seems to be that they are, in some sense, mandatory. That is to say, a stimulus triggers its automatic response regardless of whether we wish it to or not. When we look at a familiar printed word we usually cannot help experiencing its meaning. We find it almost impossible to experience it just as a set of letters. Similarly, we find it almost impossible not to recognize a familiar face as a person we know and to see it instead as a set of individual features.

The tendency of automatic skills to be called into play 'despite ourselves' can sometimes lead to embarrassing and amusing occurences which have been studied in the context of 'absent-mindedness' (e.g. Reason and Mycielska, 1982). The mother of a large family tells of the time when she was at a dinner party and found herself cutting into small pieces the dinner of her surprised neighbour while holding a conversation with someone else. If we laugh then we should laugh with rather than at the unfortunate mother since diary studies have shown that most people are able to record large numbers of slips of this kind in their everyday lives. The outcomes need not always be as embarrassing but the principle is the same. Slips of this nature seem to be an inevitable consequence of the automatization of skilled behaviour.

Simultaneity

I still remember with horror my first driving lesson. My instructor was trying to teach me how to change gear. This involved a complicated sequence of movements involving clutch, accelerator, and gear lever simultaneously. If this was not enough, my instructor kept shouting 'keep your eyes on the road, keep steering'. The multiple demands on my attention seemed impossible to fulfil. Now, some 20 years later, it all seems so trivially easy. Changing gear is a fluent and coordinated movement sequence which I can do without losing any of my attention on the road. I can do all these things whilst maintaining an intellectually demanding argument with my passenger on some unrelated topic.

Simultaneity is a characteristic of skill in two senses. First, the components of a skilled activity can be executed simultaneously (as in conjoint movements of hands and feet for gear changing). Secondly, because of the high degree of automaticity, it is often possible to carry out an unrelated activity at the same time as performing a skilled activity. One way that psychologists test how automatic a skill has become is to measure the effect on performance of adding a second, simultaneous task for the subject to perform.

One of the most strikingly counterintuitive demonstrations of simultaneity was provided by Allport, Antonis and Reynolds (1972), in an experiment where they examined performance on two skills, sight-reading of piano music and prose 'shadowing'. Subjects were experienced sight-readers. They were first asked to perform each task alone. For the sight-reading test, an unfamiliar piano piece was placed in front of the subject who was required to perform it on the piano without rehearsal. In the shadowing test the subject heard a prose passage through headphones and was required to speak it out as it was being heard. The two tasks were then combined. A subject was asked to continue as best she could with both tasks together.

After a very small amount of practice, subjects were able to perform the two tasks together. They did not break down in either of them. Even more surprising was the fact that the two tasks did not seriously affect one another. Each task was performed in the dual condition almost as well as each task was performed alone.

There has been a lengthy debate in psychology about whether or not it is possible to attend to two things at once. Some theorists have proposed that attention is like an indivisible beam which can only be pointed at one thing at a time. Dual task performance must then be explained in terms of rapid switching of attention between the two tasks (Broadbent, 1982). Others have seen it more as a *quantity* of resource which can be devoted entirely to one task or split up between several. Proponents of both views broadly agree that automatic tasks require little or no attention to be allocated to them. Therefore, when at least one of a pair of simultaneous activities is automatic, then there is enough attentional capacity to maintain both tasks. In the above experiment it seems likely that sight-reading had attained a high degree of automaticity.

Knowledge

When I get into a dispute about some topic close to my heart, I don't always win. As I nurse my wounds afterwards I often come up with the perfect response that I *should* have made to my opponent's apparently devastating blow. In the heat of the debate, however, I was just unable to gain access to the appropriate piece of knowledge, the argument I wanted to bring out. In a similar manner, examination candidates often realize what they *should* have written minutes after walking out of the examination room.

I use these examples to make the point that skill is not simply a matter of having knowledge. It involves this knowledge being readily available at the appropriate time, in response to the situation that demands its use. For instance, what is important for driving is that I should immediately slow down when I see green traffic lights turning to amber. It is no use having the conceptual knowledge that amber means 'stop' unless I can apply it in the driving situation. Recently, cognitive psychologists have paid increasing attention to the possible role in skilled behaviour of what are called *associative pattern-action pairs*. Such associations are like rules which an organism can apply to particular situations. They have the form: '*If Condition X Applies Then Carry Out Action Y*'. They look rather like the stimulus-response bonds which have had a venerable history in behaviourist explanations of animal learning. However, in these so called 'production rules', X need not be a simple external stimulus, and Y need not be an overt behaviour. We can include such things as internal mental states and goals as well. So the rule, 'If you see a police patrol car in your rear-view mirror, then feel panic' is a production rule, though one we would perhaps like to be without.

A set of production rules sufficient for carrying out some coherent task can be incorporated in a *production system*. One of the major reasons why psychologists have begun to think about skills in terms of production systems is the fact that such systems can be very easily simulated on a computer, and we shall return to discuss the utility of this in Chapter 16.

Production system theory provides a useful way of understanding how knowledge may be organized in the service of skill at several different levels. First is the level of individual actions. Particular environmental patterns can trigger immediate knowledge about the right thing to do in that circumstance. In driving, for instance, a green light turning to amber triggers an immediate application of the brakes. Two significant facts about such knowledge stand out.

One is that the knowledge may be completely inaccessible (or 'out of mind') until the circumstances which demands its use occurs. Do you know without trying, for instance, which muscle you would use first when standing up from a seated position? The second fact is that our capacity to acquire new pattern-action pairs seems limitless.

The point about accessibility is made nicely by a study on taxi-drivers (Chase, 1983). Experienced Pittsburgh taxi-drivers were called into the laboratory and asked to describe the best routes between pairs of points in the city. This they were able to do. It turned out, however, that their routes were not always the best routes or the routes that the drivers would actually take. This was shown by repeating the study in real life; actually asking the drivers to *drive* from A to B. When this happened the drivers would often remember better short cuts than the ones they had produced in the lab. These short cuts seemed to be triggered by the experience of arriving at particular locations. A driver would realize 'of course, if I turn left here I can cut round such and such a bottleneck'. This is, of course, completely adaptive. Taxi-drivers need to find good routes when on the job, not when thinking about it.

A complex cognitive skill such as chess playing is also amenable to production system analysis. We may suppose that the chess master has many thousands of production rules which link each commonly-occurring pattern or chunk to a good move associated with the pattern. In this way, masters experience good moves 'just springing off the board' at them. Poor players have to work through the consequences of many bad moves before stumbling on a good move.

The Structure of Skills

We can also use the notion of a production system to elucidate the nature of planning and structuring in skill, and the ability to keep track of where one is at. For this, in addition to production rules, we must postulate a working memory-system in which a goal stack may be held (see Chapter 5). A simple example of a common skill much quoted in this context is the ability to travel around an industrialized country. If I am in a rural location and need to get to a big city quite quickly then I could set the goal of, for instance, 'getting to London'. This goal can act as the X condition of a production rule which might be, *'If The Goal Is To Get To London Then Set The Goal Of Getting To The Nearest Railway Station'*. So the goal of getting to London is 'pushed down' the stack and the second goal of 'get to the station' sits on top as the current goal. You can imagine a goal stack to be rather like the spring-loaded plate racks found in canteens. Now the operative goal is 'get to station'. This may well call up a further rule which says, *'If The Goal Is To Get To The Station Then Set The Goal To Call a Taxi'*. So now 'call a taxi' becomes the current goal, with two unachieved goals stacked beneath it. This may call up further goals such as 'look up telephone number'. At some point there will be a goal which calls into play a production rule involving behaviour which achieves the topmost goal. When this happens, this goal can be jettisoned from the stack and the previous goal becomes current. This can then be achieved, and so on through the stack until there are no further goals left. The goal stack gives structure and direction to the total behaviour.

Without the structuring of a goal stack behaviour would tend to be uncoordinated and entirely driven by the current situation. Indeed, when the retention of goals in the stack is inadequate a partial breakdown of behaviour occurs. We can observe this through a particular class of absent-minded error. This occurs to most of us. You walk into a shop, and then stand there foolishly, trying to remember why you came in. The goal of 'buying X' led to the new goal of 'go to the shop', but on your way you started to think of other things and this intervening mental activity led to the loss of the original goal from the stack.

In real life, most of us are not pursuing just one set of goals, such as described above, but many disparate goals. It is sometimes hard to keep them all in mind, and we can never be directly working on more than one or two of them. It follows that the ability to remember what one's multiple goals are, and where one has got to in achieving each of them, is an important skill in its own right. We all know people who always seem to be forgetting to do things, whilst others seem to be able efficiently to keep on top of a wide variety of different but complex commitments. The role of external memory aids seems very important here. These are such things as diaries, knots in handkerchiefs, lists of things to do, and notes to oneself (see Chapter 8). We can see the mobilization of these aids as an explicit recognition of the fact that external stimuli are the best and most reliable triggers for action. Skill in fulfilling multiple commitments seems to be skill in engineering one's own environement to provide the necessary reminders at the right place and time.

FURTHER READING

REASON, J. and MYCIELSKA, K. (1982) *Absent minded? The Psychology of Mental Lapses and Everyday Errors.* New York: Prentice Hall.

> Provides an entertaining and readable account of many of the theoretical notions underlying contemporary thinking about skill.

CHASE, W. G. and CHI, M. T. H. (1980) 'Cognitive skill: implications for spatial skill in large scale environments'. In J. Harvey (Ed.) *Cognition, Social Behaviour and the Environment.* Hillsdale, NJ: Erlbaum.

> A useful summary of research on chess and related skills. Short, clear and eminently readable.

CHAPTER 3

ACQUIRING SKILL

John Sloboda

In the previous chapter we looked in some detail at the characteristics of skilled behaviour. We now turn to a related question: what does one have to do to become skilled? The human animal is unique in the number of skills that are acquired through learning. We are also unique in the diversity of our skills. Some of us are skilled mathematicians, others are skilled musicians, yet others are skilled mechanics. How is it that people can be so different in their skill profile?

Many animals appear extremely skilful. Observe, for example, how a cat stalks a bird. It crouches low so as to be concealed by ground cover; takes care to move slowly and quietly towards its prey. Then, when it becomes difficult to remain unobserved, it springs forward with claws outstretched to give the prey minimum time to react. My cat's skill at this operation is evidenced by the number of dead birds and mice that are proudly deposited on my kitchen floor. I could learn quite a lot about hunting techniques from carefully observing my cat.

Where did the cat's skill come from? As far as we know, most animal skills are inherited rather than learned. Kittens reared in isolation still show an appropriate repertoire of stalking and hunting behaviours (Hinde, 1966). They appear to be instinctual. Moreover, all individuals of a given species appear to inherit roughly the same set of skills.

Is it possible that human skills are inherited? In the first section of this chapter we shall examine the view of skill acquisition that attributes it to 'talent' or 'innate potential'. We will then go on to contrast it with the view that talent is less important than opportunity and practice. We will conclude by looking at a case study of an exceptional skill, which shows that we really need both views to understand properly the acquisition of skill.

Talent and Skill Acquistion

It is indisputable that gifted parents tend to have gifted children. Sometimes, specific talents such as musical talent seem to run in families for several generations. Unfortunately, it has long been realized that this finding, in itself, tells us very little about how the skill was acquired. It could be that the son of a musician has inherited some special propensity for musical achievement. Equally, it could be the case that a musical parent provides more opportunity and encouragement for a child to learn musical skills than does a non-musician. In real life, the influences of heredity and environment are inextricably mixed together, and it is very hard to establish that a particular influence is decisive.

Much of the serious psychological research in this area has centred around the notion of intelligence, and has been the subject of great controversy. One controversy concerns the question of whether there is some unitary capacity or faculty that comprises the basis for intelligent action, or whether intelligence is simply the conjunction of several distinct and independent skills. Supporters of the first view point to the fact that people who are good at one type of thing tend to be good at a whole range of other things. This fact forms the basis of intelligence testing. It is precisely because many skills correlate with one another that we can obtain a useful picture of a person's ability by just sampling a few skills. But the correlation is not perfect, and we find in almost every person areas of skill that are either much better or much worse than one might predict on the basis of intelligence measures. A good example of this, to which we will return in the next chapter, is the dyslexic, who reads less well than his other intellectual achievements would predict. Gardner (1983) provides an accessible overview of the issues surrounding this general controversy.

A second controversy concerns the degree to which we can find reliable ways of measuring the separate effects of environment and heredity. This topic is fraught with methodological and theoretical difficulties. It is also a political and ideological minefield, since it is frequently linked to the issue of putative racial differences (Eysenck versus Kamin, 1981). Very few people come to the issue with an open mind. Nonetheless, I will stick my neck out and say that there are probably three ways in which inherited characteristics might have a significant effect on skill acquisition:

(a) There are some genetically transmitted conditions that cause largely irreversible mental retardation, presumably as a result of abnormal development of the brain or nervous system (e.g. Down's Syndrome). These conditions may destroy capacities that are essential for some skills. All such conditions unfortunately, tend to handicap their posessors. There are no known conditions of this sort that confer significant advantage.

(b) Inherited physical characteristics are undoubtedly a factor in determining achievement in some skills. It will depend largely on the shape of your vocal cavities as to whether you have a chance of becoming an opera singer. It will depend largely on your size and the shape of your skeleton as to whether you could become a ballerina, and so on. Inherited physical characteristics of the nervous system are also likely to be of importance.

(c) There are a whole set of what one might call dispositional or motivational factors that could have an indirect effect on skill acquisition. From very early in life, infants seem to differ from one another in their degree of activity, the amount of sleep they require, their primary mood, and so on. Research on adult personality shows significant individual differences in such factors as ability to concentrate on boring tasks for long periods of time. There is also evidence for stable preferences for certain domains of activity. Some people seem to be biased toward visual activities, others towards verbal. These preferences may be linked to very early infancy, where significant differences in developmental profile may be observed (Kagan, Lapidus, and Moore, 1978). Some children develop early language skill but lag behind in physical development. Others show the reverse trend. All of these factors could have a strong influence on both the type and level of skill acquired. We can imagine the physically precocious extrovert as being more likely to acquire football skill, whilst the verbal introvert might be more likely to develop skill at poetry. This is not so much a question of *capacity*. Rather, it represents the amount of effort that a person is likely to want to devote to particular types of activity. Some activities seem to 'go against the grain', others seem intrinsically rewarding.

Practice and Skill Acquisition

Paul Tortelier is one of the world's foremost professional cellists. He was born to poor working-class parents who had no particular background of musical accomplishment. Before he was born they decided that their child should achieve great things in the world, and that they were going to have him trained as a cellist. By hard work, saving, and self-sacrifice, they were able to buy instruments, lessons, and other forms of support; and their son achieved their intentions for him.

Such rags to riches stories strike a deep chord in many of us, and prompt the following question. Suppose the young Tortelier had been snatched from his cradle at birth and replaced by another baby, chosen at random from the population at large? Suppose further that his parents were unaware of the switch, and treated the substitute in exactly the same way. Would they have turned *anyone* into that world-class cellist?

To the extent that we are inclined to answer 'yes' to that question we are basing our answer on the assumption that skills are not acquired by virtue of what you *are* but by what you *do*. Anyone can acquire a skill if only he or she does the right things.

It is impossible in practice to run the hypothesized substitution experiment. What we can do, however, is look at people in the process of acquiring skills and ask whether there is anything that seems to be linked with successful acquisition for a wide variety of skills and for a wide range of people. It will not come as a great surprise to be told that the single most important factor that psychologists know about is practice. Just as practice is the ingredient most emphasized by sports coaches and piano teachers.

A great deal of research has looked at the effects of practice on simple perceptual-motor skills. A frequently used task is one in which the reaction time is measured for pressing a button in response to a light turning on. Sometimes there is only a single light and a single button, while in other experiments there may be several of each, with subjects having to respond perhaps to one light at a time or to various patterns of lights coming on together. A study of Siebel (1963) is representative. Subjects viewed ten lights arranged in a horizontal row. Below the lights were ten buttons, one for each light. The subjects rested their fingers on the keys and watched the lights. After a signal, a random subset of the lights would go on. Subjects were required to depress the keys corresponding to the illuminated lights (and no others). Individual subjects repeated this task for upwards of 40,000 trials.

Siebel measured mean reaction-time to depress the correct combination of keys. As we saw in the previous chapter, rapidity of response is a crucial characteristic of skill, which is why many researchers have used reaction time as a primary measure of skill level. The faster you can respond, the more skilled you are (given, of course, that your response remains accurate). Siebel found that reaction time dropped from an initial level of about two seconds down to 0.4 seconds with this large amount of practice. One can hardly imagine that this task had any interest for the subjects, yet sheer, dogged repetition caused continued improvement right through the 40,000 trials.

More detailed information can be gained by plotting reaction time (RT) against trial number, and Figure 3:1 shows the typical result of doing this. It illustrates what is sometimes called the 'law of diminishing returns'. Early practice results in quite large gains in speed, but equivalent amounts of practice later on yield only small gains. Sometimes this flattening-out of the acquisition curve occurs because one is coming up against physiological limits, for example,

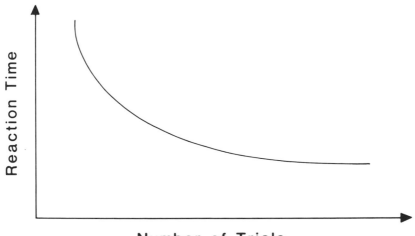

Number of Trials

Figure 3:1   A typical graph of reaction time plotted against numbers of trials.

the fixed speed at which your nerves will conduct impulses. More often, though, the flattening out begins to occur long before any such limits are being approached.

Why do we get diminishing returns with practice? One possibility could be that people concentrate less and less as they repeat a task, becoming unable to benefit from late trials to the extent of early ones. This might be a plausible explanation for decline in a single session. It would hardly account for a smooth decline over 40,000 trials spread over many days. If learning were entirely dependent on concentration, one should see many fluctuations up and down as concentration waxed and waned.

Before we consider a more likely explanation, it is important to note that experimentally obtained curves such as the one shown in Figure 3:1 frequently approximate to a logarithmic function. If they are replotted on logarithmic axes, they turn into straight lines. Figure 3:2 shows the Siebel data replotted in this way.

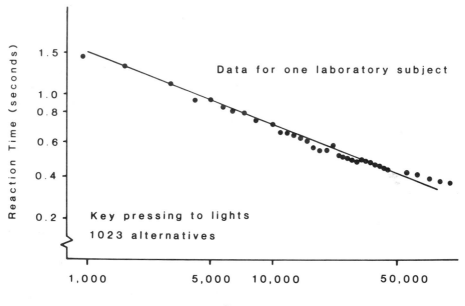

Figure 3:2   Siebel's data plotted on logarithmic axes. (After Fitts and Posner, 1967.)

Explaining The Law of Diminishing Returns

A line of explanation for diminishing returns has been suggested by Newell and Rosenbloom (1981) and is built directly on the notions of chunking and pattern-action production rules that we have already explored in Chapter 2.

They propose that, as a subject carries out some task such as Siebel's, continuous attempts are made to chunk the lights into patterns. Each such chunk will be associated with a particular finger pattern of response. To begin with, the display will be processed as ten separate lights, and a response must be made to each individually. As time passes, the subject will come to respond, say, to *pairs* of lights as single units, then to triplets, and so on, until some theoretical ceiling is reached when the complete ten-light array is seen as a single pattern (just as in reading learners progress from reading letter-by-letter to reading whole words – see Chapter 4). If we assume, for simplicity's sake, that it takes a constant time to perceive and respond to a single chunk, then we can see that the larger the chunks are, the less time it will take to respond to the whole display.

It is quite easy to see intuitively that the more chunks a person learns the quicker will be the response to any particular set of lights, because there is more possibility of detecting a familiar pattern in it. Thus, practice will increase task speed. What is less easy to see is why this notion also predicts the law of diminishing returns, but in fact it does do so. This is because a given small chunk will occur in the array more frequently than a large one, and so can be learned and put to use more quickly.

To see why this should be important, consider first the effects of chunking the display into five pairs of two adjacent lights. Each pair can take on one of four configurations (off-off, off-on, on-off, and on-on). There are five pairs, so in all there are five times four configurations, which is 20. All of these need to be learned, together with their 20 associated response patterns. If on any trial of the experiment a random half of the lights come on, then any given configuration of a pair is likely to appear once in every four trials on average. So since each of the 20 chunks appears frequently, there is a lot of opportunity to notice and learn to respond to each one. Given our assumption that it takes a constant time to respond to any chunk, then a person who has learned these 20 pair-patterns will be able to halve her response time, always seeing the display as five chunks rather than as ten individual lights. This is the reason that the early stages of practice can result in large performance gains.

Now consider what would be involved in learning to respond to the display as two chunks each containing five items. There are 32 different configurations of on and off that a set of five lights can take up. There are two chunks in the display of ten, so there are 64 configurations in all that need to be learned (32 times two). If on any trial a random half of the lights come on then each configuration of a chunk will only appear once in every 32 trials. There are more patterns to learn, and much less frequent opportunities to observe any given pattern. Thus it will take a subject a great deal longer to move from processing the display as five chunks to processing it as two chunks than it will have done to move from ten to five. The first move reduces reaction time by a half, say from two seconds to one second. The second move reduces reaction time by three fifths, from one second to 0.4 of a second. Not only will it have taken longer to bring about the second move, but this will also have yielded a smaller absolute increase in speed. This explains the phenomenon of diminishing returns, and its approximation to a logarithmic function.

Studies such as Siebel's, and the theorizing built round them, offer opportunities for mathematically precise thinking about skill. They show in a particularly elegant way why it takes so long to become really good at something. And yet such studies are lacking in several respects. First, the skills studied are very simple. They involve a single response to a stimulus rather than a coordinated sequence. Second, the stimuli themselves lack natural pattern and structure. It is very rarely in the real world that the material we deal with is so unpredictable. There are similarities between new situations and old ones that we already know about. We can make informed guesses and plans. Some patterns crop up much more often than one would expect by chance, and so on. Third, we normally have the opportunity to decide *how* we will practise a skill. In Siebel's task, subjects had to respond to all ten lights on every trial. It might be that a better strategy would be to learn the responses for each hand separately.

This leads to the fourth criticism. In such experiments as Siebel's, the subjects usually work entirely on their own, the skill is wholly without a social context. As observed in Chapter 1, this is not true of real life skills. These are usually learnt with the aid of some form of coaching. The coaching may be from an older practitioner, it may come from a book, it may amount to no more than trying to copy what you once saw someone else do. Nevertheless, there is normally available some source of comment and suggestion. For all these reasons, the rate of improvement on a task such as Siebel's probably represents a pessimistic estimate of our ability to acquire real-life skills.

Enhancing the Effects of Practice

In this section, we will look briefly at some things which have been shown to help many types of practice become more effective. These are features of practice around which any coaching programme must be constructed. The first and most important of them is *feedback*.

Feedback

Feedback is, quite simply, knowledge of what your actions have achieved. It can come in two forms, intrinsic and extrinsic. Intrinsic feedback is that provided as a direct consequence of bodily movement and sensation. If you move your arm, you can both feel the result through *kinaesthesis*, and you can see where the arm is through vision. Extrinsic feedback is that provided by some external source or agent, frequently a coach or teacher. Being told whether an answer you supply is right or wrong is a type of extrinsic feedback. Feedback of one sort or another is essential to all skill acquisition. One cannot improve unless one has ways of judging how good present performance is, and in which direction change must occur.

There are several ways in which one may harness feedback to achieve more successful skill acquisition. The first is actually to pay attention to existing feedback. This can be someting as simple as checking over what one has written when writing a letter or an essay. Many students and others omit to do this, and suffer as a result. The second is to make sure that the feedback is immediate. Comments on an essay returned after several weeks are of little use because the author has probably forgotten the precise steps taken in preparing the essay. It is no longer possible to link feedback to specific aspects of behaviour. In an ideal world the tutor would supervise every step of the essay-writing process, offering suitable comments at each stage. This means that the two persons would have to be in close and prolonged contact, with the likelihood of an intense relationship developing. And intense relationships are familiar in contexts where there is a master and an apprentice, a trainer and an athlete, or a drama coach and a student. An example from literature is the relationship between Svengali and the young singer, Trilby, in Du Maurier's novel of that name.

More exotic than ordinary feedback, are ways of helping people to become aware of internal sensations of which they are not normally conscious. By making use of a visual display which monitors some aspect of body state (such as

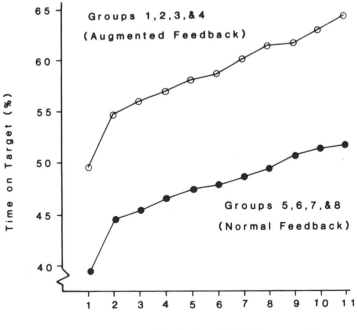

heartbeat or galvanic skin response) one can learn to identify the bodily sensations which accompany changes in these states, and some people are able to control these states even when the augmented feedback (often known as *biofeedback*) is removed.

Sometimes feedback seems to have primarily a motivating effect. It provides information which is not strictly essential but which seems to increase involvement in the task. For instance, Smode (1958) asked subjects to practise what is known as a 'tracking task', in which a randomly moving needle could be kept on a central mark by rotating a dial in compensatory movement. After each trial all subjects were given 'normal' feedback in the form of the length of time that they had managed to keep the needle centred during that trial. In addition, one group of subjects were given 'augmented' feedback in the form of a counter on which their total score over trials was accumulated. This augmented feedback had a dramatic effect on performance, as Figure 3:3 shows. The advantage also persisted after the augmented feedback had been removed. In a second day of learning where all subjects just received normal feedback, those subjects who had received augmented feedback on day 1 continued to do better.

Spacing

If you are able to devote six hours to practising a given skill should you do six solid hours of work, or six separate hours on different days? In general, it seems that it is better to *space* practice over several sessions than to *mass* it all together (Welford, 1968). There are several reasons why this might be so. One is that fatigue and lowering of attention tend to occur as a repetitive task is continued. As a result bad habits may be formed, with further practice strengthing this undesirable behaviour. Frequent rests can allow the fatigue and the bad habits to dissipate. On the other hand, when motivation is high, it is quite possible to become totally immersed in a task for many hours without any noticeable loss of attention, so the prescription to space one's practice is by no means a universally beneficial one.

Attitude

A third issue relates to the question of what mental attitude or activity should accompany practice. Should you repeat a task fairly mechanically with an essentially passive mind, intending, as it were, to stamp the skill in by sheer repetition; or should you be actively structuring the task, looking for patterns and similarities, guessing what might come next? This is a somewhat vexed question, and psychologists have not been able to supply any definite answers. It is very clear that sheer dogged repetition does have beneficial effects (see the Siebel study described earlier). There is also a lot of talk in such areas as the psychology of sport about the importance of stopping being too cerebral and letting one's body 'take over'. There is certainly plenty of evidence that we do things better if we can get them to the level of automatic control, sitting back and letting the system 'get on with it'; and it is possible that where physical movements are concerned part of such a process may be the retrieving of early, partly instinctive movement patterns which have become overlaid by maladaptive attempts to control them (Tinbergen, 1974).

Even at a more complex cognitive level, a lot of skill learning seems to be largely incidental and unintended. It sometimes seems that if you are interested enough in an activity, your involvement will, in itself, result in the acquisition of some degree of skill. It is when you attempt to acquire a skill that relates to an activity which does not intrinsically interest you that a substitute for interest must be manufactured. In Chapter 12 you will be reading about some of the ways in which educational researchers have clarified the nature of effective study strategies and skills, and the teaching strategies needed to support them. It can be helpful to see these strategies as ways of getting the unmotivated learner to do what, with motivation, would come naturally. If you think that this seems like a poor substitute for letting people study what actually interests them, and some kind of indictment of our educational system, then you would not be alone (Illich, 1973). But this view is incomplete on its own. For even when we are interested to master a particular skill, we can still benefit from advice and feedback. In the acquisition of skills, it is the function of a coach to provide these.

An Exceptional Talent – a Case Study

I would like to conclude this chapter by describing a quite extraordinary skill, which I have recently been involved in studying (Sloboda, Hermelin, and O'Connor, 1985). The subject of this study, who will be referred to as NP, is an autistic man in his early twenties. Like many autistic people, he is severely mentally retarded. He has almost no spontaneous language, shows social withdrawal and other bizarre behaviour patterns, and he requires the total care of a specialist residential institution. What makes him different from the majority of autistic people is the fact that in one small area of his life he is anything but retarded. He has an amazing capacity to memorize piano music.

In tests that we carried out, NP was able to memorize a classical piano piece (Grieg Opus 47, no. 3) lasting over two minutes, almost note-perfectly in 12 minutes. He did this simply by listening to sections of a tape-recording of a piece and copying what he heard on the piano. A day later, with no intervening opportunity for rehearsal, he was still able to reproduce the piece almost perfectly. At no stage did he observe the printed music, see anyone else demonstrating the fingering, or receive any other extrinsic feedback. He was not told what key the piece was in, but was instantly able to choose the right notes and play them with the right combinations of fingers, even though he had probably never heard the piece before, and certainly had never attempted to learn it.

This level of memory skill is very rare, even among musicians of above-average intelligence. It is probably equalled only by the legendary accomplishments of a handful of prodigies, such as Mozart or Erwin Nyerghihazi (Revesz, 1925). NP provides an ideal test case for some of the questions about skill acquisition that we have raised in this chapter.

First, we can ask whether the skill fits the notions of inherited talent that we discussed at the beginning of the chapter. There is certainly little evidence of musical accomplishment in NP's immediate family background, which is one of quite severe social deprivation. He did, however, show early precocity in music, without a great deal in the way of family encouragement. Recordings which survive from the age of six show a level of skill much above that of a normal six-year-old. It is reported that although he had no piano at home, he made a coherent performance on his very first public exposure to the instrument. Given what is known about his circumstances, the possibility of secret coaching can almost certainly be ruled out. Even today, there is a real sense in which NP cannot actually be taught. His 'lessons' consist of his teacher playing him new pieces to memorize. No one has taught him how to memorize as he does (See Chapter 6). No one *knows* how he does it, and he is not able to explain himself. Opportunities have been put in his way, but NP must be one of the purest examples of a self-taught expert that exists.

On the face of it, NP looks like providing very strong evidence for the existence of an inherited gift for music. His lack of achievement in any other area of skill makes it look like a quite *specific* gift for music. But appearances can be deceptive, and we would do well to examine this 'gift' a little more closely. The first thing to notice is that the measure of the gift is equalled by the measure of what one can only call NP's obsession with music. Whenever he has a free choice of activity, he almost always chooses either to listen to music (on radio, record, etc.) or to play it. It also seems that when not doing either of those things, he is turning music over in his mind. It would not be unreasonable to suppose that his mind is engaged with music, in an intensely concentrated way, for five or six hours each day. Like Mozart, music is his life and his love. It is hard to know where this obsessive fascination with music came from. It could be a genuinely inherited disposition, or it could come from some crucial early experience. One general aspect of the autistic personality seems to be obsessiveness, and there are in existence people who have similar exceptional skills in other areas, such as mental calculation. Maybe the autistic mind is primed to latch onto an obsession, but the particular obsession may be determined entirely by circumstance.

A second argument against treating NP's skill as a specifically *musical* gift comes from a closer analysis of the way he memorizes music. As well as playing him some classical pieces such as the Grieg, we tried him on a piece which broke many of the rules of 'normal' music. This was an atonal piece by Bartok. Although this Bartok piece (Mikrohosuios, Whole Tone Scales from Book 5) had many fewer notes than the piece composed by Grieg, NP found it almost impossible to memorize. We interpret this as showing that NP's memory skill is based on the ability to chunk conventional musical input into higher-order patterns. When, as in the Bartok, these patterns are absent, performance is severely disrupted. This is just like the chess studies reported in Chapter 2, where the master player's memory for the positions of pieces was superior only when the board was taken from an actual game, not randomly constructed. This is confirmed by an analysis of the few errors NP made on the Grieg piece. They were nearly all structurally plausible errors, in which one musically appropriate chunk was replaced by something similar and equally appropriate (much as one might misremember a sentence by substituting synonymous expressions).

All the evidence we have (see also the description of Steve Falloon's memory skill acquisition in Chapter 7) is that extensive practice is the only and inevitable route to the formation of chunks which can make such impressive skills possible. But, as Siebel's random light data show, this chunking process operates on any material whatsoever, and seems not to be essentially different for music or any other specialized material. NP provides strong corroboration for the general equation that *Motivation + Practice = Skill*. The roots of specific motivations are almost entirely mysterious, but could easily have an inherited component. Practice can be accomplished, however, without any particularly strong motivation, and it seems that our cognitive system will respond by chunking both the inputs and outputs of any task that we practice enough. Nonetheless, amounts of practice of the sort required to attain expertise are almost always unsustainable without strong motivation. Given the most supportive and enriched environment in the world, most of us would fail to acquire many skills, not because we are, in some ultimate sense, incapable of doing so, but rather because, to us, they just don't seem to matter that much.

FURTHER READING

VERNON, P.E., ADAMSON, G. & VERNON, D.F. (1977) *The Psychology and Education of Gifted Children.* London: Methuen.

This provides a level-headed account of the 'talent' view of skill and its acquisition.

FITTS, P.M. & POSNER, M.I. (1967) *Human Performance.* Belmont: Brooks/Cole.

Despite its age, this is still one of the best introductions to the psychology of perceptual-motor skills and their acquisition.

ANDERSON, J.R. (1982) Acquisition of cognitive skills. *Psychological Review*, *89*, 369–406.

This paper, although somewhat technical, provides a clear overview of recent thinking.

CHAPTER 4

READING: A CASE STUDY OF COGNITIVE SKILLS

John Sloboda

In Chapters 2 and 3 we have looked at some general characteristics of skill using examples chosen from a variety of specific skills. This has provided a broad picture of what most skills share. Each skill is in some respects, however, unique and poses unique psychological problems. In this chapter we subject one very important skill to a rather more detailed scrutiny than has been possible up till now. Such scrutiny is necessary to remind us that human skills are more various and complex than any general statements about skill.

There are several good reasons for taking reading as a representative skill. First of all, it is vitally important for anyone living in our culture to know how to read. Despite this, many people experience difficulties in learning to read and an even larger number of people feel that they do not read as well or as quickly as they would like. An understanding of what is entailed in skilled reading may well point to some remedies for reading difficulty.

A second reason for choosing to discuss reading is that a vast amount of research on reading has been carried out. This partly reflects its cultural and educational importance, but it also reflects the relative ease with which one may construct precisely controlled textual material for experimental work. Modern technology allows us to exert almost total experimental control over the relevant features of a reader's environment and to test specific hypotheses about how people process these features during reading. This is not true of many other skills such as playing football.

Thirdly, reading also presents, in a particularly acute form, a problem which besets much cognitive research. This is that silent reading entails hardly any observable overt behaviour. Psychologists have had to devise ingenious ways of tapping mental processes without disrupting or changing the behaviour being studied. The difficulty is compounded because, for most of us, a lot of the sub-processes in reading are not open to conscious inspection. Reading processes are rapid and automatic. We are aware primarily of the meaning that 'spring out of the page' at us, not of the process by which we acquired it. As you read this sentence, see if you can answer, from your own observations, any of the following questions:–

(a)   Do your eyes move smoothly along the line of text as you read it?

(b)   How much time is needed between seeing a word and identifying it?

(c)   Do you discover the sound of a word before its meaning, or *vice versa*?

(d)   To what extent do you use prior knowledge to assist word identification?

Unless you are a very unusual individual I doubt that you will be able to use your own introspections on what you are doing to answer such questions, although you may have some opinions about plausible answers. This inscrutability of the reading process makes it very hard for you, or any other proficient reader, to offer much useful advice to someone without your skills. Typically, an honest reader will say 'I don't know how I do it – it just happens'. As cognitive psychologists we need, and indeed we can provide, better answers than that.

Eye Movements in Reading

The study of eye-movements is a useful place to start because it concerns the one sure piece of overt behaviour which accompanies almost all reading. By using various combinations of photographic and electrical recordings it is possible to measure the direction of gaze at any moment without restricting normal eye-movements. Such studies have shown that when we view any stationary scene (whether it contains objects or text) the eye moves in small rapid jerks (know as *saccades*) with longer pauses (known as *fixations*) in between. Each saccade lasts about 50 ms (one twentieth of a second) and a fixation typically lasts for 200–250 ms (one fifth to one quarter of a second). Most useful vision occurs during fixations, so we may think of the experience of reading as a series of 'snapshots' of small portions of text.

Figure 4:1 shows how fixations were distributed along a single line of text when read by a good and a poor reader. The upper numbers show the order of fixations; the lower numbers their durations. This illustrates several typical features: good readers make fewer regressive eye-movements; good readers make larger saccades; good readers make shorter fixations. Each one of these features means that a good reader will read the same passage more quickly than a poor reader. Can we conclude from this that differences in eye-movement patterns are *responsible* for differences in reading ability? Unfortunately not. Making fewer and shorter fixations will only be possible if a reader is able to handle information from fixations more efficiently. Otherwise, increasing eye-movement speed will just lead to loss of comprehension. Speed reading systems which concentrate on training people to make economical eye-movements (e.g. straight down the centre of a page rather than from side to side) rarely lead to any lasting improvement in speed which is not coupled to a loss of comprehension (Crowder, 1982; Gibson and Levin, 1975). Later in the

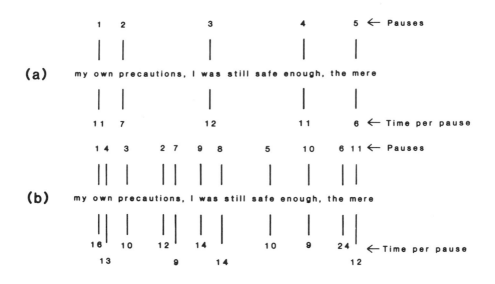

Figure 4:1   The distribution of fixations for a good and a poor reader. (After Tinker, 1965.)

chapter we will look at additional evidence which shows that good readers excel over bad readers at some reading tasks where eye-movements are not required. Economical eye-movements are a symptom of reading skill, not its cause.

Reading as an Application of Knowledge

When we read we are not simply *acquiring* fresh knowledge from the page, we are making use of many different forms of knowledge that we already possess. In Chapters 2 and 3 we saw that all skills depend on the mobilization of appropriate knowledge. In reading, our knowledge of the language allows us to recognize words in which not every letter has been identified. We 'fill in' what we expect to see, as the well-documneted phenomenon of 'proof-readers' error' shows. This is the failure to spot typing or spelling errors in text (such as the one in the previous sentence). Luckily, the *redundancy* of language renders most of such errors harmless. Look, for instance, at how easy it is to read the following sentence. Pxssiblx wxrds cxn bx xxsxly xdxntxfxxd xvxn thxxgh nx vxwxls xrx prxsxnt. Here, the context allows us to supply what the text does not.

   Morton (1964) provided one of the classic demonstrations of the role of context in word indentification. He showed people sentences with a single word missing (e.g. 'He went inside and hung up his —'. The missing word was then displayed very briefly in a tachistoscope (a simple piece of laboratory equipment for presenting visual stimuli for precisely controlled brief durations). The exposure duration was gradually increased until the word was correctly recognized. Morton found that words consistent with the preceding context (e.g. 'coat') were recognized faster than words that were inconsistent (e.g. 'boat').

In order for context to be effective, a person must possess knowledge about the situation being referred to. His knowledge must lead him to make some form of inference about likely continuations. The more he knows, of the subject being referred to, the better will be his inferences, and the more efficient his reading. Other things being equal, the psychology graduate is likely to read this book faster than the beginning student. At every stage he is able to use his existing knowledge to make sense of what he reads. Some material will be already familiar, and he will be able to 'skim' over it. Other passage will use familiar types of argument or terminologies which already have a well-articulated meaning for him. Good reading teachers know this, and they help their pupils by choosing early reading materials which relate to situations with which the pupils will be familiar. In this way pupils will be able to make intelligent guesses from the context as to the identity of words they cannot actually recognize; the success they achieve then serves to bolster their confidence.

The role of knowledge in reading is well illustrated by a series of studies carried out by Sanford and Garrod (1981). In these studies, readers saw simple stories, presented on a computer console, one line at a time. Each reader paced his own reading by pressing a button each time he required a new sentence. In this way it was possible for the experimenters to measure the time spent reading each sentence. Here is an example of the type of story they used:

John was on his way to school.
The bus trundled slowly along.
He was not looking forward to teaching maths.
After all, it was not a usual part of a caretaker's duties.

Most readers experience a mild sense of confusion and disorientation on reading the third and fourth lines. We expect John to be a schoolboy, not a teacher. When we have readjusted to the new information, we then learn that he is the caretaker. Sanford and Garrod showed that this readjustment takes a measurable time. The third sentence in this story took longer to read than an alternative, 'He was not looking forward to the maths lesson', which is consistent with John being a schoolboy. Normal well-constructed prose does not set out to violate expectancies in the way that Sanford and Garrod chose to. Their results show that making appropriate inferences from text can help us read later sentences more quickly, assuming that, on the whole, expectancies will not be violated.

Reading-Specific Knowledge

The sources of knowledge that we have just discussed are not specific to reading. They are concerned with the ways that language in general and the world both work, and they come into play when we listen to speech, or try to interpret a visual scene, and much else. Some sources of knowledge are more specific. For instance, readers come to acquire knowledge about the usual way in which letters are put together in their language, and this is knowledge that is obviously specific to literacy. An English reader knows that BRACK is a possible word whereas CKABR or BRCAK is not. Gibson, Pick, Osser, and Hammond (1962) showed that such knowledge affects reading efficiency. They presented skilled readers with stimuli made up of strings of letters and asked them to report as many of the letters as they could. The subjects were able to report the letters of regular stimuli (like *BRACK*) at briefer exposure durations than those of irregular stimuli (like *CKABR*).

Another area involving reading-specific knowledge is in making use of gaps between words. Hochberg (1970) reports an experiment in which children of varying reading abilities were asked to read either normal texts, or texts where the gaps between words had been filled in by 'x's, as follows. Hexusedxtwox-groupsxofsubjects,xgoodxandxpoorxreaders. Although good readers were faster overall poor readers, their reading speed was significantly slowed by 'x's. In contrast poor readers went at roughly the same (slow) speed for both types of text.

Why do gaps help the good reader? Data supplied by O'Regan (1979) show that experienced readers make larger saccadic eye movements when the word to the right of fixation is large than when it is small. These readers use the gap at the right end of a word in the periphery of vision as a marker for planning the subsequent eye movement. This is, of course, done completely automatically. A reader has no conscious awareness of the constantly fluctuating saccade size, or of the information which controls the saccades. As with many skills, our cognitive system seems able to learn complex yet adaptive rules without our conscious intervention. All we have to do is to supply it with the opportunity to build these rules through frequent exposure to a wide range of relevant situations.

The most reliable, if unexciting, advice that one could give to anyone wishing to improve their reading (or any other skill) is 'do a lot of it, often, for a long time'. At a level of greater detail (and rather less reliability) however, there is rather more to say than this, especially if one were devising a programme of practice for a particular individual. I want to centre the remainder of this chapter around three topics, each of which supplies information relevant to possible causes of reading failure; the role of speech in reading; reading disabilities; and the particular strategies that people adopt when reading for study.

The Role of Speech in Reading

The widespread ability to read silently has not been with us all that long. In medieval times many people found silent reading to be such an inexplicable accomplishment that they were tempted to believe those that could do it were possessed by the devil. It seemed incredible to assert that black marks on the page could yield their meaning without first being converted to the speech sounds which they represented. Such a view would probably be shared by some beginning readers today, especially those coached within an educational philosophy called 'phonics'. According to this philosophy, one learns to read by learning the typical sounds of letters and letter groups. Stringing these sounds together produces word sounds, which can then be recognized by 'the mind's ear'.

Others receive instruction under different philosophies, one of which has been called 'look and say'. In this approach, children learn object-word pairings by direct visual encounter, without systematic teaching on letter-sound correspondences. Thus, the walls of a 'look and say' classroom will be covered with pictures of familiar objects, each paired to the appropriate word. Rapid word recognition follows on constant rehearsal of these pairings.

The argument between adherents of these two philosophies has raged long and fierce. Proponents of phonics have argued that 'look and say' provides the child with no resources for working out the sound (and thus the meaning) of words which have not been seen before. Proponents of 'look and say' argue that English spelling is not regular enough for simple letter-sound translation to work reliably. Both points are valid. Consider, for instance the following sentence. 'Moast cahs hav foor weels'. Although the sentence does not contain a single English word, it is nevertheless comprehensible as representing an English sentence. Unless we were able to perform letter-sound translations comprehension would be impossible.

On the other side of the argument, we know that letter-sound rules cannot always be invoked in reading. There is nothing in such rules to tell us that 'tough' and 'bough' are sounded in a completely different fashion. There are other words which it is impossible to read by the letter-sound route because we need to establish their meaning *before* we can assign the correct sound. Consider for instance:

(a)   She wiped a tear from her eye.
(b)   She noticed a tear in the fabric.

The way the word 'tear' is sounded depends upon whether it denotes a drop of fluid falling from the eye or a rupture in a surface.

Reading With and Without Sound

Although it is obvious that skilled readers do not have to voice the words on the page, the question remains as to whether the 'sounds' are necessarily derived internally. In fact, experimental evidence exists for reading 'without sound'. Green and Shallice (1976) showed that the time taken to make a meaning-based decision about a word does not depend on the number of syllables it contains. For instance, readers took the same time to press a button to show that they had judged GRASSHOPPER to be an insect as they did for WASP. Green and Shallice argue that if sound were involved, GRASSHOPPER should have taken longer because of its greater number of syllables.

As with many controversies in psychology, increasing sophistication in our knowledge has shown that we cannot make a simple conclusion in favour of either sound-based or visual-based reading. The real situation is too complex for that. A far as teaching methods go, research has been unable to show a consistent advantage for any one method. Instead, it is the individual teacher who is the greatest factor in success (Williams, 1970). The good teacher probably uses a pragmatic mixture of approaches, coupled with the ability to empathize with and encourage children. As far as skilled adult readers are concerned, the consensus is that both a sound-based and direct vision-to-meaning process are available, the choice of which route to use being made from moment to moment according to the demands of the task. On top of this, it is now believed that there is not just one type of 'sound based' involvement in reading. Rather there may be *both* an overt form of speech involvement associated with laryngeal movements *and* a more covert form of speech-like imagery operating at an entirely subvocal level. This is best seen by looking at studies of the effects on reading of what is called *articulatory suppression*.

Kleiman (1975) asked subjects to 'shadow' digit sequences played to them over headphones. This involved saying the digits out loud as they were heard. Arguably, such a task ties up the sound-speech system. While shadowing, subjects were asked to make various types of judgement about words visually presented to them. One task involved subjects judging whether visually similar pairs of words rhymed with one another (e.g. TICKLE-PICKLE yes, LEMON-DEMON no). Although shadowing slowed subjects down, they were still able to make correct judgements. This strongly suggests that the overt sound-speech system is not necessary for making sound-based judgements. There appears to be some more deep-seated 'inner' process. As Baddeley (1979) has observed, 'It is very clear to me that when I read, my reading is accompanied by something akin to an auditory or articulatory image of the words being processed. This occurs with or without articulatory suppression'.

The fact that some sound-based aspects of reading can take place without overt involvement of the speech system does not mean, however, that the speech system is unimportant for all reading. Consider a study by Hardyck and Petrinovich (1970). They used biofeedback (see Chaper 3) to train people to suppress articulation. It was found that articulatory suppression had no adverse effect on the comprehension of easy reading material, but that it disrupted the comprehension of difficult material. We may conclude that overt (if silent) speech assists comprehension of difficult passages. Most of us are probably aware of this from our own experience. With difficult texts we may be inclined to sound the words out loud. But why should this be? Crowder (1982) suggests that such speech is useful for maintaining early words of complex sentences in short-term memory while the rest of the sentence is being read. This is necessary because one frequently needs to read the end of a sentence before the meaning of its earlier portion becomes clear (see Chapters 5 and 10).

This finding also has a converse side. If articulation is not particularly useful for reading easy material then it could be a hindrance to faster reading. The maximum rate of speech is perhaps four or five words per second. Reading with articulation cannot therefore proceed at a faster rate than about 300 words per minute. There is, however, considerable evidence that accomplished readers can read simple material at over twice this speed without loss of comprehension. This can only be done if articulation is suppressed. If your impression is that you articulate during reading then you might find it worthwhile to train yourself to read without vocalization. One simple way of forcing yourself not to vocalize what you read is to repeat some word over and over as you read (e.g. 'double–double–double' etc.).

Reading Disability

Reading difficulties can occur for many reasons. Some psychologists believe that we should make a distinction between people whose reading difficulties are accompanied by a range of other intellectual difficulties, and those whose disability seems confined to reading alone. They argue that the term *dyslexic* should be reserved for people in this latter condition. Therefore, a dyslexic is defined as a person of average or above average intellectual achievement with reading difficulty. Curiously, about 80 per cent of such people are male. Other poor readers, who tend to perform less well than average right across the intellectual spectrum, are as likely to be female as male (Jorm, 1983).

Other psychologists distrust such a neat categorization, and would find it hard to make a distinction between dyslexics and other poor readers. In any case, much research fails to make this distinction in selecting its subjects. I will use dyslexia here to mean any chronic reading disability that is resistant to normal teaching methods.

Is there a specific thing that tends to go wrong in dyslexia? It seems that many dyslexics find it hard to work out the sounds of words they are trying to read: the sound-based route to meaning. Thus, for instance, dyslexics are particularly poor at working out the pronunciation of nonsense words like BLEN, PORSUN, or THELD. An experiment by Perfetti, Goldman, and Hogaboam (1979) showed that dyslexics tend to compensate for this difficulty by relying much more heavily on context than do normal readers. Children were timed for how long it took them to pronounce printed words. In one condition the words were presented alone. In a second condition the words were embedded in a story. Table 4:1 shows the mean reading times per word for the two groups of subjects in the two conditions. Although both groups gained from the context, poor readers gained the most. It seems that the poor readers try to compensate for their difficulty with the sound-based route by assigning greater weight to contextual information.

Table 4:1   mean reading times per word (ms.)

	No Context	Context
Good Readers	786	665
Poor Readers	1069	751

The reading deficit in the sound-based route seems to be part of a wider difficulty that dyslexics have in making use of short-term (or working) memory, which we know to be specialized for holding verbal information in an acoustic form (see Chapter 5). They seem to be less able to recall the precise wording (as opposed to the gist) of short stories they have just heard, and their short-term memory span is often lower than average. We argued in the previous section that the ability to hold verbal material in short-term memory aids comprehension of difficult material. Therefore a deficit in the ability to use short-term memory may well lead to comprehension difficulties.

What causes dyslexia? There is some suggestion of a genetic component. The unequal sex distribution is characteristic of some genetically transmitted characteristics. The condition also tends to run in families, and the joint incidence of dyslexia in identical twins is higher than that in fraternal twins (Hermann, 1959). Although it is never possible to rule out environmental explanations for these facts, it is telling that dyslexic children often have brothers and sisters who are very good readers despite growing up in the same environment.

The question of most pressing practical importance is – can dyslexics be helped to improve their reading, and if so, how? The answer to the first part of the question seems to be a cautious 'yes'. Although few people are able to overcome their disabilitiess completely, some training programmes allow dyslexics to achieve lasting improvements when compared to control groups who did not receive the training. The most successful approach seems to be one that offers the reader an opportunity to practise precisely those skills in which he or she is deficient, namely sound-based processes (Naidoo, 1970). Some people have argued, however, that success is also possible by encouraging poor readers to make better use of their existing strengths (such as the ability to make use of context). Unfortunately there have not been enough good evaluation studies to provide a definite judgement on this point.

Reliable scientific knowledge in the area of dyslexia is hard to come by because the instructor/researcher is faced with a dilemma. Should a pupil be offered what, in considered but subjective judgement, is the best and most workable approach for that instructor? Or should a pupil be offered something which is not well tested (or, indeed, nothing at all as a 'control' condition for purposes of comparison) in the interests of advancing scientific knowledge? Those who choose the former course cannot be blamed. Dilemmas such as this are common in many branches of psychology. They explain in part why, despite all the research, there are fewer definite answers in this area than one would like.

Reading Strategies and Study

Suppose that you are an experienced reader who reads reasonably rapidly, without excessive vocalization. You have a wide vocabulary and good general knowledge. Are there any reasons why you might cope poorly with the demands of reading for study? Unfortunately, there are. Smith (1967) asked good and poor student readers to read texts for (a) general impressions, and (b) details. She found that good readers adjusted their procedures according to the instructions. When reading for details they reread factual materials like names and dates. When reading for general impressions they stopped to evaluate ideas at the ends of paragraphs, and if they reread, read whole sections rather than single items. Poor readers, in contrast, varied their procedures much less in the two conditions. (This is an example of the importance of *metacognitive* skills – see Chapter 12.)

A key to efficient reading seems to be the notion of economy. Poor students waste time reading inessential material at a too great level of detail. Good readers are much more likely to 'skim' through material, noting what is irrelevant to their purposes and what they should go back to and read in more detail. Such behaviour presupposes a clear idea of what the purpose of the reading is. When you are asked by a tutor to 'read Chapter 5' you should be able to formulate some concrete ending to the additional clause 'so that . . . .'

As regards skimming, a word of caution is in order. If you are asked to read something 'just to get the basic ideas', skimming will not of itself do the job. Claims of speed-reading advocates aside, it is not possible to follow an argument by lighting on the odd word or sentence here and there. Rather, skimming serves more as a preliminary 'survey', particularly useful if one has a very specific set of purposes in mind.

Conclusions

This is, perhaps, the appropriate point at which to end our discussion of reading. Although the question of evaluating the outcome of one's reading is of crucial importance for effective study, it will be taken up further in the wider context of learning skills (Chapter 12). We have barely skimmed the surface of the vast research literature on reading, but I hope that at least five important features of skilled reading have been illustrated. These are:

(a) Reading involves a complex interaction of knowledge at many levels, from knowledge of the world to knowledge of spelling rules.

(b) Such knowledge is largely automated and is applied from moment to moment without conscious awareness.

(c) There is not just one way to read, but a variety of processes and strategies which skilled readers may select according to purpose and circumstance.

(d) Reading difficulties can frequently be linked to deficiencies in specific subcomponents of the total process, such as the translation from symbol to sound.

(e) Improvement of adult reading skills may be brought about by elimination of unnecessary vocalization, and by greater awareness of the possibilities for tailoring one's reading strategy to explicitly formulated goals for reading.

FURTHER READING

CROWDER, R. G. (1982) *The Psychology of Reading: an Introduction.* New York: Oxford University Press.

A clear and concise introduction to the topic, and particularly good on reading-specific knowledge.

SANFORD, A. J. and GARROD, S. C. (1981) *Understanding Written Language: Explorations in comprehension beyond the sentence.* Chichester: Wiley.

Complements Crowder in dealing mainly with the role of contextual knowledge.

BRYANT, P. E. and BRADLEY, L. (1985) *Children's Reading Problems.* Oxford: Blackwell.

Offers an up-to-date and critical assessment of research on dyslexia and allied problems.

SECTION II

MEMORY SKILLS

CHAPTER 5

THE NATURE OF MEMORY

Angus Gellatly

A 'Good' Memory

Harry Lorayne, a professional memory man, regularly performed the following feat. Members of the audience would be introduced to Lorayne as they filed into the auditorium. Later on, with the audience of hundreds seated in front of him, he would point to each person in turn and accurately recall their names. Unlike most of us, Lorayne had no trouble at all in putting names to faces. Indeed his feat of memory is so astonishing that we might be tempted to assume some inborn faculty was at work here, to account for his performance simply by saying that he was blessed with a very 'good' memory. Such an explanation is, of course, no explanation at all (see Chapter 3). Lorayne himself insists that anyone who is prepared to make the effort can acquire the same skill of getting names right. How is it done, and what does it tell us about the nature of memory and memory skills? Answers to these questions will be provided in the course of the present chapter. Before those answers can make much sense, however, it is necessary to know something of how memory is studied by psychologists. For this purpose it will also be helpful to consider a very different case from that of Lorayne, one in which memory performance is much worse than normal.

A 'Bad' Memory

This example will treat the case of a typical patient, to be referred to as K., who suffers from a disease known as Korsakoff's syndrome. The syndrome is related to long term alcoholism that leads to damage to the limbic system of the brain. Korsakoff sufferers show a variety of symptoms dependent on the extent of their brain damage and on their individual personalities. Nevertheless there are a number of typical symptoms that can be attributed to our idealized patient, K.

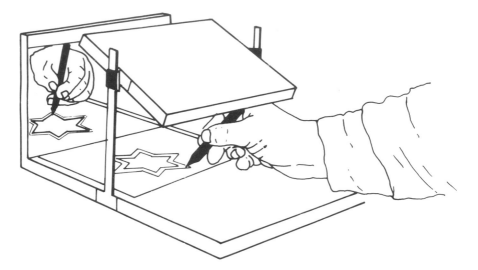

Figure 5:1   Mirror-drawing apparatus.

Imagine K. seated in the ward when a nurse comes to find him. The nurse knows K. well, but K. gives no sign of recognizing the nurse at all. When the nurse asks if K. has had his breakfast, K. replies guardedly that he does not know for sure. K. is then led to a laboratory in another part of the hospital and seated in front of a piece of mirror drawing apparatus (see Figure 5:1). He denies any familiarity with either the laboratory or the apparatus, although he has been into this room on each of the past several days to practise mirror-drawing. It is explained to him that he will have to use a pencil to trace a shape while viewing his hand in a mirror. (Because in this task people get mirror-reversed feedback about the position and movement of their hands they initially find it hard to control what they are doing, yet after a few sessions of practice they become skilled at the task and no longer experience problems.) K. shakes his head and remarks that it all sounds very difficult, then immediately starts to trace accurately round the shape. He performs like the practiced individual he is, whilst having no recollection of having attempted the task before. His memory for *how to do* mirror drawing has become dissociated from his memory of *having done it* previously.

Automatic and Effortful Memorizing

Lorayne and K. lie at the extremes of what is called 'good' and 'bad' memory but the difference between them is not merely one of degree. They are, respectively, good and bad at remembering different kinds of information. Lorayne's skill lies in having mastered a technique for fixing in memory material typically forgotten by most people, whilst K.'s most striking deficiency is for material that other people remember quite automatically and without effort.

Hasher and Zacks (1979) have proposed that there is a continuum from information that is *encoded* into memory automatically, without need for conscious attention, to that which is *encoded* only with effort. Their proposal is an application to the area of memory of the general ideas of skill and automaticity discussed in Chapter 2. The sort of information likely to be encoded automatically into memory tends to be elusive in nature, such things as smells, tastes, and emotional atmosphere. Hasher and Zacks suggest that the spatial–temporal context of events may also be encoded automatically. This is the information that enables an organism to orientate in space and time. Without memory for spatial–temporal information the smooth running of natural behaviour would be disrupted, for such behaviour requires that familiar contexts be recognized and responded to unconsciously. Errors in this unconscious processing of context can lead to the type of absent–minded behaviour John Sloboda described in Chapter 2. Encoding and subsequent recognition of spatial–temporal context is also important for that sense of familiarity which Korsakoff patients so tragically lack. Even the supposedly normal amongst us don't feel certain of having recognized a face unless we can 'place' it, identifying both the location and the occasion when we encountered it before.

In contrast to automatic memorization and recognition, which are constant and unobtrusive aspects of the natural world, effortful memory is something of an oddity. It is the characteristic of an animal that acts *on* its environment as well as *in* it. Effortful memory calls for the invention of artificial techniques to supplement the inborn skills of automatic encoding. Such techniques are the principal concern of this and the three following chapters.

More Memory Jargon

Harry Lorayne is a *mnemonist* (with the first *m* silent) and the techniques he uses to achieve his amazing feats are called *mnemonics*. The word mnemonic refers to any device for aiding memory; a common example in our culture is the ditty, 'Thirty days has September, etc.', which makes use of the mnemonic properties of rhyme and rhythm. All of us are mnemonists in various ways but few of us can match the professionals like Lorayne.

K., on the other hand, is an *amnesic* (with the m sounded). He suffers from *amnesia*, the blanket term for all kinds of memory loss. Everyone suffers to a greater or lesser degree from *infantile amnesia*, the inability to remember the early years of life, but the term amnesic is reserved for those with an abnormal pattern of memory loss. There are two major categories of amnesia. In *retrograde amnesia*, events from before the relevant trauma, or damage, are not remembered. In *anterograde amnesia*, it is memory for events following the trauma that is deficient. Frequently both kinds of amnesia co-exist but in K., as in most Korsakoff patients, the anterograde loss is much worse than the retrograde (Kolb and Whishaw, 1985). K. can remember a great deal from before he sustained brain damage but rather little of what has happened to him and the world since.

This typical pattern of loss leads to further distinctions. Many psychologists think of memory as taking place in three stages. New information must be input, or *encoded*, into memory, it must then be stored over some *retention* interval and, finally, to be of any use, it must be subject to *retrieval* when required. In cases of amnesia it is possible to ask at which of the three stages a deficit occurs. Since K. continues to be able to retain and retrieve memories for distant events it would seem that it is in the encoding of new information that Korsakoff patients are deficient. The notion of encoding will be elaborated as this chapter proceeds, but a further distinction must be made in connection with the hypothesis that anterograde amnesia results from an encoding deficit.

If K. is read half a dozen words he can repeat them back in normal fashion, yet five minutes later he will recall none of them, nor be able to remember the fact that any words were read to him. His memory over the very short term is unimpaired but it then decays drastically. Like the protagonist of Kafka's novel, *The Castle*, K. is able to make sense of the present moment but he is cut off from the longer term continuity and pattern of events. This observation brings us to the distinction psychologists make between *short-term memory* (STM) and *long-term memory* (LTM). Neither of these two terms can be defined with precision but retrieval or recognition of information more than a few minutes after it is presented is generally taken as evidence of LTM storage. The encoding deficit hypothesis proposes that although K. can encode information into STM, he is deficient at coding into LTM. This is in contrast to Lorayne who is highly efficient at encoding into LTM, at least where names are concerned.

The Nature of Short-Term Memory

Suppose you witness two men rush out of a bank, jump into a car, and race away at a furious speed. If you are quick-witted, you may take a mental note of their car registration number. But what do you do then? If you do not find a way of committing the number to some more durable form of storage, you are either going to have to keep attending to it and repeating it, or else forget it. The registration number is in short-term memory, which roughly corresponds to what we are thinking about, or are consciously aware of, at any particular moment. As traditionally conceived, STM has a limited capacity, it can hold only a fixed number of items, or chunks, at a time. Miller (1956) estimated this capacity for adults at seven $\pm$ two chunks, where the nature of a chunk depends on the familiarity of the individual with the material. For a non-reader of English F–R–I–E–N–D–S might be seven chunks, where for a skilled reader of English it would only be one (see Chapter 2).

The usual method of measuring STM is to find the greatest number of words, letters, or digits that a subject can recall accurately on fifty percent of trials. This number is called a person's memory span. Because most adults have a span close to seven items, STM tends to be thought of as some kind of box with a fixed number of slots. However, children of three have a measured capacity of only three items, the adult level not being reached until the age of about twelve. Does this mean that the number of slots in STM increases with age? Almost certainly it does not. The increase in span with age precisely parallels the increase in the rate at which children are able to speak rapidly (Hulme, Thompson, Muir and Lawrence, 1984). This suggests that a span test does not measure the number of slots in a hypothetical storage space but instead gauges people's ability at doing the test. For most people, their level of ability on span tests is in fact determined by their skill at speaking fast and hence by their maximum rate of subvocal rehearsal. (In Chapter 7 some other means by which individuals can achieve very large spans are described.)

The above point highlights a major obstacle to the investigation of cognitive abilities. Every test designed to detect and gauge a specific ability challenges the subject to develop new cognitive skills so as to boost performance on that test, often by using means unanticipated by the experimenter. Conversely, poor performance may reflect not lack of ability but, as will become apparent in Chapter 6, lack of practice at selecting and putting into effect the best strategy for tackling the test.

Working Memory

It should by now be clear that the exact nature of STM is problematic. Nobody knows quite how best it should be characterized, yet the existence of a small-capacity short term store is hard to deny. You should be able to appreciate this for yourself if you think how you would execute in your head a computation, like multiplying 36×36. A whole series of operations has to be carried our, including the storing and subsequent utilization of intermediate results. Without a short-term store of some sort, how could that be possible? And if the store did not have limited capacity why should keeping track of your place in a calculation become so difficult when multiplying large numbers? Nor is it only in mental arithmetic that short term storage requirements are encountered. All kinds of mundane cognitive activities involve short-term storage of information.

Because of the sorts of difficulty outlined above, Baddeley and Hitch (1974; Hitch, 1980) argued the STM must be more complex than had previously been supposed. Rather than a unitary store, they proposed that there must be a short term memory *system* with several components. They named this system, *Working Memory*. On the basis of experiments for which there is not the space to describe here, they decided that there are at least four components of working memory. These include a speech output system, which plays a major role in performance on tests of the span of short-term memory; an auditory input system that keeps a record of recently heard speech, so that the start of a sentence is still available by the time its end arrives; a visual input system for maintaining visual impressions in the short term; and a control system that makes use of the other components. The working memory model is obviously rather complicated and psychologists are still evaluating it. The important point in this context is that, whatever the complexities involved, there does seem to be some kind of system for the short term storage of information.

The Nature of Long-Term Memory

Given that STM turns out to be a non-unitary entity, it should come as no surprise that the same seems to be true of long-term memory (LTM). Indeed, we have already seen that for K. the ability to learn, and therefore remember, how to execute a motor task has been dissociated from memory of having encountered the task before. Our discussion of the sub-classifications of LTM can start from this observation.

Motor Memory

Motor memory underlies all types of motor skills from typing to house painting. Its nature and organization have been most fully investigated in terms of the acquisition of motor skills, like those described in Chapter 2. The most striking feature of motor memory is its durability. Skills like riding a bike or driving a car once learnt seem not to be forgotten. For this reason, motor memory has sometimes been thought to differ fundamentally from other kinds of long-term memory. Yet the thing to notice about most motor skills is that they become heavily practised, or overlearnt, and this is really the reason they are so resistant to forgetting.

When a person finally masters riding a bike or driving a car, they do not usually then abstain from the activity. Rather they engage in it repeatedly, so that it becomes overlearnt. The same is not always true of more cognitive types of learning. In this case, material is often rehearsed up to some criterion, such as the feeling that it can be trotted out in the next day's exam, and thereafter dismissed from mind. When some months later it is required once more, it turns out to be unavailable. But this does not have to be the fate of cognitive material. Overlearning can take place for cognitive skills as well as for motor skills. Overlearnt cognitive skills like understanding speech, recognizing the identity of human faces, or doing long multiplication sums do not get forgotten.

Because overlearnt cognitive and motor skills share the features of durability, chunking, fluency and so on, they can be grouped together as examples of *procedural* knowledge, or procedural memory (Ericsson, 1985). Both are examples of *remembering how* rather than *remembering that*. In this respect they contrast with the next type of long-term storage to be considered.

Episodic Memory

The term 'episodic memory' was introduced by Tulving (1972, 1984) to refer to memory for events, or episodes, in daily life. This is an autobiographical memory in the sense that it is the record of our own life and the things of which we have been aware. In K.'s case it would seem that no – or only a few – additions to this record have been possible since brain damage occurred. Episodic memory is what most people probably mean by having a 'good/bad' memory, or what they think of when coming across the term LTM. When earlier it was stated that Lorayne is especially skilled at encoding information into LTM, it was episodic LTM that was being referred to.

A characteristic of episodic memory is that information, whether encoded automatically or effortfully, is stored in terms of spatial–temporal context. This was remarked on earlier. Another characteristic of the information in episodic memory is that it is generally encoded in terms of its meaning rather than of its surface form. The record of an episode during the day will be in terms of the gist of what was said (or not said), it will not be equivalent to a tape recording. This is in contradistinction to STM, where accurate retention is judged in terms of *verbatim* recall. In fact, information in episodic memory is often *reconstructed* more than recalled. Accounts of past events are put together on the basis of how they were interpreted at the time, how they may since have come to be interpreted, and using for a framework the 'scripts' we all have for how familiar events usually proceed. This is not to deny that people do on occasions produce faithful renditions of poems or speeches, which of course they do. But such feats are built up through extensive practice and are exercises in procedural memory. As K.'s mirror drawing demonstrates, procedural and episodic memories can be quite separate from one another.

Semantic Memory

Tulving (1972) contrasted episodic memory with semantic memory. Where episodic memory is personal and contextual in nature, semantic memory is conceptual and abstract. It holds a great many kinds of information in varying kinds of relationships: the meaning of words, the rules of grammar, empirical facts, like that water finds it own level, the 'scripts' referred to above, the names of the months in the year, and so on.

All uses of episodic memory involve a semantic component, and performance on an episodic task is determined by the richness of the semantic structures for the relevant domain of knowledge (Ericsson, 1985). To put it simply, most people find a list of meaningful words easier to remember than a list of nonsense words like MAFER, just as chess masters remember real-game configurations of pieces better than random configurations (Chapter 2). Nevertheless, episodic and semantic memories can become dissociated, as they are in both retrograde and anterograde amnesia. In K.'s case, he remembers how to talk and think, which must involve semantic memory, yet his episodic memory is grossly deficient.

Baddeley (1984) has questioned the way the distinction between episodic and semantic memories is made. He argues that the information in semantic memory is *procedural* knowledge on which cognitive skills like talking, listening, and thinking are based. Procedural knowledge may have the form of production rules – as described in Chapter 2 – which cannot be stated in words by the individual concerned. By contrast, Baddeley claims that the information in episodic memory is *declarative* knowledge. Declarative knowledge is knowledge that can be verbalized, it is knowledge *that* so and so is the case rather than knowledge of *how to do* something. At present, it is not clear whether LTM is best thought of as having three components, motor, semantic, and episodic memories, or as being dichotomized into procedural and declarative memories.

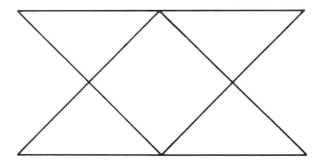

Figure 5:2   An ambiguous figure.

Encoding and Retrieval

The encoding of information refers to the form in which it is retained. The influence of encoding on subsequent memory is readily demonstrated by examining Figure 5:2, then turning the page to Figure 5:3. Recognition of the shape in 5:3A tends to be much faster than of the shape in 5:3B. Although both shapes were present in the original, 5:3A is more comparable with the usual encoding, or interpretation, of 5:2. As noted earlier, encoding of words in STM tends to be acoustic, while in episodic LTM it tends to be in terms of meaning, semantic coding. Craik and Lockhart (1972) theorized that perhaps there was no difference between STM and LTM except in the forms of encoding used. They hypothesized that the durability of memory for events or words or faces was a function of the 'depth of processing' the items originally received, and that an acoustic code was less deep than a semantic one. Craik and Tulving (1975) questioned subjects about (a) the physical structure of a word ('Is it in capitals?'), (b) the sound of a word ('Does it rhyme with BAIT?'), or (c) the meaning of the word ('Would it fit the sentence: "He met a   in the street?"'). Subjects were then given an unanticipated memory test for all the words they had seen, and performance improved across the three conditions in accordance with the supposed depth of processing, thus supporting the original hypothesis (see Chapter 12).

Craik and Tulving (1975) also showed that if all presented words were semantically encoded then recall depended on the elaborateness of that coding. When subjects were asked to judge whether the word WATCH fitted the elaborate sentence, 'The old man hobbled across the room and dropped the valuable — ', they remembered it better than when asked if WATCH fitted the less elaborate sentence, 'He dropped the — '. The wider the network of associations within which the word is embedded at encoding, the better the memory for it. So both depth and elaboration are important.

Memory performance, however, depends on more than encoding. It also depends on the context of retrieval, on how many retrieval cues are available to prompt memory. Smith (1979) presented subjects with lists of words and then tested for recall a day later in either the same or a different room. Recall was much better in the same room, showing the importance of external cues (see Chapter 2). Internal cues are also important. Eich (1980) discusses evidence to show that retrieval is more successful when mood or state (e.g. of intoxication) is the same as it was at encoding. What is more, even the value of deeper processing is dependent on the type of memory test employed. Morris, Bransford and Franks (1977) replicated the Craik and Tulving finding that deeper processing gave better performance on a straightforward recognition test. However, on a test in which subjects had to choose words that rhymed with previously presented words, best results were obtained when the original encoding had been in terms of rhyme and not of meaning.

To summarize: what, ultimately, will be the optimum encoding for information depends upon what it is to be used for, and therefore upon the conditions under which it is to be retrieved. Nevertheless, it is broadly true that deeper and more elaborate coding is liable to be the most effective. We can see how this generalization is supported in the case of Harry Lorayne's amazing memory for names.

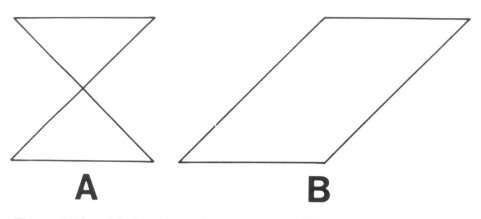

Figures 5:3A and 5:3B   Alternative components of Figure 5:2.

A System for Remembering Names

In one of his books (Lorayne and Lucas, 1974) Lorayne spells out in detail his system for remembering names. Like many mnemonic systems, it relies upon the use of visual imagery and it can be broken down into stages (see Chapter 8). The initial stage is straightforward enough, having to do with ensuring that the name you want to remember is heard in the first place. Very often the name of someone to whom you have just been introduced is not forgotten, rather it was never registered at all. So the first golden rule is to make sure that you attend to and correctly perceive the name, even if that means asking that it be repeated, or repeating it yourself, as in, 'Nice to meet you, Mr *Harrington*'.

The second stage is to *substitute* a similar sounding and easily imageable word(s) for the person's name. So Harrington could become Herring-ton. Then, in the third stage, it is necessary to examine the person's face and pick out its most distinctive feature, large ears for example. Finally, in the fourth stage, the selected feature must be linked to the substitute word(s) with as vivid an image as possible. In this instance you might image a shoal of enormous herrings, each with 1–TON printed on its flank, swimming in one of Mr Harrington's ears and out the other. Having done this, then the next time you encounter Mr Harrington and again notice his ears the image will come to mind, and you will be able to recall his name.

Lorayne's is a simple system that anyone can make use of. To manipulate the system effectively, however, requires more than a cursory acquaintance with its component stages. The key here, as elsewhere, is to engage in extensive practice. Lorayne's book lists substitute words for nearly six hundred of the most common names in America. If the pairings are committed to memory, so that each name immediately elicits its associated substitute, then one stage in the process will have been automated. Similarly, experience will facilitate the generation of images to link substitute words with facial features.

Lorayne's system for remembering names affords a particularly pertinent example of memory skill. First, the system itself is simple and easily understood. Second, the need to remember names is a common one and yet few of us ever reflect on the task demands and how they can be met. Third, not only is remembering names a cognitive skill, it is a socially important cognitive skill. It has been said that one recent American president owed his electoral success less to political acumen than to the loyalty he inspired by recalling the names of humble party workers. Here then is a simple and important memory skill at which nearly everyone can improve their performance. Sadly, it is also one at which our patient, K., is strikingly deficient.

Anterograde Amnesia

A variety of approaches have been taken to the explanation of anterograde amnesia. Many of these include the proposal that there is a deficit in the encoding abilities of amnesic patients (Mayes and Meudell, 1983; Squire and Cohen, 1984). At various times it has been claimed that amnesic patients cannot encode at all into episodic (or declarative) memory, that they encode only at shallow and not at deep levels, and that they encode events but not their spatial–temporal contexts. Evidence has been produced for and against all of these positions. Part of the difficulty in deciding between them is that the performance of patients like K. is highly dependent on the task they are given, and also on the instructions as to how it should be tackled. For example, Cermak, Butters and Moreines (1974) found evidence that patients given short lists of words to remember failed to encode semantically, i.e. at a deep level. Yet Winocur, Kinsbourne and Moscovitch (1981) discovered with a similar task that patients *could* encode semantic information when instruction emphasized the importance of doing so. It seems that the limits on amnesic performance are not fixed. There does not appear to be an absolute loss of any particular encoding ability.

In the face of this confusing pattern of data, Hirst and Volpe (1984) have hypothesized that what is disrupted in amnesics such as K. is automaticity of encoding. Information that is normally encoded automatically, such as spatial–temporal context, comes to require effort if it is to be retained. But expenditure of effort in this direction can only be at the cost of other kinds of information that might normally be effortfully encoded. What gets encoded, and so remembered, depends on where effort is placed. A normal subject presented with an array of pictures of simple objects can attend to remembering the identity of the objects, their spatial locations will be recorded automatically. For amnesics, however, this is not the case (Hirst and Volpe, 1984). It seems that amnesics have to make a choice as to how effort should be distributed across the different kinds of information that might be remembered.

This suggestion by Hirst and Volpe remains very much a hypothesis that waits to be assessed in the light of further investigations. For the very reason that automatic processes are not open to conscious inspection, it may be hard for the reader to envisage how such processes could fail in a subject who was attending to the experimental material. Some insight into how this might happen may be gained from the next chapter in which we will examine the development of mnemonic skills. Some of these can become so highly automated that it may take us by surprise to discover that not everyone possesses them.

Summary

A great deal of information has been covered in this chapter. The notions of automatic and effortful memory skills have been explored with reference to the mnemonic accomplishments and failings of Lorayne, the mnemonist, and K., the amnesic. Some of the terminology and distinctions employed in the study of memory were also introduced. Special attention has been given to the varieties of short-term and long-term storage that are recognized by psychologists, and also to the importance of encoding variables and retrieval factors for memory performance in different circumstances.

FURTHER READING

WINGFIELD, A. and BYRNES, D. C. (1981) *The Psychology of Human Memory*. New York: Academic Press.

Gives good coverage of the experimental investigation of memory.

NEISSER, U. (ed.) (1982) *Memory observed*. San Francisco: W. H. Freeman and Company.

An interesting selection of papers concerned with memory in natural contexts.

CHAPTER 6

ACQUIRING MEMORY SKILLS

Angus Gellatly

Memory: What Develops?

Although young children are sometimes credited with exceptional ability on certain types of memory test – see below – it is generally the case that memory improves as a child grows towards adulthood. We can ask, why should that be? What is it that tends to improve with increasing age?

This question was posed by psychologist John Flavell in 1971 when he convened a symposium with the title: 'What is memory development the development of?' In brief, the answer that emerged from the symposium was that memory development is part and parcel of general cognitive development. There are, of course, specialized memory techniques (*strategies*) but memory development entails more than just the acquisition of these. Memory cannot be divorced from thinking and understanding, from knowledge about the physical and social worlds and about one's ability to act in these worlds. Memory development is both dependent upon, and also feeds back into, development in other areas of cognition. It reflects the child's growing control over the direction of her attention, her dawning awareness of herself as a social actor, and her increasing grasp of the importance of planning for active memorization.

Flavell's question and the terms in which it was answered have shaped much of the subsequent research on memory in children (Chi, 1983). In large part, this chapter will be given over to expanding upon the roles played in memory development by strategies, knowledge, and understanding of one's own mnemonic abilities. Before proceeding further, however, it will be as well to consider some very basic memory process with which Flavell's symposiasts were little concerned. Their interest centred on the active memorizations of children who have already acquired language. Yet these are relatively sophisticated achievements which have their origin in non-linguistic potentialities that can be attributed to other animals beside humans. The phenomena of associative learning such as *conditioning* and *habituation* are of this nature. They can be observed even in cases where the term 'memory' scarcely seems applicable. The point to be taken is that in both evolution and in individual development memory develops from the simple to the complex. In its simpler forms memory is passive and automatic. Increasing complexity comes with the intervention of intention and effort, as noted by Flavell (1971). To begin this chapter, however, we can start by looking at some of the least intentional examples of remembering.

Habituation

Habituation is a term used to denote an organism's loss of responsiveness to a repeatedly, or continuously, presented stimulus. For example, placing an unfamiliar object in a mouse's cage can elicit fear and avoidance responses, yet within a short while the mouse will habituate to the object and show no overt response to it. At a cellular level, repeated electrical stimulation of a single neuron can lead to diminished responsiveness to further stimulation (Kandel, 1976). Such cases of cellular habituation may be explained in terms of altered cell biochemistry, and probably will not attract the label 'memory'. At the level of whole animals, however, habituation is usually defined in terms of loss of interest in, or attention to, a repeated auditory or visual stimulus. The effect is generally explained with reference to the establishment of some internal representation of the stimulus that allows unconscious recognition on later trials, and here the term 'memory' seems called for.

The technique of selective looking is often used to demonstrate habituation in infants. The infant is first allowed to view a pattern, such as a bull's-eye, for some extended period. Then, after a delay, the same bull's-eye is presented alongside a new pattern, such as a checkerboard, and a count kept of how long each stimulus is fixated. It has been shown in studies like this that infants as young as one to four days old exhibit a selective preference for a novel over a previously seen stimulus (Kail, 1984). Even newborns, then, can have memories lasting over the short time spans typical of selective looking experiments, and other studies have indicated that effects lasting over hours or days can be observed in infants at least as young as two months. It should be noted, however, that although this simple and passive form of memory *can* be discerned in the very young, the effect becomes more noticeable with increasing age.

Conditioning

Classical conditioning refers to the way in which a natural response to one stimulus can come to be associated with a second, neutral stimulus, which predicts the arrival of the first. The most famous example is of Pavlov's dogs, which learnt to salivate to a bell that preceded their being given food. Can similar effects be obtained with infants? At times it has been thought that infants aged below six months had a deficit in classical conditioning, held to be

due to cortical immaturity. In the last twenty years, however, it has been shown
that under properly controlled circumstances classical conditioning of the infant
is little different from that of the adult (Rovee-Collier and Lipsitt, 1982). So
once again the potential for passive memory is seen to be inherent in the very
young.

A more active form of learning and memory is that involved in *instrumental
conditioning*. This term refers to the fact that if an animal is rewarded for some
action, then that action is likely to be repeated. In this case the most famous
example is provided by Skinner's rats, which learnt to press a lever to obtain a
food reward. Instrumental conditioning is the basis for most animal training and
at least some human learning, but is it discernible in newborn infants? Again,
the answer is yes. Siqueland and Lipsitt (1966) were able to condition head
turning in two to four day old infants using a dextrose solution as the reward.
Rovee-Collier and her colleagues (cited in Kail, 1984) were able to increase the
frequency of leg kicking in infants by contingently rewarding kicks with the
movement of a mobile attached to the leg by a ribbon (see Figure 6:1). Two
month olds 'remembered' this contingency for three days, and three month olds
did so for eight days.

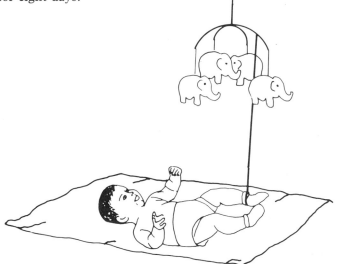

Figure 6:1   The arrangement for conditioned leg kicking. (After Kail, 1984.)

To conclude this section: infants are capable of more than one kind of learning
from very soon after birth, and therefore they must come equipped with the
potential for simple forms of memory. However, in all three cases we have
examined – habituation,   classical   conditioning,   and   instrumental
conditioning – memorization has been unintentional on the part of the infants.
Even in the case of instrumental learning, where there appears to be an intention
to gain the renewal of nutrient or of movement of the mobile, there seems to be

no intentional memorizing. The child does not *choose* to remember that leg kicking can produce movement of the mobile. The memory is a by-product of trying to produce movement. It is in progressing from passive and automatic to effortful and intentional memorizing that infants, like adults, encounter difficulties.

Strategies of Rehearsal and Categorization

Suppose you were shown a list of nameable and categorizable items, say four animals, four foods, and four colours, and told that you would be asked to recall them within a few seconds. You would almost certainly do two things in that time. You would repeat the items to yourself, and in doing so you would group them according to their categories. Rehearsal and categorization are such obvious and automatic mnemonic strategies that you might almost feel they should not count as intentional strategies at all. In that case you may be surprised to learn that young children in our culture, and much older people in some other cultures, do not make spontaneous use of rehearsal and categorization.

Flavell, Beach and Chinsky (1966) used lip reading to index rehearsal in a task requiring the recall of pictures. They found that 10 per cent of five year olds, 60 per cent of seven year olds, and 85 per cent of ten year olds engaged in rehearsal. Later studies further demonstrated that such failure to utilize rehearsal need not imply inability to profit from it. Six and seven year olds who do not show spontaneous rehearsal can be trained to follow the strategy and as a result their recall performance rises to the level of same-age spontaneous rehearsers. Although perfectly able to use the strategy, the non-spontaneous rehearsers are, however, inclined to drop it when no longer receiving encouragement from an experimenter. By failing to make use of an available strategy when it is appropriate, they exhibit what is known as a 'production deficiency'.

Other experiments show that even when young children do produce spontaneous rehearsal they are not very good at it (production inefficiency). With non-categorizable items there is a tendency to repeat only a single word at a time rather than to chant successions of words that could become rhythmically linked to one another (Ornstein, Naus and Stone, 1977). It is interesting, too, that Korsakoff patients also show inefficient rehearsal of this sort.

When pictures of categorizable pictures are used as stimuli to be remembered, a similar pattern is observed of production deficiency followed by production inefficiency. Children below the age of ten have little tendency to group the items into categories while studying them for later recall, (Moely, Olson, Halwes and Flavell, 1969). In addition, when provided with retrieval cues similar to category names, younger children do not use them efficiently to organize recall (Kobasigawa, 1974). Whereas eleven year olds try to recall all the members of one category before moving on to the next, six and eight years olds tend to recall only a single category member before moving on. The younger children know to which categories the items belong but *they do not know how to utilize their knowledge* so as to improve performance on the memory task.

All of the above might be taken to suggest that failure to employ mnemonic strategies is largely a matter of motivation. After all, most of us know that taking notes can help with remembering the content of a book we are studying, but we do not always bother to take them. In a like manner, some children may not be motivated to excel at a psychologist's meaningless recall task.

Although this is a possible explanation of production deficiencies and inefficiencies, there are a number of reasons why it probably does not hold in the majority of cases. First, many young children appear keen to do well on the tasks they are set. Second, even financial inducements produce little improvement in performance. Third, there is an alternative explanation that will account for cultural as well as age differences in memory skill.

Cultural Differences in Memory Performance

All the experiments referred to in the last section investigated the performance of children brought up in a Western culture. Studies have also been made of the recall of categorizable lists by unschooled and non-literate people of the Kpelle tribe in West Africa (Cole and Scribner, 1974). In these studies it was found that recall was poor and little use was made of categorization. There was no sign of the dramatic improvement with age typical of Western subjects, Kpelle adults performing little better than young children of either culture.

That even adult Kpelle make little use of categorization in recall is a particularly salutary discovery. In our culture categorization is taken to be such an obvious way of going about remembering things that failure to group items automatically into categories is sometimes interpreted as evidence of brain damage (Goodglass and Kaplan, 1979). Korsakoff patients exhibit precisely this deficit (Hirst and Volpe, 1984). Yet an altogether different explanation is required to account for why the Kpelle do not show spontaneous categorization in recall.

The answer to the puzzle has been summarized by Hunter (1985). In line with Cole and Scribner, he argues that people develop the mnemonic skills that are useful in their own cultures, and thus in their everyday lives. Recall for its own sake of a set of arbitrary items is the kind of task Western-educated people meet repeatedly in school. As a result, Western-educated people develop the appropriate strategies of rehearsal and categorization to the point where these become automatic. The same is not true in the case of the Kpelle. On the other hand, storytelling is a much practised art in Kpelle culture and the people can be expected to have proficient storytelling skills. When Cole and Scribner embedded to-be-remembered words in a story, rather than presenting them as an isolated list, the Kpelle were able to recall at a high level and also recalled items by category. It can be seen that unschooled people are able to recall strings of words and to make use of category information, but in different circumstances from those in which schooled people do the same.

Another cross-cultural study of memory, reported by Kearins (1981), was carried out with desert-living aboriginal children and city reared white children. In this experiment, a child spent 30 seconds viewing a five by four array of squares on which were 20 simple objects and then, when the objects had been disarrayed, the child was required to place them back in their original positions. At all ages from six to 16, and with various types of objects, the performance of aboriginal children was markedly superior. But not only did the aboriginal children replace more items correctly, they also approached the task in a different manner. White children tried to remember the positions of the objects by rehearsing their names in order; when allowed to start reconstructing the array they began in great haste, as if afraid they might quickly forget the relevant information; and after placing an object on the board they frequently changed its position. Aboriginal children, by contrast, did not engage in verbal rehearsal, were in no hurry to start reconstruction of the array, and once they had placed an object in a square very rarely changed its position. Kearins proposed that, unlike the white children who sought to apply a verbal strategy, the aboriginal children relied on a visuo-spatial strategy.

For present purposes, two points from the Kearins study are of particular relevance. First, as stated earlier, the tendency automatically to adopt a strategy of verbal rehearsal is not universal, nor does it always confer an advantage. Second, memory strategies we don't understand are much more intriguing than those we use readily ourselves. How the aboriginal children fare so well on Kearins' task is not well understood and so their ability appears quite remarkable. It can be surmised, however, that the Kpelle might be equally impressed by the ability of Western-educated individuals to recall relatively large numbers of categorizable words for an isolated list, especially if rehearsal was conducted silently and without lip movements. The message is that people develop those mnemonic skills in which they are drilled by the everyday life of their culture.

The Concept of Metamemory

The last two sections have stressed the importance of strategies of memorization to adequate performance on a number of laboratory tasks. It has been found that young children, not having yet mastered these skills, tend to perform poorly on the tasks. Yet it would be a mistake to exaggerate the failings of the very young. As Kail (1984) remarks, pre-school children frequently exhibit excellent memory for events in their own lives. And many parents have experience of the child who insistently remembers facts and remarks in socially awkward circumstances. So why should there be this discrepancy between the young child's memory for naturally occurring episodes and for items presented in experiments?

Kail points out that four year olds score highly on tests of recognition even though their performance on recall tests is appalling. It may well be that many of the naturalistic settings in which young children exhibit their memory capabilities involve recognition, as when the child points out a previously-visited building or part of town. Even when recall is involved – as in, 'You *did* say Mrs Smith drinks' asserted in the presence of Mrs Smith – there may be multiple cues in the physical and social context to elicit the recall. What these suppositions are intended to suggest is that when young children demonstrate good recollection, it is likely to be passive in nature. Most frequently, memories happen to the child. When, on the other hand, the child is required to store or retrieve information intentionally performance will be poor (Flavell, 1985).

If this argument is accepted, then the discrepancy between laboratory results and daily experience is accounted for. At the same time, the question still remains as to why young children are so poor at intentional remembering. We know that they do not make spontaneous use of basic strategies, but also that they *can* do so if instructed appropriately. So why do they show production deficiencies?

The answer proposed by Flavell was that the young child is deficient in *metamemory*. Metamemory means knowledge about anything to do with memory. It refers to our personal knowledge of how remembering works in various circumstances. Even four and five year olds have some grasp of metamemory. They understand the difference between guessing and remembering (Johnson and Wellman, 1980), and they know about using external memory-aids, such as leaving an object you want to take with you in a visible place (Kreutzer, Leonard and Flavell, 1975). Yet, not surprisingly, young children are lacking in many aspects of metamemory. They are particularly bad at predicting the difficulty of any but the simplest of memory tasks. Like the Kpelle, the four year old has little experience of recalling arbitrary strings of words and so does not know how beneficial rehearsal and categorization can be. This lack of metamemory, the ability to diagnose the mnemonic requirements of different tasks, is a cause of production deficiencies. It can lead in some cases to bizarre discrepancies. Thus Istomina (1982) found that children could recall more items as part of a game of shopping than when asked simply to recall items as an isolated activity. Shopping was something the children understood and it automatically elicited attempts to remember. The bare recall task, however, was strange and purposeless to the children. It did not elicit automatic rehearsal, and because the children knew little about the function of rehearsal and the requirements of recall tasks, they could not arrive at the strategy by conscious thought.

Metamemory development probably continues throughout life, and we ought to be able to feel some sympathy for the child facing a recall test. Given a week to do so, few adults would know how to set about learning the part of Hamlet.

Yet actors can manage feats of this kind; as a result of experience they have discovered the mnemonic requirements of learning parts, they have the necessary strategies and metamemory.

The Nature of Metamemory

Metamemory is a complex area of study in its own right and only the briefest outline of it can be presented here. Flavell (1977) distinguishes two main categories of metamemory. One of them is *sensitivity* to the mnemonic requirements of different activities. The child has to learn that for items to be recalled later it is necessary to put effort into memorizing them. The second category is *knowledge of your own abilities*, how they function in different tasks, what strategies you use most efficiently. In this category is the ability to monitor your own experience, to know that something not presently recallable is nonetheless available, or to foresee that although you can now repeat the instructions just given you, the same won't be possible in an hour's time. Metamemory includes being able to predict one's own future performance.

As remarked above, memories can happen to us because external cues dictate that they should. There can be cues to input, or encode, information and cues to retrieve it. The requirement to judge a face to be honest or otherwise acts as a cue to encoding; it results in improved recognition of the face later on, even though there was no intention to memorize it at input (Bower and Karlin, 1974). The smell of a particular perfume can act as a cue for unintended retrieval of all manner of memories.

All of us are at the mercy of memory cues in the physical and social environments, including the implicit demands of social roles ('remembering our places'!). These provide an external scaffolding for our experience. Mnemonic skill resides in the ability additionally to furnish our own internal and external scaffolding, and thereby to exercise some degree of intentional control over present and future experience. The acquisition of metamemory is part of this process.

Metamemory is intimately connected with the kinds of mnemonic demands that everyday life makes upon the individual. In a schooled culture one becomes sensitive to the memory requirements of school-type tasks and learns about one's own capabilities in respect of them (see Chapter 12). In a hunter-gatherer society, or a culture in which storytelling is a significant activity, rather different tasks will be explored. People develop the memory skills called for by their way of life and the metamemory corresponding to those skills. Current research is investigating how the development of metamemory can be accelerated by the provision of suitable learning experiences (Flavell, 1985).

Memory and Knowledge

Performance on memory tests is determined not only by memory strategies and metamemory. As with other skills, knowledge plays an important part (Chi, 1985). The point is strikingly made in an experiment of Piaget's in which children were asked to reproduce a picture they had been shown an hour earlier (See Fig. 6:3A). Children below the age of eight often fail to draw an accurate reproduction of the original. They make a number of characteristic errors, one of the most frequent of which is illustrated in Fig. 6:2B. Here the water level has been drawn parallel to the bottom of the bottle and therefore at a slant rather than horizontal. In trying to remember the appearance of the original the child reconstructs on the basis of inadequate knowledge of the physical world. However, if the same child is again asked to draw the picture some months later, the new reproduction may well be accurate. Memory has, paradoxically, *improved* over time. The improvement is due to an increased understanding and this, according to Piaget and Inhelder (1973), has resulted from the development of the cognitive structures said to underly the child's thought.

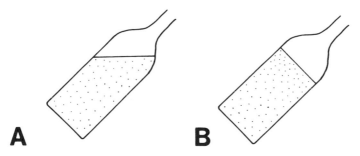

Figures 6:2   Original picture and one type of reproduction obtained in Piaget's experiment.

The water-level test is a good example of the role of reconstruction in memory. It is because reconstruction is involved that we sometimes misremember events, or find ourselves disagreeing with one another when recollecting recent episodes. Remembering is frequently a matter of piecing together partial information, of using logic and empirical knowledge to decide what *must* have been the case. As Luria (1973) remarked, the child initially learns to think by remembering, then later learns to remember by thinking.

Another experimental demonstration of the importance of knowledge for performance on memory tests was reported by Chi (1978). She used both a digit-recall test and the chess reconstruction task described in Chapter 2. A group of highly-educated adults with no knowledge of chess and a group of children who were skilled at chess acted as subjects. With digit recall the usual adult superiority was observed but when it came to reconstructing meaningful configurations of chess pieces the subjects who knew about the game, although younger, were much more proficient. This result is hardly surprising, it is precisely what would be expected on the basis of the work on expertise at chess. Nonetheless, it does provide a forceful example of the fact that knowledge is often the factor determining mnemonic ability. Adults generally do better than children on memory tests both because they have had more practice on such tests, and are therefore more skilful mnemonists, and also because they usually have more knowledge of the domain for which memory is being tested.

Special Memory Abilities in Children

It was remarked at the start of this chapter that young children are sometimes credited with exceptional ability on certain types of memory test. The subsequent discussion emphasized memorial deficiencies in the young, and how these are an inevitable concomitant of insufficient knowledge and practice. So how is the claim of exceptional ability to be squared with the picture that has been drawn of the child as an apprentice mnemonist? We will attempt to answer the question in this section by examining two tasks, both involving visuo-spatial memory and both said to show younger children in a more positive light.

The first task is not one invented by curious psychologists but is a game often enjoyed by adults as well as children. The game is variously known as pelmanism, pairs, concentration, or simply as the memory game. In a straightforward version of it, a pack of cards is shuffled and then spread face-down on a table. On each go, a player has to turn over two cards for all to see. If the cards form a pair the player keeps them and has another go, if not they are replaced face-down in position. The winner is the player who ends up with most pairs, and clearly the game calls for memory of which cards are in which locations. A number of authors (e.g. Meacham, 1972; Gardner, 1982; Wood 1983) have written that children often outperform adults on the game, but in no case has any data been presented to support the claim. To rectify this omission, studies were carried out in which five, seven, and nine year olds and university students played a solo version of the game, with time and number of goes taken as indices of performance (Gellatly, Jones and Best, 1988). The results showed that five and seven year olds fared markedly worse than the others, with no significant differences between the older groups. What was more, the poor showing of the five and seven years olds was seen to result from a failure to implement reliably a strategy typical of older children and adults. Of course, occasional five years olds are indeed good at the game, but the evidence shows that performance on the task improves with age in the same manner as it does on other memory tasks, and because of a similar kind of development. No special ability need be attributed to the very young in this case.

The second special ability said to be found in very young children – and sometimes cited as an explanation for the putative high performance at pelmanism (Gardner, 1982) – is that of *eidetic* imaging. An eidetic image is a particularly vivid and detailed memory image for a recently viewed picture or scene. Such images are experienced as being 'out there' rather than in the head and can be projected on to a wall or screen. They are described by the imager in the present not in the past tense, they can be visually scanned, and pairs of images can be superimposed to form a composite containing information not present in either alone (Haber, 1979). Eidetic imagery is almost non-existent in adults but is found in about 5 per cent of six to twelve year olds. Its nature is not well understood but it does seem to represent a genuine instance of young children exhibiting better memory than adults.

Although interesting in its own right, eidetic imagery is unlike the kinds of memory with which this chapter has been mostly concerned in that it is an incidental registration of information rather than an active and intentional form of memorization. Although its disappearance prior to adulthood remains something of a puzzle, the existence of eidetic imagery is not inconsistent with a view of memory development as the acquisition of intentional strategies of memorization, the growth of metamemory, and the accumulation of knowledge.

Conclusion

In this chapter we have examined the development of intentional memorization from its origins in passive memory. Emphasis has been given to the manner in which a way of life is associated with the acquisition of particular memory skills. Acquisition in this sense has been seen to be more or less fortuitous, the actual skills acquired simply following from the round of daily activities. In Chapters 7 and 8, we will examine how mnemonic skills can be developed through intentional coaching and practice.

FURTHER READING

HUNTER, I. M. L. (1985) 'Memory development: the cultural background'. In: J. A. Branthwaite and D. R. Rogers (Eds.) *Children Growing Up*. Milton Keynes: Open University Press.

A brief account of the cultural factors that influence memory development.

KAIL, R. (1984) *The Development of Memory in Children* (2nd edition). San Francisco: W. H. Freeman and Company.

A very readable survey of the experimental study of memory development.

CHAPTER 7

EXCEPTIONAL MEMORY SKILL

Ian M. L. Hunter

This chapter is about people who achieve remarkable feats of memory. The aim is to emphasize the role played in such feats by previously acquired knowledge and skill.

Consider a real example. An artist visits the Louvre Museum in Paris, inspects Holbein's portrait of Erasmus, and later makes from memory a close reproduction of the portrait. This feat is described by Boisbaudran (1911) whose book includes photographs of the original portrait and the reproduction. We may well comment that the artist 'has an amazing memory'. If, by this, we mean simply that his feat is uncommon and not achievable by most people, then our comment is correct. But if we mean that he is gifted by nature with a special faculty of visuo-spatial memory, then we imply something that goes far beyond the evidence and we ignore that, in fact, the artist has undergone prolonged training in the craft of examining pictures so as to be able to copy them from memory.

The general point is this: unusual feats of memory do not, of necessity, imply that the person is constitutionally abnormal, i.e., endowed by nature with a qualitatively special gift or faculty or aptitude. Such biologically-given gifts may exist, although their existence is difficult to establish with certainty. But two things are certain. First, extended practice can lead to truly astonishing memory skills. Second, people who accomplish unusual feats of memory have often had an unusual amount of previous, relevant practice.

In order to put flesh on the above general remarks, I shall focus on one investigation in which an American university student, Steve Faloon, became astonishingly expert in the digit-span memory task (see Chapter 5). The fullest account of this investigation is by Chase and Ericsson (1981) and the wider implications are elaborated by Chase and Ericsson (1982), Ericsson and Chase (1982), and Ericsson (1985).

Steve's Feat of Memory

Steve listens to a succession of digits read out at one per second. They have been selected at random, so he cannot know which digit will come next. He listens until 80 digits have been presented. Then he recites back all 80 digits. He makes no errors, gets the sequence correct, leaves none out.

This feat is clearly exceptional. When most normal adults tackle the digit-span task, the number of digits they can repeat back correctly is, on average, seven plus or minus two digits. It is also known, in broad terms, why the digit span is normally so small. We have two kinds of storage system in which we can hold information (see Chapter 5). One is short-term memory (STM) which is temporary and has very limited storage capacity. The other is long-term memory (LTM) which is more durable and has virtually unlimited storage capacity. When we perceive and attend to new information, we can keep it available for a very short time but then we lose it irretrievably unless we attend to it again, i.e. rehearse it in some way. If, for example, we look up a phone number, we can hold it by attentive rehearsal until we reach the phone, but if something distracts us, we lose the number. By contrast, if we commit the number to long-term memory, it is more durably available without needing constant attention. In the digit-span task, people normally rely heavily on STM and their severely limited span is mostly due to the small storage capacity of STM.

When we try to discover what lies behind someone's feat of memory, there are two important questions to explore. First, the social-biographical background, and, second, the processes used in carrying through the feat. The next two sections consider these issues as they relate to Steve's feat of memory.

Social and Biographical Background

Steve developed his feat of memory in the social setting of a psychological laboratory investigation, conducted in the late 1970s at Carnegie-Mellon University in the USA. Three people were involved: William Chase and Anders Ericsson, both experimental psychologists, and Steve Faloon who acted as subject. Steve was a student in his early twenties. He made high university grades but showed no abilities which were out of the usual for bright university students. He was, however, a keen long-distance runner. This gave him a striving, record-breaking attitude and also a knowledge of running times on which he was to capitalize in dealing with the digit-span task. To indicate his athletic prowess, he belonged to track and cross-country and marathon teams. He trained by running 10 to 13 miles a day and, for the previous nine years, he had competed in many long-distance events. His best events were the three mile, five mile, and marathon; and his best times in these events were respectively, 14 min 39 sec, 25 min 40 sec, and 2 hr 39 min 36 sec.

When the investigation started, the aim was to give Steve a couple of weeks of practice on the digit-span task and find what effect this had. As it turned out, practice had such interesting effects that all three collaborators were keen to continue. The investigation kept being extended until it ran for over two years. Throughout that time, Steve attended the laboratory for a one-hour session on two to five days per week.

In each session, the usual routine was to test Steve's digit span by the up-and-down method. He heard a list of random digits read at one per second, then tried to repeat the list. If he succeeded, the next list was longer by one digit: if he did not succeed, the next list was shorter by one digit. This method kept him working near the limits of his ability

Immediately after trying to recall a list, he was asked to talk about the procedures he had used. At the end of each one-hour session, he was asked to recall as much as he could about the lists given during that session. On some days, the usual routine was replaced by experimental sessions which explored aspects of his performance. The entire proceedings of this extended investigation were tape recorded.

Steve was not specifically coached in what to do but he was constantly striving to increase his digit span. Like an athlete in training, he met barriers to progress and tried ways of overcoming them. If a way worked, he stayed with it, gained mastery of it, and made headway until the next barrier presented. If a way did not work, he tried some other way. Thus, for him, the digit-span task was an exciting challenge and, as he gained experience with the task, new features opened out and the challenges became even richer and more absorbing. On top of this, he regularly reported details of his working and got informed comments from the experimenters who were greatly interested in these details and in his progress. In short, the laboratory investigation created a social setting which encouraged Steve to gain extended, creative experience in dealing with the digit-span memory task.

Steve's progress is charted in Figure 7:1 which shows that, in 215 practice sessions, his span increased from seven to 80. The indications were that, had practice continued, he would have made yet further progress. Digit span, it seems, can be increased indefinitely.

The key point of this section is that Steve's feat of memory arose in a social and biographical setting which encouraged him to gain unusually extended experience and practice of a kind relevant to the feat. The accomplishments which people acquire are typically those that are useful in their everyday life. For most people, a large digit span is useless and they have neither opportunity nor incentive to engage in activities which would lead to improvement. But imagine a social world in which record-breaking achievements in digit span are valued as highly as, say, record-breaking achievements in athletics. In such a setting, there is no doubt that large digit spans would be achieved by lots of

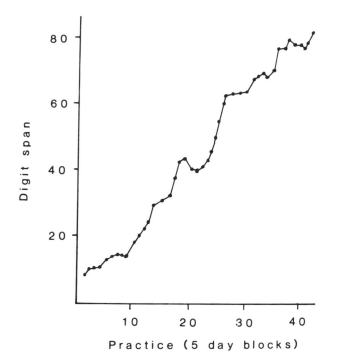

Figure 7:1   Improvement in Steve Faloon's digit span with extended practice. The 43 blocks of practice shown here represent about 215 hours of practice. Interspersed among these practice sessions are approximately 75 hours of experimental sessions (not shown). (After Chase and Ericsson, 1981.)

people. (Chase and Ericsson worked with a second subject, also a long-distance runner, who reached a digit span of 100 digits.) What is most exceptional about Steve's memory still is that he had the opportunity, motivation, and persistence to acquire it. He reminds us forcibly that human capabilities develop out of the interactions of individuals with environments that afford the opportunities and incentives needed to nurture the capabilities in question.

THE PROCESSES INVOLVED

During the investigation, Steve developed new ways of dealing with the task. This section sketches four key developments:

   (a) Meaningful encoding.
   (b) Structuring.
   (c) The greater role of long-term memory.
   (d) Speedup.

Notice, incidentally, that these four developments are essential ingredients of all known mnemonic systems, of which the best known is the Method of Loci (see Lorayne and Lucas, 1974; also Chapter 8).

Meaningful Encoding

At the outset, Steve dealt with the task in the same way most people do. He tried to hold the digit sequence phonemically, rehearsing until recall. He noticed occasional patterns, such as a run of ascending numbers, but he relied mostly on attentive rehearsal (STM) and achieved a span of seven. For the first four sessions, his span remained at seven. In Session 4, he commented at length about how he had reached his limit and no further improvement was possible.

Then in Session 5, his span jumped to ten and, for the first time, he reported meaningful encoding. To illustrate, consider 4131946273. He would treat the first four digits as a group and think of it as 'four thirteen point one, a mile time', that is, 4 min 13.1 sec, the time taken by some athlete to run a mile. He would then think of the second group of four digits as 'nine forty-six point two, a two-mile time'. To his delight, he found he could now remember a ten–digit list as two encoded four–digit groups with an extra two digits tacked on at the end.

In Session 5, then, Steve started treating groups of digits as numbers which were meaningful as running times. He went on to build a larger and larger repertoire of meaningful numbers – mostly running times but, later, people's ages and historical dates. He used these numbers to encode almost any presented sequence of three or four digits. His use of meaningful encoding became distinctly purposeful. In listening to incoming digits, he did not wait until four digits had come and then search for a meaningful encoding: on hearing the first digit, he started homing in on a possible encoding and, with each incoming digit, he narrowed the field of search until, with the arrival of the fourth digit, or shortly after, he had a suitable encoding.

Structuring

By Session 30, he was recalling 18 digits by encoding three four–digit groups and holding the final six digits as an uncoded group of two triplets. But now he met a barrier. When he increased the number of encoded groups from three to four, he could not hold the sequential order of the four groups. In Session 32, he broke this barrier when, for the first time, he grouped the groups. Let us call a group of groups a 'supergroup'. Consider his new technique for dealing with 20 digits. He thought of two four–digit groups as belonging to a supergroup; then two three–digit groups as belonging to a second supergroup; and then a final unencoded group of six digits.

In the following weeks he improved his use of the supergroup technique. He went on to use supergroups containing not two but three encoded groups. His span gradually increased to 40 digits. Now came another barrier. When he tried using supergroups containing not three but four encoded groups, he could not hold the sequential order of the four groups. In Session 109, he broke this barrier. He used supergroups containing only three encoded groups, and he introduced a new, higher-level grouping, which contained two supergroups.

For people not immersed in the details of Steve's performance, his use of supergroups and higher-order groups is perhaps difficult to grasp. But the general principle is simple. He was imposing a hierarchical structure on the list. Consider how, as an expert, he dealt with a presented list, and remember that he always knew how long each list would be.

Before he even heard the first digit, he decided the exact and complete structure he would impose. With a list of, say 30 digits, he might impose the structure represented in Figure 7:2. This has six four-digit groups combined into two supergroups, and an unencoded six digits at the end. As the digits came in, he fitted them into this predetermined structure. When he later recalled the list, he did so by systematically searching through the sturcture, using it to provide retrieval cues (see also Chapter 8).

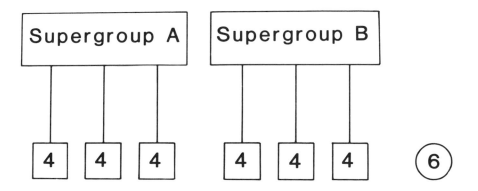

Figure 7:2   Representation of a list structure. Groups of four digits are combined into threes to form supergroups. The circle represents six uncoded digits.

By the end of the investigation, Steve was familiar with structures which could accommodate up to 80 digits. He used these structures adroitly. He could report on the structures and make schematic drawings of them. Furthermore, his structures were reflected in the pace at which he recalled lists. When recalling a list, he did not say the digits at one per second but in bursts of three or four digits with pauses of varying lengths between bursts. The bursts corresponded to the digit groups, and the lengths of pause to the list structure, e.g. he paused longer when crossing between supergroups than when crossing between groups within a supergroup.

Greater Role of LTM

Did Steve increase the storage capacity of STM? There is no clear evidence that he did. Essentially, he increased his digit span by acquiring resources of LTM which enabled him to side-step the persisting limitations of STM. As a novice, his digit span relied almost entirely on STM because he had no LTM resources applicable to the task. He built, through practice, LTM resources which could apply. As an expert, his digit span relied mainly on LTM, as is shown by the following two pieces of evidence.

First, at the end of each one-hour session, he tried to recall the lists presented in that session. As a novice, he could recall virtually nothing. As an expert, he could recall virtually everything. He could recite the lists presented. He could report again on how he had dealt with the lists, e.g. structures imposed, groups formed, encodings made. If given any four–digit group from the list, he could usually say how he had encoded it and where he had located it in the list structure, e.g. in the first or third or middle position in a supergroup. If asked to recall selected portions of the list, he could recall them without having to run through the list from the beginning. He used the list structure to range selectively over the list.

The second piece of evidence arose from what he did immediately after a list had been presented. As a novice, he lost no time in starting to recite the list back. As an expert, he waited for 30 seconds to 2 minutes before beginning to recite. During this pause, he was consolidating his grasp on the list, reviewing it, tidying up its details and structure.

The two pieces of evidence just mentioned showed that Steve the expert, committed presented lists to LTM. He did this by using the body of knowledge he had built during practice. This knowledge – of codes, structures, and techniques – was stored in LTM and he had it 'at his fingertips', available rapidly and without fumbling. He used this ready knowledge to side-step the limits of STM which, nevertheless, continued to impose restrictions on his performance. For example, Steve never encoded a group of more than five digits: he never constructed a supergroup containing more than four groups: he always worked in small segments and, as quickly as he could, he committed each segment to LTM and attended fully to the next segment of the ongoing task.

An important finding about the LTM resources on which Steve's expertise depended was that they were domain specific, i.e. they related only to the subject matter of digits and not to other subject matters. When, for example, he was given memory-span tasks involving randomly selected letters of the alphabet, his span was six letters – no more than normal. Clearly, Steve had not acquired a general-purpose 'super-power memory' applicable to any and all domains.

Speedup

Through practice, Steve got progressively faster at carrying out component processes. The process of encoding, for example, sped up dramatically and continued to speed up throughout the entire duration of the investigation. Such speedup is, of course, enormously beneficial because it allows the person to plan and execute more complex manoeuvres (see also Chapters 2 and 3).

Deliberate and Incidental Improvement

At the start of this chapter, I made two general points. First, extended practice can lead to exceptional memory skills. In other words, if we start with someone who shows no unusual memory abilities, then that person may, with practice, develop memory abilities that are distinctly out of the ordinary. This point is illustrated by Steve Faloon, and further examples are given by Ericsson and Chase (1982) and Ericsson (1985). Second, people who show unusual memory abilities have often had unusual amounts of previous, relevant practice. In other words, if we start with someone who shows exceptional memory ability, we often find that they have a background history of extended practice in the relevant domain. This section is concerned with this second point and, in particular, the distinction between deliberate and incidental memory improvement.

Steve's memory skills developed while he was deliberately trying to increase his memory span. In the course of pursuing this explicit goal, he acquired in LTM a repertoire of codes, structures and techniques which enabled him to increase his digit span. However, it can happen that people develop memory skills incidentally, as a byproduct of pursuing goals which are not aimed explicitly at memory improvement. Such incidental memory improvement is a feature of what can be called the 'memory effect of expertise', i.e. experts are good at learning and remembering material in the domain of their expertise.

There are many domains in which people may become expert, e.g. chess, bridge, music, law, entomology. People become expert in a domain by prolonged experiences with it: the material of the domain becomes meaningfully familiar. Now, suppose that we, as psychologists, select material from one domain and use it to test how well people can learn and remember this type of material. What do we find? People who are experts in that domain usually outperform people who are not experts.

For example, when experts in mental calculation are given digit-span tasks, they achieve spans that are two or three times larger than normal. Such experts have not deliberately practised with digit-span tasks. But, in the process of becoming expert in mental calculation, they have developed bodies of knowledge and skill which enable them, as a byproduct, to do well in digit-span tasks. To give specific examples, Hatano and Osawa (1983) tested the memory abilities of three people who had won the championship of the mental calculation division at the nation-wide abacus tournment in Japan. Given memory-span tasks involving letters of the alphabet, the three champions had spans of 5, 8, and 5. With memory-span tasks involving words (the names of fruit), their spans were 5, 9, and 5. But with memory-span tasks involving digits, their spans were 15, 16, and 16. There was no reason to suppose that they had large digit spans before they became experts in mental calculation.

The 'memory effect of expertise' can also work in reverse. Let us go back to the artist mentioned early in this chapter. He was one of many pupils trained by the French art educator Horace Lecoq de Boisbaudran. The pupils went through training aimed deliberately at becoming able to copy complex pictures from memory. Pupils were given experience and practice in decomposing pictures into familiar components and in using these components so as to reconstitute the pictures from memory. In pursuing this goal, pupils acquired knowledge and skill which they could subsequently employ when they turned to creative work in the pictorial domain. The long-term goal of artistic expertise was approached through the short-term goal of memory training in art.

The Case of S.

A somewhat different kind of memory expertise is provided by the case of S. V. Shereshevskii (usually referred to as S.), a Russian man whose exceptional memory abilities were studied by the Russian psychologist, Luria (1969). S. illustrates how challenging, and sometimes frustrating, it is to get clear what is involved in the case of someone who comes to notice on account of their exceptional memory. S. was almost thirty when Luria first met him. At that time, in the mid-1920s, S. was a newspaper reporter.

> Each morning the editor would meet with the staff and hand out assignments for the day – lists of places he wanted covered, information to be obtained in each. The list of addresses and instructions was usually fairly long, and the editor noted with some surprise that S. never took any notes. He was about to reproach the reporter for being inattentive when, at his urging, S. repeated the entire assignment word for word. Curious to learn more about how the man operated, the editor began questioning S. about his memory. But S. merely countered with amazement: was there really anything unusual about his remembering everything he'd been told? . . . The editor sent him to the psychology laboratory to have some studies done on his memory. (Luria, 1969, pp. 7–8).

Luria tested S. by giving him lengthy sequences of words, nonsense syllables, and numbers to learn. Provided the items were presented slowly and clearly, S. would, at the end of the sequence, pause to review the material in his mind and then recall the sequence without error. S. could also recall the sequence in reverse order and, if given any item from the sequence, he could readily say which item preceded or followed it. During a single presentation, S. had taken the sequence into long-term memory.

However, when Luria tried to discover how S. carried out his feats of learning and remembering, he made relatively little headway. S. reported encoding material in terms of *perception-like characteristics*. A word, for example, could trigger complex mental images which were not merely visual but also auditory, tactile and gustatory (to do with taste). Yet S. could say little about the processes involved. Nor could he report anything about the past development of his memory processes – so far as he knew, he had always had his unusual abilities. In brief, at this juncture in the investigation, Luria was unable to determine whether S.'s present abilities were due to an inborn peculiarity or to an acquired disposition to deal with experienced events in ways which led, as an incidental byproduct, to these events being remembered in detail. In real life, there are some questions to which clear answers cannot be found.

Sometime after his meeting with Luria, S. decided to capitalize on his memory abilities by becoming a professional mnemonist and giving public displays of his ability to learn and remember material which, for most people, is meaningless and hard to remember, e.g. lists of randomly selected words or numbers. Luria discovered that, in order to meet the demands of these public performances, S. developed significantly modified ways of working – which, interestingly, involved the four developments mentioned in connection with Steve Faloon. In short, S. developed with practice bodies of knowledge and skill which enabled him, more rapidly and efficiently, to encode and structure presented material.

Basically, in his public performances, S. used the Method of Loci (see Chapter 8). For example, he would imagine himself walking down a familiar street with familiar landmarks, such as Gorky Street in Moscow, and he would visualize each successively-presented item in association with each successive landmark. One development in the direction of greater efficiency concerned simplifying the visualization involved.

> Formerly, in order to remember a thing, I would have to summon up an image of the whole scene. Now all I have to do is take some detail I've decided on in advance that will signify the whole image. Say I'm given the word *horseman*. All it takes now is an image of a foot in a spur . . . So my images have changed quite a bit. Earlier they were more clear-cut, more realistic. The ones I have now are not as well defined or as vivid as the earlier ones . . . I try just to single out one detail I'll need in order to remember a word. (Luria, 1969, p. 42).

The fact that S. was able to adapt his imagery abilities to meet the circumstances of his new profession tells us something about the nature of his skills. We still are not able to conclude that his facility with imagery was either inborn or acquired, but it is clear that the facility could be brought under some degree of control and put to intentional use.

Conclusion

To conclude this chapter, we know something about people who show exceptional memory abilities. We know that such people exist. We know about the importance of rapid, meaningful encoding and structuring. We know that their astonishing accomplishments can sometimes be matched by normal people who have undertaking extensive practice. However, the fuller elucidation of exceptional memory skills is, at present, a wideopen challenge to psychologists.

FURTHER READING

ERICSSON, K.A. & CHASE, W.G. (1982) Exceptional memory. *American Scientist*, *70*, 607–615.

A succinct account of the experiments with Steve Faloon and their wider implications.

LURIA, A.R. (1969) *The Mind of a Mnemonist*. London: Cape.

A marvellous case study of the memory of S.

CHAPTER 8

HOW CAN MEMORY SKILLS BE IMPROVED?

Angus Gellatly

Each of the last three chapters has, in one sense or another, had something to say about the improvement of memory skills. The present one differs mainly in presenting a prescriptive account in place of a merely descriptive account. Previously the focus was upon observing individuals as they tackled memory tasks, the aim being to describe the cognitive process in which they engaged. On the whole, subjects were not instructed how to accomplish their task and when instructions were given the aim was a theoretical one, to explore the limits to the subjects' capabilities, rather than to bring about improved memorization for its own sake. In the present chapter, the balance of interest swings in the opposite direction. Emphasis is to be given to the improvement of memory rather than to the theoretical understanding of it. We shall be looking less at the psychologist as scientist, more at the psychologist as coach. Of course, this is a shift in emphasis only, and it is still to be hoped that applied and theoretical work on memory will be mutually sustaining.

The Mnemonic Tradition and Memory Therapy

Courses on memory improvement have long been available to the paying public. Nowadays, newspapers carry advertisements for them but the practical and commercial exploitation of the art of memory has a venerable history (Yates, 1966). Mnemonic systems were an important component in Greek, and later in Roman, education. At a time when literacy was confined to the few, and telecommunications had yet to be invented, the social importance of public speaking was much greater than it is now. The best orators avoided speaking from notes and therefore methods of committing information to memory were highly valued, and continued to be so until the modern era. Indeed, living in a culture of pens and paper, of photographs and tapes, it is scarcely possible to imagine the vital role of mnemonic techniques in pre-literate societies, or in societies with different or less widespread literate practices than our own. For this reason research into the cognitive 'side-effects' of literacy and its social uses has proved a source of intriguing insights into the nature of memory and thought.

The traditional art of memory and its modern descendants, the courses advertised in the newspapers, have concentrated on the acquisition of mnemonic techniques (and what we now call metamemory) by normally healthy persons. In contrast, and with the exception of work like that described in Chapter 7, modern research into the improvement of memory has come to focus on the mnemonically disadvantaged. The retarded, the head-injured, and the aged have all been studied in terms of mnemonic therapy. This means therapy aimed at reducing the life problems consequent upon abnormal memory failure. In this work, there is a general acknowledgement of the ideals of controlled study and theoretical analysis, but in practice a heavy dependence upon commonsense solutions is necessary. Memory therapy is designed to assist individual patients with problems that are often profoundly mundane. The difficulties faced by the disadvantaged prove to be those of the normal person magnified on a grand scale, and the solutions called for can be correspondingly prosaic. Nevertheless, although current laboratory and practical work do not dovetail neatly together, there is much to be learnt about memory processes from their dissolution in the organically damaged. Memory therapy may ultimately prove of aid to theoreticians as well as to patients.

Internal and External Memory Aids

As little can be done in the way of enhancing the retention stage of memory, improvements have to be implemented either at encoding or at retrieval. Some mnemonic aids, such as rote repetition, have their effect at the former stage, while other techniques, such as the matching of contextual and state conditions to what they were at encoding, can be counted as influencing the retrieval stage. In practice, however, many of the best known mnemonics operate at both encoding and retrieval. Typically, a known structure is employed to organize the information at encoding and then the same structure is called upon to key retrieval (see Steve Faloon's techniques described in Chapter 7). An example is categorization. Words to be remembered are grouped into categories for rehearsal, then at recall they are retrieved by category.

Related to, but not fully overlapping this encoding/retrieval dichotomy, is the distinction between *internal* and *external* memory aids (Wilson and Moffat, 1984). Internal aids are indeed mnemonics, such as the images in Lorayne's system for remembering names. They are internal to the mind of the individual and can function at encoding, retrieval, or both. External aids, on the other hand, exist out in the environment. They include written notes to oneself, cooker timers, knots in handkerchiefs, and manipulations of the environment such as leaving a parcel by the front door so as not to forget to take it along. Although some external aids may act as cues to retrieval, their more frequent purpose is to prompt actions rather than the retrieval of information.

External aids remind you that something needs to be *done*, perhaps indicating only indirectly if at all what the something is. Internal aids *can* serve as prompts to action (Lorayne and Lucas, 1974), but that is not their usual function, in our own culture at least.

External aids are commonly employed in everyday life to help with remembering to do things. Only recently, however, have experimental psychologists turned their scrutiny on the use of external aids and on the methods by which people help themsleves to remember to do things (Harris, 1980a; 1984). This has in part come about because of the relevance of these two topics for memory therapy. It is also an indication of the trend towards studies of practical memory performance (e.g. Gruneberg, Morris and Sykes, 1978).

Having now established a background to the study of memory improvement, let us move on to examine some of what is known about the subject.

Improving the Normal Person's Memory

As stated earlier, improvement in the memory of normal persons has most often relied upon the use of mnemonics of one sort or another. Yet mastery of a set of mnemonics is not all there is to intelligent memorization. Equally important as the ability to employ strategies, or mneonics, is an understanding of the appropriate circumstances in which to press them into service – what has already been called metamemory in Chapter 6. Improving memory performance in some area of activity entails first of all a careful appraisal of the memorial demands of the activity, attention to the nature of the material, the likely conditions of recall, and so on. Once this task analysis has been completed, it becomes possible to start formulating a plan of action, assessing the viability of different strategies and the ways in which they might fruitfully be adapted to the task in hand. Actual utilization of a mnemonic strategy is the last step in the process of intelligent memorizing. For example, learning a foreign language calls for memorization at many levels from individual words, to rules of conjugation, to principles of grammar. In addition, the aims and requirements of learners will vary with their purposes. Do they wish to read the language, speak it, or both? Will they need to converse socially or are they prepared to restrict themselves to certain technical matters? Without such an appraisal mnemonic techniques can provide no more than piecemeal assistance. In conjunction with thorough task analysis, however, systematic application of the techniques can be an effective aid to language learning (Gruneberg, 1985).

Verbal Mnemonics

The structure imposed upon material by verbal mnemonics is frequently that of rhyme or rhythm, as in the ditty for remembering days of the month (Chapter 5). Another example of the use of rhythm is in the lines 'Richard of York, gave battle in vain', where the first letters of the words give the order of colours in the spectrum (red, orange, yellow, green, blue, indigo, violet). Rhythm is a natural principle of organization, it is spontaneously adopted by many subjects in digit-span experiments, with items that are presented at a constant rate being grouped for rehearsal into threes and fours. Rhythmic groupings were purposefully built into the design of British postal codes, the majority of which have the form letter-letter-digit, digit-letter-letter.

The most striking use of rhythm and rhyme for mnemonic purposes is found in the oral histories and genealogies of non-literate cultures, like the epics of Homer (Lord, 1982; Bateson, 1982). Skilled bards are able to give performances of many hundreds, and even thousands, of verses. They do so, it turns out, not by remembering their songs in word-for-word fashion but by composing them afresh at each performance in accordance with formulaic and thematic principles. By constraining the process of reconstruction, the metre of the verse acts as a guide to memory. Prose epics are not found in oral societies precisely because prose lacks the mnemonic properties of verse.

Of course, storyline itself is also an important mnemonic ingredient of the epic song. The educational virtues of narrative have always been recognized and fables, parables, and morality tales abound in all cultures. In the absence of metre narrative takes on a less than epic scale, but still the structure of even the simplest story (beginning–middle–end) confers mnemonic power. Just as the Kpelle exhibited better memory when words were embedded in a story rather than presented in an isolated list, so Western subjects will recall more words when instructed to create stories linking the words together than when the words are simply rehearsed (Bower, 1972).

Besides rhythm and narrative, some verbal mnemonics substitute words or consonants for numbers that are to be remembered. These systems were developed especially to deal with the memorization of such things as dates, although in some cases they can be generalized to other materials also. Hunter (1964) and Norman (1976) give examples and some historical background.

Visual Image Mnemonics

Visual image mnemonics are amongst the commonest and most widely utilized. Perhaps the simplest is the one named by Hunter (1964) as the system of successive comparisons. It can be used to remember any list of items, such as words, so long as each is capable of being represented by a visual image. To begin with, the first and second items must be imaged together as vividly as possible. Then a new image is produced to link the second and third items, and so on. This is a very simple method of chaining and any type of association between items is acceptable. The method can be generalized to items other than words so long as they can be represented in imagery, so a sequence of ideas or actions can be memorized in this fashion.

Successive comparison is the least structured of the visual image mnemonics, having only the linear structure of connections devised by the individual. Another system is the 'peg-word' mnemonic, for which it is initially necessary to learn the following rhyme. 'One is a bun; two is a shoe; three is a tree; four is a door; five is a hive; six is sticks; seven is heaven; eight is a gate; nine is wine; ten is a hen'. The first item to be remembered is then imaged in interaction with some kind of bun. So if the first item was WINDOW, you might imagine an enormous stale bun topped with massive sugar crystals like lumps of Iceland spar, breaking through a picture window. The images produced should be as vivid and detailed as possible. Following this step, the second item is imaged in connection with a shoe, and so on. This method involves some structure, enlisting as it does an overlearnt sequence of numerals. Hunter (1964) demonstrated that subjects instructed in the method recalled many more words than uninstructed control subjects. As with successive comparisons, the method is generalizable to any material that can enter into visual imagery.

The most extensively reported visual imagery mnemonic is also the most structured. It is known as the method of loci after the Latin word *locus* meaning place, as in 'location'. The method, which was developed in great detail by the orators of Rome, relies upon knowledge of the layout of a particular building, or the landmarks along a familiar walk. If a list of items, or a succession of ideas in a speech, is to be committed to memory, all that is necessary it to take an imaginary walk through the building depositing, so to speak, an image of each idea in one room after another. So long as the order in which the rooms are entered is a routine one, then the ideas can be retrieved serially by repeating the imaginary walk. The richer the imagery employed the more reliable the method becomes, and if a room is imaged in detail, more than one idea may be deposited within it, so long as each goes next to some prominent feature. The essence of the system is that an already well-known sequence of places provides a framework onto which new information can be fitted.

The method of loci has a number of points in its favour. Most important of these is that it is highly effective, even when employed for the first time. Nevertheless, as with all memorization, practice with the method makes for radical improvement.

Why Mnemonics work

In this section two questions relating to mnemonics will be given brief attention. First, why is it that mnemonics work? Second, why are stories and visual images such potent mnemonic devices?

The answer to the first question is that mnemonics work because they impose organization on the material to be remembered. The structure of the mnemonic system provides a retrieval plan that directs the search for the desired information, it acts as a framework.

This leads us to the second question – why are storylines and visual images such good methods for securing information to a framework? One possibility is that, in creating or comprehending a story, people automatically generate images of the material, so that the two methods are really the same. Whether or not the two *are* distinct, it seems likely that the reason they are effective is because both methods involve deep and elaborate processing which, as we saw in Chapter 5, is an important determinant of memorability. One reason to believe that this may be the important function of imagery instructions is that, although there are large individual variations in reported ability to form visual images, the effect of imagery instructions are fairly uniform.

Improving Memory in Educable Retarded Children

Recent attempts to bring about improvements in the memory performance of educable, or mildly, retarded children have been closely connected with the research into memory development in normal children (see Chapter 6). Whereas previously the retarded had been thought to differ neurologically from normals in that information once encoded was less well retained by the brain, the newer approach has been in terms of a deficit in encoding itself (Kail, 1984). Mildly retarded children usually perform on recognition tests of memory at, or close to, the level of normal children. It is when they are required to carry out the more active type of memorization suited to recall tests that a decrement is observed. It has been found that retarded adolescents are not inclined to engage in spontaneous rehearsal in preparation for recall (Belmont the Butterfield, 1971), and that they do not frequently organize their recall by categories (Spitz, 1966). In other words, on these tests educable retarded adolescents exhibited the same lack of mnemonic strategies as did very young, normal children.

As in the case of young normal children, the next question to be asked was whether the retarded adolescent could be trained to employ strategies. Once again, the answer proved positive. Belmont and Butterfield were able to coach the retarded in how to engage in rehearsal, and to achieve improved performance as a result. However, after an interval of a week, the effect of the training had been totally lost.

More durable effects of training can be obtained when the training is extended rather than brief, and strategy use becomes automated, or overlearnt (Brown, Campione, and Murphy, 1974). So the performance of the retarded can be boosted in the long as well as in the short term. Even better results follow when, instead of simply being given practice with a strategy, its purpose is explained to the retarded children and they are taught the self-monitoring habits that normal children seem to acquire spontaneously (Wong and Jones, 1982; see also Chapter 12). Such methods also yield better transfer of training.

Transfer refers to seeing new problems as analogous to old problems and realizing how existing skills can be brought to bear upon them. Effecting transfer is a perennial problem of all education and training but with retarded individuals transfer is particularly poor. Early studies found that even simple rehearsal skills did not spontaneously generalize to tasks differing only slightly from the original. However, when strategy training is accompanied by discussion, hints, and training in meta-cognitive skills like self monitoring, better transfer is observed (Campione and Brown, 1984; Wong and Jones, 1982). The same is also true for ordinary children and adults but in the case of the retarded transfer tends to be more limited, requires more and more explicit help from others, and may fail altogether.

To summarize this section: the term retarded is aptly applied to the people we have been considering. Their course of development is a normal one but much slowed down, and for the most part arrested at an early stage. The development of cognitive skills is inhibited at all levels and especially so for higher-order skills. Enhancement of performance on simple memory tasks is possible and fragile insights into their own cognitive functioning can be brought about, but these successes are hard won and remain difficult to consolidate.

Memory Therapy for the Head Injured

In response to laboratory findings, head-injured patients have been taught to encode information deeply, to make use of peg-word systems, to employ the method of loci, to chunk information, to apply first-letter verbal mnemonics to shopping lists, to try to remember names with Lorayne's system, and to draw upon study techinques developed to assist school learning. All these methods appear to be of benefit to some patients on some tasks, and their effectiveness has been assessed by Powell (1981) and by Wilson and Moffat (1984).

Part of the therapist's expertise lies in fitting a particular method to a particular patient. Wilson and Moffatt suggest that patients with injury to only one of the cerebral hemispheres, as is common in strokes, can be selectively matched to appropriate mnemonic systems. Those with left-hemisphere damage and a consequent verbal impairment can be encouraged to adopt imagery mnemonics, while those whose imageing ability has been reduced by right-hemisphere injury can be taught to make use of verbal mnemonics. A similar kind of matching to modality of impairment is also suggested for patients who are impaired specifically for auditorily- or visually-presented materials. In both sorts of matching, advantage is taken of the fact that what helps normal subjects to remember will, by and large, also assist the head-injured. This is not always the case, however. For instance, several studies have found that Lorayne's system for remembering names is too complex to be learnt by patients who are severely deficient on naming.

Those who have no experience of patients with head injuries may have difficulty imagining the magnitude of the problems that sometimes have to be faced. An example may help in this respect. Wilson and Moffat describe a patient who could recall the names of three of his physiotherapists only if given the appropriate initial letter. A fourth therapist with the name Anita proposed that he remember her name because she had '*a neater* way of doing her hair', at which she shook her hair at him. Subsequently the patient was always able to articulate 'Anita' when she repeated this gesture. Unfortunately, he did the same when any woman shook her hair at him. The name had become linked to the action rather than to the individual.

Where incapacitated individuals are involved, minor innovations can sometimes yield surprisingly large benefits, both for patients and for those who care for them. Harris (1980b) describes how in one unit – for geriatrics rather than the head-injured – the rate of incontinence was decreased by the expedient of painting lavatory doors a different colour from all other doors. This environmental cue elicited appropriate behaviour that would not otherwise have taken place. In a similar vein, hospitals and rehabilitation centres frequently rely on chalk lines on walls and floors to guide patients from one part of the building to another. Environmental cues of this sort are no different in principle from those which facilitate many automatic and semi-automatic behaviours in daily life. They act as communal external memory aids (see Chapter 2).

Wilson and Moffat suggest that external memory aids are particularly applicable in cases of global amnesia. Some 'obvious' aids, such as pocket diaries, are of reduced value for such cases because the patient forgets to consult the diary. One way around this obstacle is to have a timer which is set to bleep occasionally and so remind the patient to consult his or her list of things to be done. Fowler, Hart, and Sheehan (1972) found that after several weeks the habit of consulting the list had become ingrained and the timer could be dispensed with. Electronic memory aids, which can store permanent information such as the patient's name and address and so on, as well as being programmable with relevant messages on a daily basis and providing auditory reminder signals, are now commercially available. Such aids have been evaluated by Jones and Adam (1979). In many respects, they show little advantage over less technologically-sophisticated aids, but improvements are expected that will bring them more closely into line with three criteria that Harris has set for effective aids to remembering to do things. These are (a) that the aid should have its effect as close as possible before the desired action; (b) that it should be an active rather than a passive reminder; (c) and that it should specify the required action (unlike, for instance, a knot in a handkerchief).

Improving Legal Testimony

An important area of applied memory research is that of legal testimony. Psychologists usefully contribute in at least two ways to the legal processes of evaluating evidence. First, they attempt to influence general police and court procedures in the light of research findings. Secondly, psychologists can appear as expert witnesses who advise the judge and jury on the factors which may have influenced testimony in a particular case. In practice, these two functions overlap, and between them they cover an enormous range of topics only a few of which can be accorded brief mention in the present context.

Improving the System

Davies (1981) has reviewed the history of face-recall kits, such as identikit, and remarked upon their generally low reliability. In part he attributes this weakness to reliance on memory for features rather than for whole faces. Newer techniques, based on 'whole face' methods and made flexible by computer graphics, promise better for the future.

Identification from either kit 'mock-ups' or 'mugshots' typically leads to the holding of an identity parade, and this is perhaps the legal procedure most studied by psychologists. The probability of a correct or an incorrect identification being made in a line-up is subject to the influence of many factors (Deffenbacher and Horney, 1981). It is trivially the case that the composition of the line-up can influence an outcome. Any tall blonde male in a collection of otherwise small dark females is likely to be picked out by a witness seeking a tall blonde male! But when such obvious absurdities have been avoided, the composition of the line-up still remains a far from trivial matter. For instance, a suspect who differs from other members of the line-up along more subtle dimensions, such as clothing, posture, or gait is in danger of possibly incorrect identification. The number of people taking part in the line-up also affects the numbers of true and false detections, as does whether the witness believes the line-up 'definitely does' or only 'may' contain a suspect. In the latter case there is less pressure to arrive at a positive indentification than in the former case, and this may be especially important when witnesses are looking for a member of a different ethnic group for whom their powers of discrimination may be less acute.

Deffenbacher and Horney (1981) report that in Sweden, if the original sighting took place in less than optimal visibility, then the identification procedure is conducted under similar conditions. In addition, the parade may take the form of having the witness walking about in a room full of people who are carrying on conversations amongst themselves. In this way there are not only facial and postural characteristics to prompt the witness's memory but also gesture, facial mannerisms, and voice quality. Both these departures from traditional procedures amount to reinstatement at the time of recognition of greater numbers of retrieval cues. By providing extra information to the witnesses, they should ensure that guilty suspects are more likely to be recognized and innocent suspects more likely to be detected as differing in some way from the original criminal.

The Expert Witness

Rather than seeking to influence the processes by which evidence is collected prior to a trial, the psychologist may contribute to the trial itself. Factors that may have influenced the testimony of a witness can be pointed out to the judge and the jury. For instance, it has been found that subjects in experiments who (a) witness a 'crime', (b) see a series of 'mug-shots', and (c) are asked to pick out the 'criminal' from an identity line-up, were more likely to pick from the line-up an 'innocent' individual whose face had appeared in the 'mug-shots' than they were to pick an individual whose face had not appeared. In other words, faces that are familiar from the 'mug-shot' session get confused with the face(s) from the crime. Thus the identification of a defendent by a witness who, in the time since the crime, has seen a mug-shot or a newspaper photograph of the defendant is less to be trusted than the identification of one who has not.

The psychologist may also instruct the court about research which shows that the confidence of experimenal 'witnesses' in their testimony bears no relation to its literal accuracy (Deffenbacher, Brown and Sturgill, 1978). There may also be occasions, over and above those to which any competent counsel would draw attention, when it can be necessary to point out ways in which a witness's reconstruction of events has been 'led' by the form of the questioning employed. For example, Loftus and Palmer (1974) showed that subjects' recall of the speed at which cars were travelling towards each other in a filmed car crash depended upon whether they were asked how fast the cars were going when they *smashed* (40.8 m.p.h.), *collided* (39.3 m.p.h.), *bumped* (38.1 m.p.h.), or *contacted* (31.8 m.p.h.) each other.

Memory Aids for Examinations

To conclude this chapter on the improvement of memory skills we turn to a topic likely to be of relevance to many readers of the book: how to improve examination performance.

Beard and Hartley (1984) review the research about preparing for and taking examinations. For the purposes of this chapter the relevant points that these authors make are:

(a) that students should *organize* their revision activities;
(b) that students should revise *actively* rather than passively; and
(c) that students need to *practise* taking examinations if they want to improve their skills in this respect.

In terms of organization, it is suggested that students study previous examination papers in order to see what are the requirements of particular exams – in terms both of format and content. Beard and Hartley also advocate that students should construct revision timetables in order that they may plan how to space out their revision systematically rather than cramming in material the night before. (The advantages of spacing out practice were discussed in Chapter 3.) Last minute revision can be useful, (especially if there has already been spaced revision), because

• loose ends can be drawn together;
• perspectives on the whole course can be obtained; and,
• the final refreshing of memory from notes is most efficient.

However, spaced revision
• ensures a more complete coverage of the syllabus;
• makes a daunting task easier by splitting it into manageable parts; and,
• overcomes the problems of strain, ill health, etc. which may intensify or strike towards the end of a course   (James, 1967).

Beard and Hartley also provide a list of active, as opposed to passive, revision strategies. These include the well-known ones of underlining, summarizing, and writing out answers to examination questions in note form or in full. Some less common strategies that they suggest include explaining topics to fellow students who are unfamiliar with them, and meeting in small groups to review particular areas, to work out how particular questions might be answered, and to prepare outlines on specific topics. The argument for employing strategies such as these, is, of course, the one outlined in Chapters 5 and 7: the more deeply one processes material, the more thoroughly organized and interrelated it has been, the better it will be recalled.

Finally, Beard and Hartley note that simply allowing students to practise examinations can improve their performance and that it is possible to regard taking examinations as a skill. Like all skills, there are certain useful subroutines to practise, of which thoroughly reading the question and retrieving the appropriate material are only two. Practice, and the automaticity which follows from it, is particularly important because examination candidates are frequently anxious, and anxiety disrupts the fluent execution of subroutines (see Chapter 2). Table 8:1 below suggests some valuable techniques for examinees to practise on the day.

Table 8:1 *Notes on examination technique (based on suggestions by A.B. Hill)*

1. Do not arrive more than ten minutes before the start of the examination unless required to do so.

2. After arriving for the exam, do not talk to friends about the revision you or they have done.

3. Check the instructions and then read *all* the questions on the paper twice, slowly and carefully before choosing those you will answer.

4. Work out how much time you have for writing each answer. For example, three questions in two hours gives you 40 minutes per question. *Keep strictly to this time limit.* If you have time left over after answering all your questions, complete any you have had to leave unfinished because of your time limit. If you finish all your questions early, read over your answers and check them.

5. Make *sure* you answer any compulsory questions.

6. Check carefully what your selected questions require you to do. For example, if the question says 'Evaluate . . . .' or 'Give a critical account of . . . .' make sure your answer *does evaluate* or is a *critical* account. It is easy to give an answer which is not properly relevant to the question if you do not make sure *exactly* what is required of you.

7. To keep your answer relevant and coherent, and to make sure you say all that you can or want to say in your answer, make a list of important points *before you start to write the answer.* Number these in the order they are to be made and cross them off as you cover them in your answer.

8. Make *sure* you answer *all* your questions, i.e. if you have to do three questions make *sure* you attempt three, not two or two and a half. Answering only two out of three questions gives you a maximum possible mark of (for perfect answers) 67 per cent.

9. If there is a choice between questions requiring specific knowledge and questions of a rather general sort, do the specific questions unless you are fully confident of your ability to cope with the general ones. It is easier to keep your answers relevant on these.

10. If you become nervous or panicky calm yourself down with two or three minutes of relaxation practice.

11. After leaving the examination room, do *not* discuss with your friends what questions you did or what answers you gave.

Summary

This chapter has examined how what is known about human memory can be applied to improve the memory performance of different groups of people in their different circumstances. Mnemonics used to amplify the memories of ordinary people can be understood within the skills framework of memory presented in this book, and the data on the performances of the educable retarded also fits well with theory. In the area of memory therapy for the head injured, theory provides some understanding of acquired deficits but aids to improvement have to be improvised for individual cases. In a similar manner, the performance of eye-witnesses is influenced by multiple factors, only some of which have yet found theoretical accommodation.

FURTHER READING

LORAYNE, H. and LUCAS, J. (1974) *The Memory book*. New York: Stein and Day.

Provides an intriguing discussion of ways in which we can all improve our memories.

HARRIS, J.E. and MORRIS, P.E. (1984) *Everyday Memory, Actions and Absent-Mindedness*. London: Academic Press.

A collection of chapters on aspects of everyday memory, including work with head injured patients.

SECTION III

COMMUNICATION AND COMPREHENSION SKILLS

CHAPTER 9

THE SKILLS OF THE SPEAKER

Don Rogers

In many ways, speaking is the characteristic human skill. It is uniquely human and, in addition, it shows in strong form many of the characteristics of other motor and intellectual skills which are discussed elsewhere in this book (see especially Chapters 2 and 3).

There are hundreds of different languages spoken on the earth. Some have only a few hundred native speakers, while others have many millions. Some of these languages are very different from others: for example, those with a well-developed literary tradition have large numbers of seldom used words which most speakers of the language do not know (as you can see by looking at any large dictionary of English); some have a well-developed specialist vocabulary which others lack (e.g. Eskimo languages have numerous words for different types of snow which languages from tropical regions have no need for!); and some languages employ rather different grammatical devices from others: for example, languages such as English indicate grammatical relations such as subject and object by word order – *John liked Mary* is different from *Mary liked John* – while for languages such as Russian or Latin, word order is much less important, subject and object being indicated by variable endings to nouns.

While languages display differences from one another, these are comparatively minor. There are a number of important points which apply to language generally and which will form the subject matter of this discussion of speaking skills. Before that, two preliminary points are worth making. First, all humans can learn to use language. This needs qualification since some forms of developmental abnormality can be associated with inability to use language, but it is nevertheless astonishing that children who are profoundly deaf can learn to use sign language; that there are cases of children who have learned to communicate linguistically although blind and deaf; and that there are cases of children who have been locked up and not spoken to for the first five or six years of their life, but who upon contact with a normal environment have quickly learned to talk in a relatively normal manner. (See Clarke and Clarke (1976) for details of a number of such studies.)

Second, no non-human species seems to be able to use language. Parrots can imitate speech, dogs are good at expressing emotion and indicating desires, but these are far from language. The closest that any non-human seems to have come to language is in those cases in which chimpanzees and other primates have been taught to use American sign language – the communication system used by the deaf and dumb in America. At first, these studies fuelled hopes that the animals would learn to use language fully, but at the moment it seems that, while chimpanzees can certainly learn a few hundred signs (more or less equivalent to 'words'), they cannot readily combine these signs to produce new 'sentences' (Terrace *et al.*, 1980).

It is this combinatorial productivity that is the most striking fact about language. Language is creative. We can easily produce a sentence that neither we nor anyone else has heard before; and we are not surprised if that sentence can be understood.

Language derives this productive resource from the way it is structured. Any spoken language has a small number of sounds, which can be combined to produce many thousands of words, which in turn can be combined in accordance with the grammar of the language to produce an infinitely large set of sentences. Speakers of the language can easily produce sentences which are 'lawful' in terms of the grammar of the language, and can easily understand such sentences.

Language users, then, can be both speakers and hearers: producers and comprehenders of language. We will look at these aspects in turn, at speaking in this chapter and at comprehending in the next.

Speaking as a Skill

Having seen that the language is a uniquely human characteristic, let us look at some of the ways in which speaking can be said to be skilful. Remember that in Chapter 2 it was pointed out that the skilled individual can be said to act fluently, rapidly, automatically (i.e. without thinking consciously about all aspects of the task), that he can integrate different components of the activity together simultaneously, and that he can (usually!) produce the right component at the right time. Similar points can be made about the skilled speaker.

Fluency

When young children begin to speak, they typically start off by producing one word at a time. For instance, a child of around 18 months seeing a dog pick up a ball might say 'Doggy' or he might say 'Ball'. With more experience of speaking, both words might be used, but not run together into a single utterance, so the same scene might find the child saying 'Doggy . . . ball'. With time, words can be put together into a single utterance 'Doggy ball', 'Doggy bite' etc. The older child can put together into a single utterance, with a single intonation contour, several words to express a thought: 'The bad doggy licked my hand'. As we shall see in this chapter, the fluent speech of adults is not without hesitations and pauses – according to Goldman-Eisler 'two-thirds of spoken language comes in chunks of less than six words' (See Beattie, 1983), but nevertheless, while not perfectly fluent, the speech of an adult shows many more words occurring between pauses than does the speech of a young child. And of course, as discussed in Chapters 2 and 3, this chunking of output is a typical feature of skill of all sorts.

Rapidity

Hesitations apart, the speaker of English normally produces two to three words a second. Since each word has around five sounds on average, this means that the speaker is producing about 12.5 sounds per second. If each of these sounds were independent of one another, this would require an impossibly fast decision-rate. But, of course, they are not independent: sounds are grouped together as words, words grouped as phrases, and phrases as clauses (a sentence can be broken down into one or more clauses, each containing a verb). The sounds within a word and the words within a clause are related to one another in such a way that, together, the sounds produce a meaningful word or the words a meaningful clause: and as we shall see, rather than making a separate independent decision about each sound, the speaker plans ahead, displaying the anticipation seen in all skilled activities.

Automaticity

A characteristic of skilled performance is that the performer is unaware of the details of his performance: he is concerned only with high-level planning, and details are dealt with by an 'automatic pilot'. As we shall see, speaking has precisely this hierarchical character; the speaker is concerned with telling a story, conveying information, convincing someone of his innocence or whatever – he does not consciously plan to produce the particular form of the plural which is appropriate to the noun he is using. Rather, this is left to a well practised subroutine; and, in the absence of agitation, intoxication or some other disturbance, this generally proves adequate.

Simultaneity

Just as in driving a car, speaking involves doing several different things at the same time. This can be seen when a speaker talks and simultaneously moves his hands, his body, his eyes, and changes facial expression – it has been said, 'We speak with our mouths, but converse with our whole bodies' (see Chapter 11).

Simultaneity can also be seen in the way in which we anticipate what we are going to say as we say something else. Sometimes this leads us into error, saying 'The golly green giant', instead of the 'jolly green giant', but usually it does not; since anticipation is always present, this is fortunate. A simple example will show you one sort of anticiaption: try saying 'strew', then say 'string'. You will find that your lips are already rounding to form the 'ew' sound as you say the 't' and even the 's' in 'Strew', while your lips are spread out to say 'ing' as you say the 't' and 's' of 'string' (Fodor, Bever and Garrett, 1974).

Since you can plan ahead what you are going to say while saying something else, this clearly shows some form of simultaneity just within different aspects of language skill. In addition, of course, people can talk while walking, cooking, driving and engaging in all manner of activity.

Knowledge

The last aspect of skill to be mentioned in Chapter 2 involved the common observation that the skilled individual can produce an item from memory in the course of executing a series of actions, but might well not be able to produce it at another time. This, of course, is equally true in the case of speaking. Despite hesitations and the odd occasion when we just cannot remember a word, speech proceeds quite fluently with the right word being produced at the right point in a sentence on most occasions. But this is far from the case if you are asked to produce a word given only its meaning. As I write this, my daughter is trying to finish a crossword puzzle, and occasionally asks, for instance, 'What's an eight-letter word meaning disaster, ending in T?' I usually cannot answer.

Producing the right word at the right moment when speaking a sentence requires us to plan ahead. In Chapter 2, this was discussed in terms of a 'push down goal stack'. You might care to work out the goal stack involved in, say, telling the story of Cinderella.

Speaking, then, is skilled behaviour, not too different from other forms of skilled behaviour. Skills, of course, take a long time to acquire: it has been suggested that around 10,000 hours of practice are required to produce an expert, be it a chess master or a composer. But after all, 10,000 hours is less than three hours a day for ten years, so that by the end of primary school children have had adequate practice to be experts at the skills of language.

The Art of speaking

There are several problems in studying speech, and in particular in observing the cognitive processes involved in a speaker's deciding what he is going to say. It is clear that the speaker has a great many choices open to him. These range from choices over the topic; through choices over the selection of relevant points to be made; how these points are to be ordered and linked together to tell, let us say, a story or a joke; through choices over how to express a particular point, and how a particular choice will affect the listener; the choice of particular grammatical structures; the choice of particular words and phrases among many that will convey the same meaning; and the choice of tone of voice, accent and so on. We will see in the next chapter that speakers need to take account of what their listeners know and believe, they have to frame their speech in terms of the needs and purposes that they attribute to the listener, and they have to try to make their speech socially appropriate (not telling jokes at a funeral, for instance). For the moment, though, notice that the choices a speaker makes affect not only the extent to which a listener can comprehend what is said, but also the extent to which the listener will be interested, the extent to which he will like the speaker, the social status he will attribute to him and so on.

Precisely because there are so many choices open to speakers, and so many factors affecting the choices they make, it is extraordinarily difficult for the psychologist to understand the underlying processes. We will look in this chapter at three techniques which have been employed to examine the cognitive processes involved as speakers speak.

In the first technique, individuals are given some task to perform – describing their apartments, retelling the story of a film, giving route directions, or whatever, and the content of their accounts is examined. In the second technique, it is assumed that the processes involved in making choices will be reflected in hesitations and pauses in speech, so these are examined to discover how frequently they occur, and in what sort of circumstances. In the third technique errors of speech are examined, in the hope that by looking at cases in which something goes wrong in the performance of a skilled action we can draw inferences about the normal case where things go right. It turns out that these three techniques rather naturally match different levels of planning in speech: analysis of content is most useful in examining choices made at an overall level of strategic planning in which decisions are made about which points will be made and the order in which they will be mentioned; analysis of hesitations turns out to be most useful at an intermediate level of planning; and analysis of errors is in the event useful for examining local planning at the level of the phrase or clause.

Long-range Planning

A speaker embarking upon a descripton is in some ways like an explorer: he needs to plan his route in advance. In particular, some thought needs to be given to (a) what points should be mentioned, (b) in what order they should be mentioned, and (c) what level of detail is appropriate. This can be a highly deliberate and well-structured process, as in writing an essay plan (see Chapter 12). But more usually it is not; the thinking involved seems to be extremely rapid.

A classic study of planning is that of Linde and Labov (1975), in which a number of New Yorkers were tape-recorded while replying to the question 'Can you tell me the layout of your apartment?'. This study is an attractive one, because it was not artificial: although the data lent themselves to linguistic analysis, they were recorded as though they were part of a survey of life in New York City.

Virtually all of the respondents solved the three problems mentioned above in the same way. Ninety-seven per cent of responses involved an imaginary tour through the apartment, which began at the front door, proceeding systematically through the apartment, looking into each room in turn, and going through the room only if there was another room on the other side of it. The major rooms were emphasized more than the minor rooms, which were seen as appendages: 'Straight ahead there's a bedroom with a little closet off that'.

The respondents in this study then all asumed that the question called for a particular level of detail – that of rooms. This partially determined the content of the descriptions, but some rooms were seen as more important than others. Finally, the problem of ordering the contents was solved by imagining a walk through the apartment.

Other descriptions call for different solutions, but again, an assumption about what will be most comprehensible, most useful and most interesting to the listener will affect descriptions so that, often, different people will come up with similar solutions. An account of a series of events, for instance, will generally call for a description whose order matches that of the series of events (see e.g. Levelt, 1981). This is not obligatory, and storytellers can create particular effects by failing to observe this rule.

The strategic level of planning, then involves decisions over what sort of detail is appropriate – if someone asks how to get somewhere, you don't need to describe every shop he will pass; it involves decisions about at least some of the main points which need to be included, and it involves decisions about the order in which these should be mentioned. Deviations from the expected level of detail, main points or order are possible, but they have consequences in terms of the listener's interpretation. It is part of the art of the storyteller (or indeed the joke teller) to be able to predict the effect that violations of listener's expectations will have (see Chapter 4).

Intermediate-range Planning

Developing an overall plan is important, but as every essay writer knows, it still leaves a lot of problems of detailed execution of the plan to be solved.

When writing an essay, the next step after the overall plan is finished is to pause for thought, write a few sentences, pause for thought again and so on. According to Butterworth (e.g. 1980), just so with speaking. He has found that speaking tends to occur in a cyclical manner, with a period marked by many hesitations, followed by a fluent phase, followed by another hesitant phase and so on. This can be seen in Fig. 9:1. Typical cycles, Butterworth says, 'last about

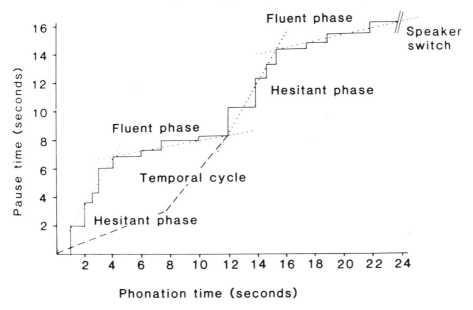

Figure 9:1   Temporal cycles in speech. (After Beattie, 1983).

18 seconds, but some as long as 30 seconds, which means that they will contain, on average, five to eight clauses, i.e. generally two or more sentences.' He argues that each of these cycles coincides with a single 'idea'. To examine this, he asked judges to divide transcripts of spontaneous speech into separate 'ideas', and found that there was a good (though not quite perfect) correspondence between the beginning of a hesitant phase and the beginning of an 'idea'.

Planning the expression of ideas seems to take time, but once a plan for expressing the idea is developed then speaking can proceed more fluently.

When pauses occur, they appear especially in between clauses and before content words (Butterworth, 1980; Beattie, 1983).

A sentence can be divided up into one or more clauses, the essential character of each clause being that it contains a verb. The pauses which appear between clauses probably have three functions. First, they enable the speaker to breathe; second they may well help the listener to break up the speech he hears into appropriate units; and third, they are probably important in planning the detailed articulation of the clause. Since clauses are the major units of a sentence, they need to be planned as a unit so that stresses can appear at the appropriate places. It is worth noting, however, that by no means all clauses are preceded by pauses – less than one half in the hesitant phase and around one quarter of clauses in the fluent phase have pauses before them (Beattie, 1983).

Hesitations also appear before 'content words' – the nouns, verbs, adjectives and adverbs which carry the meaning of the sentence. They tend not to occur before 'function words' – articles, prepositions, conjunctions, etc. which indicate the grammatical framework of the sentence. These pauses are often associated with gestures which seem to represent the meaning of the word when it is eventually forthcoming (Beattie 1983). In other words, when speaking, even in a fluent phase, we sometimes find a word on the tip of our tongues but can't quite grasp it, though we can indicate its meaning by a gesture. Phenomena such as these have suggested to a number of people that when we plan speech, we plan the overall meaning of an idea, plan the grammatical framework of the sentences and clauses, and a specification of the words involved. Proceeding through the framework we come to a slot which needs to be filled by a word with a particular semantic specification. We search our memory for a specification of a sequence of sounds to match the meaning, but cannot immediately find it, though we clearly know its meaning since we can indicate it by a gesture. It might seem surprising that a sentence framework could be set up in advance of selecting the words comprising the sentence, but in fact this is quite consistent with common experience – it is, after all, easy enough to fill in words to fit in with the framework of a limerick:

> There was an old lady of Kent,
> Who wobbled wherever she . . .
> One leg was long
> And not very . . .
> And the other was little and . . .

Looking at hesitations, then, provides us with evidence about two aspects of speech planning. First, about planning how to express ideas, which involves planning a few sentences at a time; and second, study of hesitations begins to give us some hints about how clauses are planned in detail. It looks as though the speaker plans a clause in advance, at least as far as the main structure is concerned, and knows the meaning of the words involved, but not always precisely how these words are to be spoken.

However, in order to examine in more detail some of the processes involved in producing clauses, we need to look at errors that people make when they speak.

Short-range Execution of Speech Plans

There are several different kinds of speech error, as can be seen in Table 9:1. Speculation as to why these errors might arise has been quite informative about the process involved in producing speech. First, as might be expected, the process of finding words produces errors – sometimes words take time to find, which produces hesitations, sometimes the wrong word is found which may be *similar in sound* to the intended word, e.g.

1 'No I'm amphibian' (instead of ambidextrous).

or *similar in meaning*, e.g.

2 'He rode his bike to school tomorrow' (instead of yesterday).

and very occasionally two words are pulled from memory at the same time and inadvertently *blended together*:

3 'a slooth move' (smooth + slick)
4 'That's torrible' (terrible + horrible)

Table 9:1 *Some types of speech error (examples from Garrett, 1980)*

---

1 *Substitutions*
   (a) Of similar sounding words,
        e.g. It doesn't sympathize
             (intended: synthesize)

   (b) Of similar meaning word
        e.g. Ask me whether you think it will do the job,
             (intended: tell me)

2 *Blends*
   e.g. Have you ever flivven at night?
         (intended: flown or driven)

3 *Anticipations*
   e.g. The song called Yankle Doodle Dandy,
         (intended: Yankee Doodle Dandy)

4 *Exchanges*
   e.g. We completely forgot to add the list to the roof,
         (intended: roof to the list)

         on a sot holdering iron,
         (intended: hot soldering iron)

These errors in word finding tell us something about the processes involved in fitting words into a framework. The story they tell is consistent with that derived from hesitation studies: it looks as though the speaker reaches a point in the sentence framework where he has the intention to produce a word. Seemingly, his plan contains a specification of the meaning of the word, as can be seen by the fact that sometimes a word of nearly the right meaning is produced in error, and also by the fact that two alternative words can sometimes be blended together.

However, at some point the speaker needs to retrieve from memory a word having the right sounds as well as the right meaning, and it seems that sometimes this process can slip: it is as though there is a process which fills in a specification of the appropriate sounds for a word having a particular meaning. Usually this then leads to the right word being spoken, but sometimes it happens that another word fits the sound specification rather well, and is spoken instead: hence the substitution errors involving words of similar sounds (as in example 1 above).

However, word-finding errors do not tell us about how the clause is planned: for that we need to turn to anticipation errors and, particularly, exchange errors.

Three points can be made as a result of study of these errors: First, if we anticipate the sounds of one word when we are speaking another, saying, 'golly green giant' instead of 'jolly green giant', then the specifications for 'g' and 'j' must be simultaneously present in our minds. Similarly, if we switch around two words, as in 'Is there a cigarette building in this machine?', both words must have been present at once. Hence, we can see once more that speaking does not proceed one word at a time, but is planned ahead.

Second, if we look at the words that are exchanged, we can get some idea of the duration of speech which is planned in a detailed way. It turns out, according to Garrett (1980), that words are most often exchanged within a clause, and that only a small proportion (20 per cent) of exchange errors involve a longer stretch of speech than a single clause (remember that sentences can be divided up into one or more clauses, each containing a verb). It rather looks, then, as though the clause constitutes some sort of articulatory unit. This of course is much shorter than the intermediate term planning cycles which Butterworth described, which contained five to eight clauses. However, it seems likely that what is planned at that level is a pretty abstract specification of the meaning of what is to be said, and that it does not have sufficient detail to be actually articulated. The 'articulatory program' itself deals with a shorter stretch of speech, and seems to involve a detailed specification of how to say a particular clause.

The third, and most interesting, point is that examination of exchange errors has suggested to several authorities (e.g. Fromkin, 1973; Garrett, 1980) that it is possible to deduce a sequence of processing stages in the formation of an articulatory program. To look at these ideas, we need to examine exchange errors more closely.

Exchange errors are, of course, classically known as Spoonerisms, after the unfortunate Dr William Spooner who was noticed sometimes to exchange parts of words in his speech. Many of the better-known examples attributed to him are probably not authentic but were very likely made up by his students. For example:

You have hissed all my mystery lectures.

The lord is a shoving leopard to his flock.

Take the flea of my cat and heave it at the louse of my mother-in-law.

If we look at *real* exchanges we find that there are several different sorts.

(a) Exchanges can involve *words*:
'Is there a cigarette building in this machine?'
'You should see the one I kept pinned on the room to my door'.

(b) They can involve *syllables*:
'[He] favours pushing busters' (busting pushers).
'I've got a load of cooken chicked'.

(c) Or they can involve *sounds*:
'We have a lot of pons and pats to wash' (pots and pans).
'The rage of eason' (age of reason).

There are three aspects of these exchanges that provide useful pointers in working out the processes which may be involved in producing a clause: notice first that exchanged items tend to be very similar to one another, in that words exchange with words, syllables with syllables, sounds with sounds; and in that exchanges tend to involve items in similar positions – e.g. sounds which exchange come from similar positions in their respective words.

Notice second that many exchanges leave the grammatical structure of the clause unaffected:

'I went to get a cash checked' (cheque cashed).

'You have to square it facely' (face it squarely).

'It waits to pay' (pays to wait).

Notice finally that if a speaker intended to say 'It pays to wait' the verb would have formed the present tense so that it sounded like a 'z' (pays). When 'wait' and 'pay' got shifted round, the 'z' sound would have been wrong for the new verb: wait needs an 's' sound for its present tense, and this is what the speaker gives it.

Observations such as these have been used by Fromkin and by Garrett to build up suggestions about how a succession of processes might be involved in articulating a clause. Some of these suggestions can be summarized as follows.

(a) *Selecting a meaning.* The first stage is presumably that of deciding the idea to be expressed in the clause: for instance, that an action of a particular kind is being performed by a particular person to a particular object.

(b) The second stage appears to be that of *selecting a grammatical framework.* As was remarked earlier, it seems rather surprising to choose a grammatical framework before picking the words which will fill the slots in that framework, but this seems to be the only way of making sense of some of the characteristic ways in which exchanges work: specifically that the framework nearly always remains intact. For example, when someone means to say 'He favours busting pushers', but instead says 'He favours pushing busters', it looks as though the framework 'He ——s ——ing ——s' was set up, and then the words were popped into the wrong slots.

(c) The third stage, then, is that of *selecting content words* to fill in the slots. As we saw earlier, this stage too can go wrong – a word similar in sound to the intended one can be selected in error, a word similar in meaning can be chosen, two appropriate words can be blended together, or there may be difficulty in finding the right word at all.

(d) Finally, there is a stage in which *details of pronunciation are specified.* The evidence that this stage comes after the previous one lies in the observation that when an exchange occurs, the pronunciations of plurals, tenses and the like are appropriate for the words which *actually* fill the slots, rather than the words which were intended to fill the slots. Consequently, the speaker who intends to say 'It pays to wait', but fills in the wrong words to the slots says 'It waits to pay', with an 's' sound after wait. Presumably, the framework built up at stage (b) contained only a specification that there should be a present tense indicator in the second slot; only after a word was filled into the slot in stage (c) was it possible to flesh out, at stage (d), how this tense indicator should actually be pronounced. As with the stacking of goals illustrated by example in Chapter 2, specifications increase in detail as you move down the hierarchy of control, or planning.

Conclusion

For a human, but only for a human, years of practice will result in a skilled individual who can talk effortlessly, planning ahead and producing sentences which he has never spoken before nor heard spoken. Three main techniques have been employed to study this extraordinary skill: examining the choices speakers make, examining the points at which speakers pause for thought, and examining the (surprisingly rare) occasions when speaking goes wrong. These techniques have been employed to begin to sketch in a fairly detailed picture of the processes involved in speaking. However, *listening* is also a matter of skill, one to which we will turn in the next chapter. A number of points will be made there about how speakers' choices affect listeners, and these can usefully be considered when thinking about either speaking or listening.

FURTHER READING

BEATTIE, G. (1983) *Talk: An analysis of speech and non-verbal behaviour in conversation*. Milton Keynes: Open University Press.

An interesting book which examines real-life instances of conversation.

AITCHISON, J. (1989) *The Articulate Mammal*. London: Hutchinson.

A useful, sensible and readable introduction to the whole field of psycholinguistics.

CHAPTER 10

LISTENING SKILLS

Don Rogers

Comprehension of Language

When we think about the processes of comprehension, one very obvious theory of how they work comes to mind: that comprehension works 'from the bottom up'. That is, we hear and recognize individual speech sounds (or, when reading, recognize individual letters); that we recognize particular combinations of those sounds or letters as words; that our knowledge of grammar enables us to comprehend particular combinations of words as particular sentences; and finally that we understand combinations of sentences as a narrative, a conversation or whatever.

However, while there must obviously be a good deal of truth in this proposal, there also seem to be some senses in which the processes of comprehension work 'from the top down': in that we work out what the letters, words and sentences must mean on the basis of the context and of our own knowledge.

We will look at this phenomenon with respect to several different linguistic levels, beginning with the simplest, that of sounds or letters. Rather than dealing with speech sounds, we will discuss reading, simply because the effects are easier to illustrate on the page – understanding of speech sounds presents exactly the same problems. This, of course, relates this chapter to the discussion of reading in Chapter 4.

Recognizing Letters

While letters are often quite easy to recognize, we all know that sometimes – particularly when we are trying to read handwriting – there may be difficulties. However, it is striking that we are often able to read without difficulty letters which are very badly formed. Have a look at the examples in Fig. 10:1. You will see that there are numerous cases in which a given letter is very hard to recognize *unless you can see the rest of the word* in which it occurs. You will also

Figure 10:1   Individual letters may take a variety of physical forms. The same is true of speech sounds.

find cases in which *quite different forms can be recognized as examples of the same letter*. It also happens that in some cases *The same form will be recognized as indicating different letters* in different contexts, as in Figure 10:2.

In general then, there are occasions on which a decision about what letters are present within a word is dependent upon a decision about an overall reading of the word. That is, the preceding and succeeding context is taken into account in recognizing letters. Much the same holds for the recognition of the sounds that make up speech. For example, the same vowel will take very different forms depending on the accent of the speaker. And, especially where the accent is unfamiliar, the identification of particular sounds – or even whole words – will depend on context.

Understanding Words and Sentences

Just as letters are easier to recognize in context, so context greatly facilitates recognition and comprehension of words. Several points can be made here. First, as experienced listeners to language, we have the impression that speech is segmented into words, with pauses between each word, just like a printed page. In fact this is not the case: as we saw in the last chapter, the pattern of pauses in

Figure 10:2   The same stimulus can be given different interpretations
according to context.

speech is much more complex. If you try speaking a sentence or two with gaps
between each word, you will find that it sounds very odd. The impression of
gaps that we have arises because we understand the sentence and imagine there
to be gaps between the words. It is an enjoyable pastime to work out sentences
which can be divided into words in different ways, so shifting the positions of
apparent gaps. Here is a well known example from a children's chant:

> I chased a bug
> Around a tree
> I'll have his blood
> He knows I will.

If you read this aloud quickly you may find that it can be broken up into
different words, with apparent gaps in different places. Likewise, children's
riddles may rely for their effect on dividing sentences up in different ways. For
instance:

A.   There were four tea-cups on the table. One broke. How many left?

B.   Three.

A.   No, there were thirty-nine cups left. (Opie & Opie, 1959, p. 71).

(Of course, if B had answered thirty-nine, it would have turned out that the
answer was three!)

A second function of context at the level of word comprehension concerns the fact that many words have more than one meaning, and in many cases different words sound alike. In order to decide which particular meaning is involved, and which particular word is involved, the meaning and the grammatical structure of the whole sentence needs to be taken into account – and often surrounding sentences too.

Another children's punning story illustrates the point that different words can sound the same:

> There was a man in a house and he couldn't get out. The only furniture was a table. He rubbed his hands until they were sore. Then he sawed the table in half. Two halves make a whole. He shouted through the hole until he was hoarse, jumped on the horse, and rode away. (Opie and Opie, 1959, p. 29).

In general, it is very easy to think of examples in which a word can have one meaning in one context, and another meaning in another, simply because so many words have several different meanings. For instance:

'He banked at Barclay's' or 'He banked at 45 degrees'.

Hunt (1984) gives an amusing example: 'The sentence "Grasp the red block and put it on the green block" has five content words (grasp, red, block, put and green), none of which has fewer than seven distinct meanings and one of which (block) has twenty-two, according to an unabridged dictionary; hence [. . .] there could be nearly three million interpretations of the sentence, many of them as senseless as this one: "Understand the communist obstruction and blame it on the immature coalition".

Third, when listening or reading, we need to decide the parts of speech and grammatical function of each word. This is not a straightforward or mechanical procedure as can be seen by examining a few sentences. For instance:

> *Time flies like an arrow* is superficially similar to
> *Fruit flies like a banana*,

but clearly in the first 'flies' is a verb and in the second a noun, while 'like' is a verb in the second sentence but in the first a conjunction linking an adverbial phrase to its verb.

These three points – that speech is not divided into words separated by pauses, that words can have numerous different meanings, and that a given word can fulfil different grammatical functions in different sentences – suggest that we need to make considerable use of context in determining the part of speech of a word, the particular aspect of meaning it is fulfilling, and indeed what words are involved.

This has suggested to some workers that the comprehender waits until the end of the sentence before reaching a decision about its meaning. However, it looks rather as though 'bottom up' processes and 'top down' processes operate simultaneously. This arises partly because decisions have to be reached very rapidly. In normal speech, we hear around two to three words each second. Marslen-Wilson and Tyler (1981) have demonstrated that in experiments people can repeat (*shadow*) speech with a delay of only about quarter of a second – the subjects heard someone talking, and were asked to repeat the message as they heard it. The experimenters found that some of the words took as much as 375 milliseconds to be spoken, but the subjects were able to begin repeating them only 250 milliseconds after onset! That is, they began to repeat the word before they could have heard the whole of it. Furthermore, there was good understanding of the material as it was repeated – it was not just a minimal echoing without comprehension. The conclusion seems inescapable that in this situation people were able to decide correctly what word they were hearing when only half of it had been spoken. This shows a powerful effect of context, but also shows that it is not at all necessary to wait until the end of the sentence before understanding the words involved. Because of this, it is quite easy to fool the system, and numerous studies have employed sentences which (as Aitchison 1983, puts it) lead hearers 'up the garden path'. For example, in

'The elephant squeezed into a telephone booth collapsed'

we take it as we read the sentence that the elephant is doing the squeezing. It is only when we reach the hanging main verb at the end that we realize that something has gone wrong, and re-scan the sentence to discover that someone else squeezed the elephant into the booth.

Understanding the Social Significance of Sentences

However, understanding the words and grammar of a sentence still leaves the listener with a number of problems. In particular, he needs to appreciate the intentions of the speaker in order to reply appropriately.

When we hear someone speak, they are not simply uttering a string of sounds arranged in a way that we can understand as a sentence but they are also performing a social action: they may be accusing us of something, they may be warning us of something, they may be requesting something of us and so on; these have often been called *speech acts*. The question is, how do we know what they want? (See also Chapter 13.)
One way might be for them to tell us what they want:

'I'm telling you: get out of my way!'

As users of the languge, however, we know perfectly well that people do not often speak to us like that, and that if they do it is as a challenge rather than as a normal request.

Secondly, there might be specific kinds of grammatical structure associated with particular kinds of speech act. There are two problems with this. First of all, as Austin (1962) has pointed out, there are many hundreds of different speech acts that can be performed, and so the number of special grammatical forms would have to be large. Also there is indeed a special form for getting someone else to do something. That is the imperative, and appears in the following:

> 'Get out of my way!'
> 'Open the door!'
> 'Stand to attention!'
> etc.

Obviously enough, the imperative either appears in contexts where there is a large, and often institutionally based, status difference between speaker and hearer – as in an army – or it is extraordinarily rude (precisely because it suggests a large status difference).

Requests, then, are usually framed in a polite way, as 'indirect requests' – one example of the large class of 'indirect speech acts'. For example, we might say,

> 'Would you mind doing the washing up?'
> 'Isn't it your turn to wash up?'
> 'The washing up does need doing'.
> etc.

Clearly, there is a problem as to how the hearer distinguishes an indirect request from an ordinary question or statement. The philosopher John Searle has provided a useful analysis here (Searle, 1975). He points out that in order for any utterance to be a request, certain conditons must be met. In the above examples, (a) there must be a need for the action (i.e. the washing up must need doing), (b) the hearer must be capable of performing the action, and willing to do it, (c) the speaker must be sincere and want the hearer to do the action (d) the utterance must be an attempt to get the action done, (e) the speaker must have some right to make a request of the hearer.

Only if all of these conditions are fulfilled can an utterance count as a request, and it is often by pointing out one of these conditions that a request is performed. For example,

> 'Would you like to do the washing up?'

draws attention to the condition that the hearer be willing to perform the action.

If all the other conditions were fulfilled (i.e. the washing up needed doing, etc.) then this could count as a request. On the other hand

'Would you like to fly to the moon?'

is more likely to be treated as a genuine question, expecting an answer 'Yes' or 'No' but no further action (see Stubbs, 1983, for deeper discussion).

In order to respond to some requests, however, we need to go further than simply appreciating that a request is being directed to us. Often we need to put ourselves in the shoes of the speaker, considering his purposes, his existing knowledge and salient characteristics of the overall situation. As a very simple example, consider being asked where something is:

'Do you know where Harrod's is?'

The answer you give will depend on

(a)   Where you are at the time. If you are in Edinburgh the appropriate answer could be, 'London', if in London it could be 'Knightsbridge', if in Knightsbridge, 'Just down the road'.

(b)   Your assessment of why the speaker needs the information. If for instance he is looking at a map of London, then the answer 'Knightsbridge' would be more appropriate than 'London', even if you are in Edinburgh at the time. If you know that he is a stock exchange gambler and you know that he has seen you reading a financial report you might reply 'Up three and a half'.

(c)   Your assessment of the speaker's existing knowledge. Often this is something that is established in conversation prior to the appropriate reply being selected:

   A: 'Do you know where Harrods is?'
   B: 'You know Hyde Park?'
   A: 'No'.
   B: 'Ah, well if you go to the end of the road here you'll see a high arch. Across the other side of that's the park. If you take the path through that to the other side and then ask again you'll get there. Come to think of it, why not get a taxi?'

Going Beyond the Sentence

Sentences do not appear in isolation of course: they are also parts of larger texts – narratives, conversations or whatever – and they may also be used in particular physical contexts. This of course helps considerably in interpreting sentences: an ambiguous sentence such as, 'They are eating apples' has fewer alternative readings if there are apples in front of you, or if the previous few sentences have been about apples.

However, the interpretation of sentences in context does present some problems, and provides further evidence of how powerful, skilful and active the processes of comprehension are.

In a classic study, Gordon Bower (1976) read to students stories like the following:

> (Nancy) went to see the doctor. She arrived at the office and checked in with the receptionist. She went to see the nurse who went through the usual procedures. Then (Nancy) stepped on the scale and the nurse recorded her weight. The doctor entered the room and examined the results. He smiled at (Nancy) and said 'Well, it seems my expectations have been confirmed'. When the examination was finished, (Nancy) left the office.

These stories were preceded by a brief description, which could be either:

> Nancy woke up feeling sick again and she wondered if she really were pregnant. How would she tell the professor she'd been seeing? And the money was another problem.

or they could be a brief description of Jack, a young man who is worried that he is not heavy enough to become a member of the wrestling team. (Of course, when this description preceded the story, the names and pronouns in the story were changed to 'Jack' and 'he'.)

Twenty-four hours later, the students' memory for the story was tested. It was found that many distortions occurred in their recollections of the story, and that these were different according to the description before the story. For example, in the 'Pregnant Nancy' condition students misremembered the doctor's remark 'My expectations have been confirmed' as 'Your fears have been confirmed', or simply as 'You're pregnant', while in the 'Wrestler Jack' condition, the doctor was remembered to have told Jack how well he was gaining weight.

At least two points can be made on the basis of this experiment. First, it shows that comprehending narrative involves a process of active inference (see Chapters 4 and 13). This, of course, is a very general phenomenon in reading or hearing stories, and detective novelists such as Agatha Christie make considerable use of this propensity in their readers. It is only because we actively draw inferences that we are misled by the false clues strewn about by the novelist.

Second, in Bower's story as in detective stories, it looks as though we make inferences as a result of trying to fit together the pieces of information contained in the story. We seem to assume that if a point has been mentioned in a story, then it must be relevant, and must be able to be fitted in with other points in the story.

In respect of this, the philosopher H.P. Grice (1975) has pointed out that speaker and hearer operate as though they were observing a set of co-operative principles. He encapsulates some of these principles in four 'maxims':

Quantity	Be as informative as required: do not provide too much or too little information.
Quality	Be truthful
Relation	Be relevant
Manner	Be clear and orderly

These maxims are not intended simply as a recipe for aspiring conversationalists, but rather as a set of intuitive principles which any skilled and experienced conversationalist implicitly obeys. It is because of this that the reader or hearer is able to draw inferences; it is precisely because we assume that the maxim of quantity is obeyed, so that no more information is being supplied than is needed, and that the maxim of relation is being obeyed so that the information we have is *relevant*, that we are able to conclude that the doctor's remark has some connection with Nancy's pregnancy.

Violation of Grice's maxims produces interesting effects. For example, as he points out, if after a man has been treated abominably by another he says 'He's a fine friend', then he has violated the maxim of quality by saying something which is untrue. If his hearer knows this, he will be able to conclude that the remark is intended ironically.

These issues, and particularly the issue of relevance, are taken further in Downes (1984).

A further point can be made on the basis of Bower's story. We assume that Nancy's feeling of sickness is connected with her pregnancy. However, notice that this inference involves what might be called 'non-linguistic' or 'world' knowledge – it is not part of the meaning of the word 'sickness' that it is correlated with pregnancy. The point is that understanding language involves a knowledge not just of the language itself, but also a knowledge of the world. This point can be seen clearly in a rather odd experiment by Dooling and Lachman (1971). This experiment involves a story which is extremely hard to understand until a title is supplied:

> With hocked gems financing him, our hero bravely defied all scornful laughter that tried to prevent his scheme. Your eyes deceive, he had said; an egg not a table correctly typifies this unexplored planet. Now, three

sturdy sisters sought proof, forging along sometimes through calm vastness yet more often over turbulent peaks and valleys. Days became weeks, as many doubters spread fearful rumours about the edge. At last, from nowhere, welcome winged creatures appeared signifying momentous success.

Many people on reading or hearing this story find it quite incomprehensible: they can understand the words, but they cannot find a framework which makes all the points relevant. However, on being told that this is a story about 'Christopher Columbus discovers America', the relevance of the points becomes clear, and in particular the rather inflated metaphors can be interpreted. The words themselves have not changed: there is no change in linguistic knowledge, but the appropriate frame of reference can now be articulated, and the story understood on the basis of our knowledge of history, the sea, the gender of sailing ships, and so on.

Improving Skills of Speaking and Listening

Clearly, a big problem faces the listener if he finds that he has difficulty in understanding and remembering the content of, say, a lecture. Unlike the reader he cannot rest when he finds his concentration flagging, and nor can he go back if he finds that he cannot follow an argument: the rate at which he has to take in information is paced by the speaker. However, as we all know, it is very difficult to keep concentrating throughout the course of a 50 minute lecture: just as a radar operator cannot maintain the same level of vigilance constantly, so a student cannot give equal attention to every golden word which drops from the lips of his teacher. In fact, according to Wilkinson, Stratton and Dudley (1974), 'students listening to lectures have been found to comprehend half or less than half of the basic matter'. This is particularly unfortunate since, as they further point out, a great deal of a student's time is spent in sheer listening; even in the primary school, children were found to be listening for 58 per cent of each school day.

With this in mind, it is clear that a great weight falls upon the speaker to ease the task of the listener, and a great many courses and books are available to help public speakers communicate effectively – for example, George Brown's 'Lecturing and Explaining' (1978). There are of course numerous different solutions to the problem of effective speaking but all need to take account of the listener. For example, many of the devices which the good speaker uses are aimed at overcoming the listener's inability to attend all the time. Thus, the speaker may indicate in advance the main points he wishes to make; he may summarize his main points; he may draw attention to each of his main points by writing it on a blackboard; or he may supply extra information by making the same point through his speaking and through his visual aids.

In addition, it should be obvious from the earlier part of this chapter that the speaker has also to take account of the existing knowledge of the listener, and of his needs and purposes. It is often difficult to explain a new topic to a group in such a way that each member can understand it, and public speakers need to learn to estimate correctly what their audience already knows: if they overestimate existing knowledge the audience will not understand, will not remember, and will not even be interested in the talk; while if speakers underestimate existing knowledge the audience may become bored.

While the main burden of effective communication falls upon speakers, it does seem also that there are comprehension skills which listeners may exercise more or less expertly. Three types of comprehension skill can be discerned. The

Table 10:1 *Types of discourse engaged in by lecturers. (Reprinted with permission from Brown, 1978)*

Preambles	Ritualistic mutterings such as 'um – er – good afternoon. Today we are – er – going to – er – consider – um – an – er – important – er – topic.'
Orientation	The framework of the lecture. Needless to say, some lecturers do not make this explicit. Ideally, they state what they are going to talk about and write headings down. Orientations may occur at the beginning of a lecture or at the beginning of topics or subtopics (see next).
Frames	The framing of the subtopics in a lecture. They usually begin with such words as 'Now . . .', 'So far . . .', 'This then . . .'. Sometimes the lecturer simply pauses and looks down at his notes. The 'framing words' indicate a switch in topic. What immediately follows a frame is usually (not always) important.
Keys	Key statements. These are central principles, rules, facts, conjectures or questions. Watch out for them. The questions you have scribbled down will probably alert you to them.
Examples	These may be examples of the principles or facts, or may be metaphors, illustrations and analogies. A *brief* note of them will help you to understand the principle.
Summaries	These may occur at the end of topics or subtopics as well as at the end of a lecture.

first type is concerned with attention and having the will to give the speaker a hearing. Included here are such things as deciding the level at which you wish to understand and remember the speaker's material. For example, a burglar and a householder might take away very different information from a talk on crime prevention. The second type of skill is concerned with performing certain cognitive operations such as distinguishing main and subordinate ideas, keeping related details in mind, drawing appropriate inferences, or perceiving the logical structure of an argument. Thirdly, a further set of skills is involved in identifying the 'sign posts' with which speakers indicate the direction of their thoughts. These sign posts may be verbal – 'first of all', 'nevertheless', 'let me summarize by'; they may involve emphasis or tone of voice; or, finally, they may be wholly non-verbal, as in gesture, posture, and general bodily movement, all of which can supply information about how the speaker views the organization of what he is saying (see also Chapter 11).

In one interesting attempt to improve listening skills, Brown (1978) taught students to look for both verbal cues (see Table 10:1) and non-verbal cues (see Table 10:2) given by lecturers. After practice with tapescripts and videotaped talks, it was found that the quality of the students' note-taking had improved. It also seems that the students felt themselves to have benefited from the coaching they had been given.

Overall, then, a speaker will talk more effectively if he appreciates the cognitive limitations and strengths of his listeners. He needs particularly to guard against the consequences of lapses of attention on the part of listeners by providing a clear structure to his talk, by indicating what this structure is, by indicating the main points, by repeating and summarizing, and by supplying additional information through other media. In addition, he requires to engage the existing knowledge structures of the listener so that what he has to say will be comprehensible and can augment the listener's knowledge. On the other hand, the listener can help himself to understand by listening more effectively, by looking out for verbal and non-verbal cues, which indicate what the speaker is trying to do. The listener's task is the converse of that of the speaker. He needs to attend to all the same points as the speaker and to try to deduce the speaker's meaning and intentions.

Conclusion

In the course of this chapter I have demonstrated that comprehension is by no means a passive process, but seems at all levels to be active and skilful. By making use of context and expectation we can cope with highly degraded or ambiguous letter forms, and can employ fast, powerful word-recognition routines; as a result of accumulated knowledge of the social world we can get behind the forms of utterances, putting ourselves in the shoes of others and guessing at their intentions; and as a result of our general world knowledge we

Table 10:2 *Types of behaviour engaged in by lecturers. (Reprinted with permission from Brown, 1978)*

Lecturer writes on board	(next section or just lecturer restlessness?).
Lecturer steps back from board and stares at it	(just checking).
Lecturer removes spectacles	(probably a main point coming).
Lecturer removes spectacles and pauses	(probably a qualification or reservation).
Lecturer stares out of window	(lecturer thinking of what to say; maybe a pretty girl passing by).
Lecturer raises finger	(qualification coming).
Lecturer closes hand and gestures	(probably an important point coming).
Lecturer uses 'halt' sign	(qualification coming).
Lecturer looks at notes	(next section coming or he is lost).
Lecturer stares hard at notes	(he is lost).
Lecturer scrambles through transparencies	(he is lost).
Lecturer looks up from notes and stops reading	(he is about to explain a point; usually important).
Lecturer sits on desk and lights a cigarette	(you are about to be given the 'I'm a good guy' technique? Maybe a substitute for a lecture – but not always).

can bring to bear upon the task of understanding appropriate frames of reference, which enable us to make inferences that for the most part intersect appropriately with those intended by speakers.

FURTHER READING

DOWNES, W. (1984) *Language and Society*. London: Fontana.

A clear and sensible discussion of social aspects of language.

AITCHISON, J. (1983) *The Articulate Mammal*. London: Hutchinson.

A useful, sensible and readable introduction to the whole field of psycholinguistics.

CHAPTER 11

SOCIAL SKILLS

Helen Graham

In his play *Rosencrantz and Guildenstern Are Dead*, Tom Stoppard (1967) borrows his characters from Shakespeare's tragedy, *Hamlet*. The two doomed heroes are charged with the unenviable task of discovering what afflicts Hamlet, whose symptoms include:

> Pregnant replies, mystic allusions, mistaken identities, arguing his father is his mother, that sort of thing; intimations of suicide, forgoing of exercise, loss of mirth, hints of claustrophobia, not to say delusions of imprisonment, invocations of camels, chameleons, capons, whales, weasels, hawks, handsaws – riddles, quibbles and evasions; amnesia, paranoia, myopia; daydreaming, hallucinations; stabbing his elders, abusing his parents, insulting his lover, and appearing hatless in public.

Faced with these strange behaviours, Rosencrantz and Guildenstern find themselves hopelessly out of their depth. As a perplexed Guildenstern admits, 'we don't know what's going on, or what to do with ourselves. We don't know how to act' (p. 49). On this basis, a psychologist might justifiably conclude that Rosencrantz and Guildenstern are socially incompetent; that they have inadequate social skills.

Social Competence as Skill

Social competence can be thought of as 'how to make friends and influence people'. It is the ability to achieve personal and professional goals, whether through forming and maintaining relationships with others, or in professions such as teaching, selling, interviewing or psychotherapy. Argyle (1983) suggests that the interactions involved in these social behaviours can be conceived as utilizing a hierarchy of skills; the lower elements of which are automatic and habitual; whilst higher-level sequences are under cognitive control. The latter are planned and subject to continuous monitoring and corrective action in the light of feedback.

Argyle (1969) defines skill as an organized, coordinated activity in relation to an object or situation, which involves a whole chain of perceptual (sensory), cognitive (central) and motor mechanisms.

> One of its main characteristics is that the performance, or stream of action, is continuously under the control of the sensory input. This input derives in part from the object or situation at which the performance may be said to be directed, and it controls the performance in the sense that the outcomes of actions are continuously matched against some criterion of achievement or degree of approach to a goal, and the performance is nicely adapted to its occasion. (p. 180).

He suggests that during social interaction an individual is engaged in a skilled performance which involves the matching and modification of output on the basis of the information available. Overall behaviour is directed, adapted and far from automatic, although it may be seen to be made up of elements that are themselves automatized.

Elements of the social skill model are represented diagrammatically in Figure 11:1.

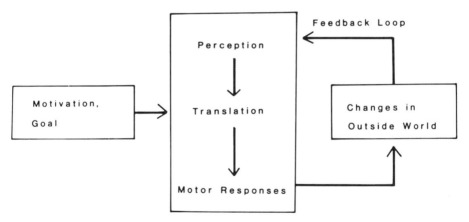

Figure 11:1   The social skill model. (After Argyle, 1969.)

The social skills model follows closely the model of perceptual-motor skills (Chapters 2 and 3). It has five stages:

(a) *The goals of skilled performance.* These may include obtaining or conveying information, changing attitudes or emotional state, supervision or collaboration. They may be professionally motivated, as in teaching, interviewing, selling or nursing, or purely socially motivated by needs such as affiliation or dominance.

(b) *Selective perception of cues.* Social perception is highly selective. Participants in interactions become highly sensitive to visual, auditory, and possibly, tactile information, learning which to attend to.

(c) *Central translation processes.* Information obtained via the sensory receptors guides the formation of appropriate plans of action. Social interaction depends on a learned store of such translations which are built up during socialization as a person learns which social techniques elicit desired responses from others.

(d) *Motor responses.* The plan is put into action, but it takes practice to achieve a smooth and accurate performance of the patterns of motor response. As such skills are perfected conscious awareness is reduced so that complex social skills such as establishing rapport or reducing another person's anxiety may become automatic for some people.

(e) *Feedback and corrective action.* Using perceptual cues, the performer takes corrective action where necessary.

Social skills are taken to be analogous to motor skills like typing or driving a car; skills which must, in part, be learned. It might be expected, therefore, that some persons acquire and develop better skills than others.

Everyday observation and experience suggests that this is indeed the case. Many people are shy and find it difficult to make friends or maintain relationships. They may be poor conversationalists, unable to assert themselves, or they may have difficulty in coping with everyday situations such as relating to members of the opposite sex or to those in authority, going to parties, or saying 'no' to the demands and requests of others. That people differ quite considerably in their ability to handle such situations is clear but what is less obvious are the possible consequences of this difference. Argyle (1984) reports on a number of recent studies which reveal that absenteeism, labour turnover, complaints, and sales from a particular counter all differ significantly between different supervisors. On a more personal level, inadequate social skills can also have serious consequences; leading to failure in making and maintaining relationships, obtaining partners, gaining and sustaining employment; and, in extreme cases, to social isolation and loneliness, mental illness, and possibly even suicide.

Indeed, in Stoppard's play it is the inability to appreciate nuances in social situations that contributes to the untimely and tragic demise of Rosencrantz and Guildenstern. As Guildenstern realizes before their execution, 'There must have been a moment, at the beginning, where we could have said – no. But somehow we missed it' (p. 95).

Social Skills

Social skills can be considered under a number of headings: communication skills, interpersonal skills, performance skills; all of which tend to be interrelated, hence any categorization is necessarily somewhat arbitrary. However, since all involve conversation to a greater or lesser degree conversational skills can justifiably be regarded as of primary importance.

Conversational skills

Conversation is essentially spoken communication which involves verbal exchange between or among persons and is therefore two-way in the sense that 'talk' or 'speaking' *per se* might not be.

> Conversation is without doubt the foundation stone of the social world – human beings learn to talk *in* it, find a mate *with* it, are socialized *through* it, rise in the social hierarchy as a result *of* it, and, it is suggested, may even develop mental illness *because* of it. (Beattie, 1983, p. 2)

Nevertheless, as Beattie points out, whilst conversation is primarily a social event, complex cognitive processes are involved in its planning and generation. (See also Chapter 9.)

In *Rosencrantz and Guildenstern are Dead* we can see extensive planning of the contents of conversation, and its rehearsal. A great deal of Stoppard's play concerns *what* Rosencrantz and Guildenstern will say to Hamlet if they are ever able to talk to him. However, like many socially inept persons, they miss numerous opportunities to initiate conversation, as the following sequence illustrates:

GUIL: I can't see for the life of me how we're going to get into conversation. (*Hamlet enters upstage, and pauses . . . Ros. and Guil. watch him.*)

ROS: Nevertheless, I suppose one might say that this was a chance . . . One might well . . . accost him . . . Yes, it definitely looks like a chance to me . . . Something on the lines of a direct informal approach . . . man to man . . . straight from the shoulder . . . Now, look here, what's it all about . . . sort of thing. Yes. Yes, this looks like one to be grabbed with both hands, I should say . . . if I were asked . . . No point in looking at a gift horse till you see the whites of its eyes, etcetera. (*He moves towards Hamlet but his nerve fails. He returns.*) We're overawed, that's our trouble. When it comes to the point we succumb to their personality . . . (p. 55)

Moreover, when Hamlet finally does speak to them, they are unable to sustain the conversation; giving short, simple answers to his questions, not reciprocating or leading the conversation forward. They merely receive Hamlet's words passively without engaging actively in the dialogue. As a result they are left with only the few words Hamlet has directed to them and what others have said about him, neither of which proves particularly enlightening. It seems to Rosencrantz that "Half of what he said meant something else, and the other half didn't mean anything at all." (p. 41).

Nonverbal Communication

Much of Rosencrantz and Guildenstern's problem arises because, in trying to gain information about Hamlet's state of mind, they rely almost exclusively on the verbal content of his speech, and their analysis focuses on the precise meanings of his utterances. As a despondent Guildenstern declares 'Words, words, words. They're all we have to go on.' (p. 31).

Psychologists also have traditionally focused attention on words, on language structure, syntax and grammar. However, as Rosencrantz and Guildenstern discover, talk isn't just a matter of words. It is the Player, the leader of a group of actors or tragedians summoned to perform before the Royal court, who disabuses them of this notion. He observes that, 'We are tied down to a language which makes up in obscurity what it lacks in style', and indicates that it is the dumbshow – the nonverbal behaviours accompanying language – that makes communication more or less comprehensible.

Several theorists (notably Goffman, 1956, and Harŕe and Secord, 1972), like Stoppard's Player, emphasize the resemblance between theatre and everyday life, viewing social behaviour as a dramatic performance under the continuous control of feedback from its audience. The social skills model takes a similar position. Accordingly, many psychologists have in recent years focused their attention on the dumbshow; on the non-spoken aspects of communication such as gaze, facial expression, posture, gesture, touch and proxemics (the way in which physical space is perceived, structured and utilized); and upon paralinguistic features of communication such as intonation, phrasing and pitch.

One consequence of this division of interest between speech and performance is that the two domains of verbal and nonverbal communication are typically kept quite separate in the psychological literature. It tends to be assumed that there are two distinct languages with two different functions, the verbal for conveying information, and the nonverbal, or 'body language' for conveying attitude and emotion. In practice, however, it is not possible to separate these two 'channels', and Beattie argues that little is to be gained from doing so in theory. He insists that both are dynamically interrelated, rather like steps and style in a dance routine.

Synchronization of Speech and Movement.

Examination of speech patterns has revealed close organizational ties binding speech and nonverbal behaviour at the most microscopic of level; ties which are probably essential for successful communication. Moreover these studies have revealed that the comparison between conversation and dance is particularly appropriate. Condon and Ogston (1967) showed in their detailed micro-analysis of a filmed three-person interaction that 'the body dances in time with speech' in the sense that subtle and fleeting changes in a speaker's body motion occur synchronously with the articulated, segmental organization of their conversation. Moreover, this 'self-synchrony', or congruence, is only one way in which speech and nonverbal behaviours are coordinated.

Condon and Ogston also discovered that, during conversation, interactants share harmonious patterns of bodily movement with the speaker. They not only move in precise harmony but change the direction of movement at the same 1/24th of a second and sustain directions across syllable and word-length segments of speech.

That these organizational ties may be essential for successful communication is suggested by their study of a schizophrenic (1966). Schizophrenics are, typically, poor communicators and it was found that although interactional synchrony was maintained between the patient and his therapist, self synchrony broke down, certain parts of the body being out of synchrony with other parts.

A more obvious form of interactional synchrony is that which Scheflen (1964) termed 'postural congruence', where two or more individuals adopt identical or mirror-image postures during conversation. For example, two or more people in a small group may sit with their legs crossed at the knee, their arms folded over their chests and their heads cocked to the right. This is not coincidence for when one member of a congruent set shifts posture the others often quickly follow suit, so that the congruence is maintained through repeated changes of body positioning. Scheflen suggests that, in a general way, postural congruence indicates similarity in views or roles in the group, or similarity in status. When one member of a group differs markedly in social status from the others this may be reflected by a posture differing from that of the others.

Shakespeare's Hamlet, despite all his alleged afflictions, clearly recognizes the importance of close organizational ties between speech and nonverbal behaviour, as he reveals in his directions to the players:

> Suit the action to the word, the word to the action, with this special observance, that you o'erstep not the modesty of nature.
> (Act III, Scene ii).

Nonverbal Cues to Deception

Congruence between verbal and nonverbal messages is not only necessary if speakers are to appear 'natural' but also if they are to achieve credibility. Freud (1905, p. 94) recognized that information can be conveyed both verbally and nonverbally, and that at times our bodies betray our speech:

> If his lips are silent, he chatters with his fingertips; betrayal oozes out of him at every pore.

It would seem that actions do speak louder than words. Ekman and Friesen (1969) suggest that convincing nonverbal 'liars' such as professional actors, skilled barristers, shrewd diplomats, proficient poker players and successful conmen, have heightened awareness of their nonverbal behaviour and have engaged in training which involves focused external feedback from a coach, director, audience, client or customer as to the effectiveness of their simulations.

Lying is thus a skill in itself, and one that Rosencrantz and Guildenstern have failed to master, as Hamlet is quick to observe:

> There is a kind of confession in your looks, which your modesties have not craft enough to colour. (*Hamlet*, Act II, Scene ii).

Turntaking

Another example of the way in which verbal and nonverbal behaviours are jointly organized is the apparently universal convention of turntaking in conversation; one person generally speaking at a time and then allowing another to speak. Various cues have been identified by Duncan (1972) as signalling the end of a speech sequence so that another person knows when to commence speaking. These cues typically include changes in intonation, pitch or loudness; drawl or stress on a final syllable; some kind of stereotyped expression such as 'right' or 'you know', or a mannerism such as the termination of a hand gesture or the relaxation of a tensed hand position during a turn.

The development of turntaking can be traced back to basic interactions between mothers and babies (Rogers, 1985, Newson, 1978). Nevertheless, although evident in the exchanges between very young children and their mothers, turntaking is an acquired skill, and some persons are better at it than others. This has important social consequences because violation of turntaking through interruption, or simultaneous speech, is generally regarded as a serious breach of etiquette.

Through our association with others, we learn their idiosyncratic use of turntaking cues, enabling us to judge with accuracy when they are about to cease or commence speaking. Such familiarity is clearly evident in the exchanges of the two friends Rosencrantz and Guildenstern, whose turn-taking is at times so dovetailed as to give the impression that each is completing the sentences of the other, as in the following deliberation on Hamlet's condition:

ROS: He talks to himself, which might be madness.
GUIL: If he didn't talk sense, which he does.
ROS: Which suggests the opposite.
PLAYER: Of what?
GUIL: I think I have it. A man talking sense to himself is no madder than a man talking nonsense not to himself.
ROS: Or just as mad.
GUIL: Or just as mad.
ROS: And he does both.
GUIL: So there you are.
ROS: Stark raving sane.

Beattie (1983) reports a number of studies which suggest that turntaking behaviour is influenced by social variables such as status and confidence. It would appear that the more confident a person is the more likely they are to interrupt another's speech, and the more socially anxious, the less likely they are to do so. Certainly Rosencrantz and Guildenstern frequently interrupt the Player, who is socially inferior to them, but they never interrupt Hamlet, who, although a friend since childhood, is nevertheless the heir to the throne and their social superior. Similarly, they never interrupt any other members of the Royal court.

Given that social status and confidence are significant factors in turntaking behaviour, it might be supposed that males, whose status in society is generally higher than that of females, might interrupt more than females. Support for this view has come from studies of conversation amongst both adults (Zimmerman and West, 1975) and young children (Esposito, 1979), but in a study of university tutorials Beattie (1979) did not find sex differences in either the frequency or the type of interuptions. However, status within universities may be sex determined to a lesser degree than in many contexts so 'normal' social conventions may be less in evidence. The results of Beattie's study suggest, therefore, that interruption is affected by social context as well as by other variables.

Certain of these variables were further elucidated in a study of political interviews (Beattie, 1982). In an analysis of two interviews televised during 1979, one with Mr Callaghan, who was Prime Minister at that time, and one with Mrs Thatcher, then Leader of the Opposition, Beattie discovered that Mrs Thatcher was interrupted twice as many times by her interviewer as she interrupted him, whereas Mr Callaghan interrupted his interviewer far more than he was interrupted. However, when interrupted Mrs. Thatcher continued to finish her point regardless of the duration of simultaneous talking required. It would appear, therefore, that it is Mrs Thatcher's insistence on being heard that has given rise to the widely held belief that she is strident and domineering in interviews, in contrast to Mr Callaghan's relaxed affability. Beattie suggests that these findings cannot be explained in terms of differing status accorded to the two politicians nor of Mrs Thatcher's status as a woman, but that they need to be considered in terms of their respective use of turntaking cues; in other words, to differences in conversational skill. He suggests that Mrs Thatcher gives turntaking cues in inappropriate places and that interviewers understandably misinterpret these cues. It may be that Mrs Thatcher is interrupted frequently because she lets her tone drop at the end of sentences, thereby seeming to signal that she has finished speaking when in fact she has not; or because she typically uses hand gestures after an interruption has begun and not before it.

However, in this connection it has to be remembered that Mrs Thatcher is highly skilful at public speaking and debate. During speeches she delivers her points in a convincing and forceful manner. It may well be that she adopts a similar manner in interviews – that of talking *at* rather than *with* her interviewer. Certainly, when interviewed she appears not to expect to give up the floor to another speaker, suggesting that she may well regard the interview as a platform from which to address a wide public and not as a conversation *per se*.

Research on Social Interaction

As the Player in *Rosencrantz and Guildenstern Are Dead* observes, 'There's a design at work in all art' (p. 59), and it falls to the psychologist to discover, identify and describe the design at work in social interaction. Traditionally, this has been achieved by comparing groups of effective and ineffective performers to determine where the difference in their social behaviour lies, and then teaching the desirable skills to those deficient in this regard. Numerous recent developments in social psychology have important implications for social skills training. During the 1970s, there was considerable research in the field of nonverbal communication, much of which related to the encoding of interpersonal information – that is, the way in which persons attempt to communicate, or in some cases conceal, their attitudes, emotions, ideas and thoughts. The findings of early research in this area (Ruesch & Kees, 1956; Davitz, 1964; Grant, 1969; Mehrabian, 1970) were popularized by Fast (1972). This research was stimulated by developments in video-recording which enabled micro-analysis of fleeting facial and bodily behaviours, and also by the need of many politicians and public figures to present themselves effectively and persuasively through the medium of television.

Studies of facial and bodily behaviours were conducted by ethologists, (such as Hinde, 1972), many of whom had been struck by the remarkable similarities in the expressive behaviour of man and non-human primates such as chimpanzees. Several of the studies focused on children under the age of five, in the belief that nonverbal behaviours are more clearly observable before verbal language has fully developed (Blurton-Jones, 1972; McGrew, 1972). Much work examined and identified cross-cultural differences in facial expression and gesture (Birdwhistell, 1968; Eibl-Eibesfeldt, 1972; Ingham, 1972; Ekman, 1972; Ekman and Friesen, 1976), and popular attention was drawn to these variables by Morris (1977) whose *Manwatching* became a best-seller.

Gaze

During the past fifteen years, a vast amount of research has been conducted on gaze, which previously had been largely ignored. Gaze is of considerable importance since, if one is not looking in the right direction at the right time, no perceptual information will be received. Gaze is also an important social signal. The first research in this field was conducted by Neilson at Harvard in 1962 and subsequently a great deal of work was carried out by Exline, in America, and by Argyle, Kendon and Cook in England. Argyle and Cook (1976) report that in general the research supports the proposition that people who look more and with longer glances create a more favourable impression and are liked more than those who do not. People who look longer are found to be more friendly and self-confident. Conversely those who look less and with shorter glances appear to others to be defensive, evasive or 'shifty' and tend to be less at ease socially.

Decoding Facial Affect

In order to respond effectively to the communications of others, accurate perception of the information conveyed is essential. This can be thought of as the decoding of interpersonal messages, and Rosenthal (1979) has shown that more socially-skilled persons are more accurate decoders. Various attempts have been made to provide a comprehensive code for the facial expression of emotion, or affect, by humans (Lanzetta and Kleck, 1970; Ekman, Friesen and Tomkins, 1971; and Cuceloglu, 1972). However, the most comprehensive system developed to date is the Facial Action Code (FAC) developed by Ekman and Friesen (1978). This was derived from an analysis of the anatomical basis of facial movement. It measures the face itself rather than the information which can be inferred from the face, which has been the traditional focus of research on facial expression since the pioneering work of Darwin (1872). Having identified the different actions of the face in terms of the muscle groups involved, Ekman and Friesen have provided a training pack, or self-instruction manual, to serve as a reference in decoding facial behaviour. This comprises textual material describing each facial action in terms of its muscular basis and appearance changes; information about combinations of movements; still photographic and motion film examples, together with details of the development of FAC; reliability and validity studies; experiments which have successfully utilized the code, and possible areas of application. FAC has been used in training different professional groups in America, and its authors report that it has been used to isolate facial signs among deaf persons using sign language, and to measure change in brain damaged children.

Social Skills Training

It is to enable people to interact more effectively and enjoyably and to avoid the undesirable consequences of poor social skills that research data on social skills have been incorporated into occupational training for many professional groups, and offered in therapeutic programmes and courses for the general public in areas such as assertiveness training and conversation. It is here that one again encounters the psychologist as coach. Psychologists are called upon to administer such training in almost every conceivable kind of setting, whether occupational, clinical, educational, social or custodial. For example, at the University of Keele, general medical practitioners receive instruction on how to conduct interviews with patients, and with society becoming increasingly multi-racial, training for various professional groups in inter-cultural differences has become widespread. So, American police are now trained to maintain a certain physical distance when stopping negroes on the street (Garratt *et al.*, 1981), whilst English business personnel receive training in Arab social behaviour.

Training for professional social skills in interviewing, teaching, supervision, and therapy is one of the main areas of interest. However, it has been recognized for some time that traditional methods of education such as lectures, discussion, and textual instruction are insufficient to affect social skills. Like motor skills such as horse riding or swimming, social skills cannot be taught in this way, and there has been a growing emphasis on role playing and various forms of group training. The most common form of social skills training is what Argyle (1969) terms 'learning on the job', in which people are given no specific training other than the opportunity to practise a skill in the relevant situation. However, as Argyle points out, this does not necessarily guarantee improvement in social skill since many people are socially incompetent to begin with and merely persist in the use of ineffective social techniques. To be effective, learning on the job requires opportunities for practice of the skill, for feedback and the generation of new responses. People can and do acquire social skills in this way but they may not necessarily learn the most effective style of performance. The method therefore has its limitations, but Argyle suggests these may be partly overcome if, in real-life situations, someone acts as coach.

Role Play and Simulation

Theatrical techniques are often employed whereby the trainees enact the part they are going to play and receive immediate feedback from a trainer or other trainees on their performance. Such techniques are commonly used in the training of salespersons and teachers, and have been greatly assisted by developments in video-recording.

T-groups

The group training idea was inspired by gestalt psychologist Kurt Lewin, who recognized that training in human-relationship skills was greatly neglected. He advocated the establishment of groups for training such skills, the first of which met in Maine in 1947, shortly after which the National Training Laboratories were established. During the 1950s, many employment commissions and business schools in the United States sent students to groups run by the National Laboratories in order to develop their managerial skills and interpersonal sensitivity. Initially, groups of up to twelve persons met once a week over a period of several weeks to observe the nature of the group process, social interaction and human relations, and gradually this experience became known as sensitivity training. The training had far-reaching and comprehensive goals which underwent a marked change as it came to be recognized that participation in T-group or sensitivity training often led to powerful personal experiences – dramatic and startling disclosures, cathartic emotional expression, heightened sense of well-being and personal change. The effects seemed similar to those claimed for psychotherapy, and indeed during the 1960s the T-group rapidly lost its identity as a social-skills training group as it developed into the Encounter. Argyle (1969) indicates that whereas some 30–40 per cent of T-group trainees have been found to benefit from the training, many others are seriously disturbed by the experience.

The most widely-used of current methods of social-skills training involve elements of group work, role play and real-life training. These include explanation and modelling, followed by role playing, feedback provided in the form of verbal comments from a coach or trainer and video playback, and then rehearsal. Nevertheless, generalization to real-life situations remains problematic and so 'homework' is often prescribed between sessions; the trainee being required to perform repeat exercises in real life settings and report back on them. Even so, role-played sessions may be too far removed from certain real-life situations for them to be effective and so in some professional training, such as for the police, on the job training has been more heavily emphasized.

There have been many evaluation studies of social-skills training and Shepherd (1983), reviewing 52 such studies, concluded that social-skills training is of some value for the socially inadequate and that it has proved to be fairly successful in occupational settings. Argyle (1984), whilst cautious in his claims for social-skills training, suggests that it is starting to meet an immense human need. Not, of course, that it would have proved of much use to the unfortunate Rosencrantz and Guildenstern, who recognized too late that 'Wheels have been set in motion, and they have their own pace, to which we are . . . condemned' (p. 44).

FURTHER READING

ARGYLE, M. (1969) *Social Interaction*. London: Tavistock and Methuen.
ARGYLE, M. (1983) *The Psychology of Interpersonal Behaviour*. Harmondsworth: Penguin.

These are standard texts that provide an introduction to the psychology of social interaction and social skills.

ARGYLE, M. (1984) Some new developments in social skills training. *Bulletin of the British Psychological Society*, 37, 405–410.

This short article provides a comprehensive up-date on developments in the area.

CHAPTER 12

LEARNING SKILLS AND THEIR IMPROVEMENT

James Hartley

This chapter is divided into two parts. In the first part, I discuss four suggestions for improving learning skills that emerge from research in cognitive psychology. In the second part, I consider implications from these suggestions for coaching in study-skills.

Cognitive Psychology and Learning

If you asked a selection of cognitive psychologists what, in their view, were the main considerations that one ought to bear in mind when discussing learning, you would receive many answers. High on the list, however, would be notions about:
- the organization of material;
- the depth to which one processes it;
- the role of prior knowledge; and
- the knowledge that people have about their own skills of learning.

This chapter begins by describing experiments carried out by psychologists that illustrate each of these four areas. In some cases, similar material has been covered in earlier chapters, and so this will be an opportunity for you to consolidate your understanding.

How does the organization of material help learning?

It is often said that the hallmark of good instruction is that it is well organized. What does this mean? And can the benefits be demonstrated? Well, compare the following passages:

> The fox looks like a dog. Sometimes he stays in a hole. The fox eats small animals. He is red. The fox lives in the forest. He even likes fruit. He has a long nose. He catches birds for food. He makes a home in the bushes. He sometimes eats fish. His tail hangs down. He sleeps on the ground.

> The fox looks like a dog. He has a long nose. He is red. His tail hangs down. The fox lives in the forest. He sleeps on the ground. He makes a home in the bushes. Sometimes he stays in a hole. The fox eats small animals. He catches birds for food. He sometimes eats fish. He even likes fruit.

The second passage presents the same information but I hope you will agree that it is better organized. The information has been grouped around three main themes : what a fox looks like, where it lives, and what it eats. Danner (1976) used passages like these to examine the effects of organization on recall. He showed that children aged seven, nine and eleven invariably recalled the second passage better than the first. Similar findings have been reported several times. (See e.g. Bransford, 1979; Howe, Brainerd and Kingsma, 1985).

Studies such as these are concerned with the organization of elements in text. Textbook writers similarly try to help their readers by organizing the materials they are presenting. Books are divided into chapters, chapters into sections, sections into paragraphs, paragraphs into sentences, and so on. At each level the sequence of elements is important if the structure is to be made clear to the reader. Devices such as contents pages, chapter titles, and sub-headings are used to make the structure more apparent, as indeed are more subtle uses such as typography and layout (Hartley, 1985).

Without devices such as these, much of the organization imposed by the textbook writer (or the teacher) may not be apparent to the learner. Learners, as we shall see below, have different prior knowledge and expectations about what is being taught, and this may affect how they perceive material presented to them. Indeed, the evidence suggests that learning is improved further if learners also impose their own structure on material they are learning.

In one influential study Tulving (1962) presented students with a list of sixteen unrelated words in a different order on each trial, and after every presentation he asked them to recall the words in any order. Tulving examined each recall to see whether groups of words began to be remembered together irrespective of the fact that they appeared in a different order on each presentation. And this was what he found for some students. Furthermore, those students who grouped sets of words together and learned them in subjective clusters did better than students who did not do so.

Studies of students organizing material in more natural learning situations – say, by re-casting information into summary diagrams and tables or by using patterned notes – have also suggested that such organizational procedures are of considerable value (Davies and Greene, 1984; Jonassen, 1984).

How does the depth to which one processes material affect learning?

In order to consider this question I would like you first to try the following experiment (based on Howe, 1984). Read through the following list of words and mentally answer each question in turn.

speech   Is this a form of communication?

BRUSH   Is this written in small letters?

cheek   Does this rhyme with floor?

FENCE   Does this rhyme with tense?

FLAME   Is this something hot?

flour   Is this a kind of house?

honey   Is this written in small letters?

KNIFE   Does this rhyme with hunter?

glove   Is this written in small letters?

copper   Does this rhyme with mountain?

SHEEP   Is this an item of furniture?

MONK   Is this written in capital letters?

I shall return to these words in a few minutes (when you have had time to forget them . . .). Meanwhile I shall consider my third area of concern.

How does prior knowledge affect learning?

Prior knowledge can be shown both to handicap and to help learning. Rosemary Driver (1983) in *The Pupil as Scientist?* gives examples to show that many pupils come to science lessons with already formulated ideas that are at variance with theories that the teacher may wish to develop – and that this can handicap learning. These ideas influence the observations that children make in their experiments as well as affecting the explanations that they give for them. Driver points out that what seems obvious to the teacher may not be at all obvious for the pupil and *vice versa*. This is why, for example, teachers have to tell pupils what to see down a microscope, and have to help them to draw 'lines of force' when, for example, they sketch patterns of iron filings around magnets.

A study by Morris *et al.* (1981) demonstrates clearly how, on the other hand, prior knowledge might help recall. Morris *et al.* gave a group of students a forty-two item test of their knowledge of Association Football. (The test contained items such as: Who is Manchester City's goalkeeper? Who plays at Brisbane Road? Who is the Manager of Celtic? Who were the last English team to win the EUFA cup?) The students completed the test on a Saturday afternoon and then at 5.00 p.m. they listened to the results of sixty-four matches played that day. They were then presented with a fixtures list and asked to recall the scores.

The results showed that students who did well on the football knowledge test did significantly better at recalling the scores than students who did badly on the test. The average recall score for the first division matches (of which there were eleven) was 7.8 for ten students who scored twenty-five or more on the test of football knowledge, whereas it was only 3.3 for eleven students who scored five or less. Overall, the correlation between the prior knowledge score and successful recall was 0.81.

If prior knowledge can help or hinder learning then it seems sensible to say that good instruction should start from what the learners already know. This is easier to say than it is to achieve but there have been some demonstrations of the principle in action. Wittrock, Marks and Doctorow (1975), for example, sought to use children's prior knowledge as the basis for new learning in a vocabulary task. In this study four groups of 10–11 year old children took part. Group 1 twice read through a passage containing a number of difficult words and were then tested on their understanding of the words. Group 2 listened to the passage twice and were then tested. Groups 3 and 4 read or listened respectively to the same passage and then took the same test but on the first occasion the difficult words had been replaced with simpler, more familiar synonyms. It was only on the second occasion on which they read or heard the passage that the difficult words were included. Nonetheless, Groups 3 and 4 did much better than Groups 1 and 2 on the subsequent vocabulary test. Their prior familiarity with the easier words enabled them to give meanings to the more difficult words.

Depth of Processing (revisited)

Let us now return to the list of words that you examined a short while ago. Consider the twenty-four words listed on the next page and pick out as many of the original twelve words as you can recognize. Don't look back.

WITCH	KNIFE	EARL
FENCE	WOOL	MONK
BRUTE	FLAME	SKULL
POND	HONEY	BODY
CHEEK	SPICE	SPEECH
NURSE	PAINTER	GLOVE
FLOUR	SHEEP	WATER
STAR	BRUSH	COPPER

With the original twelve word list you were asked to answer a question about each word. There were three different kinds of question. There were questions about visual appearances (capital or small letters), questions about sounds (what words rhymed with others), and questions about meaning (for instance, whether sheep was an item of furniture).

Experiments like this one (with much longer lists of items) have suggested that you will remember something better if you have to process it or think about it more deeply (Craik and Tulving, 1975). Thus, in this experiment, we might expect that you will have remembered most of the words *speech, flour, flame,* and *sheep* because the questions about these words were related to their meaning. It is likely that you will have remembered least of the words *brush, glove, honey*, and *monk* because the questions about these words focussed only on their appearance. Your score on the remaining group of words (*cheek, knife, fence,* and *copper*) is likely to be somewhere in between because the questions about these words involved some processing but not as much as the questions about their meaning. (Don't worry if your individual scores don't come out in this way: I am only suggesting the average pattern of results obtained when many participants take part.) Results such as these suggest that people remember material better when they think about it or process it more deeply. (But see also Chapter 5.)

The idea that the more deeply one processes information the better it is recalled is an attractive one (although it is sometimes difficult to test). Yet so far we have considered only brief presentations of unrelated materials and their recall. What about more natural learning situations? Well there are sets of experiments which do indeed suggest that various information processing strategies can markedly affect long-term recall.

These strategies (listed in Table 12: 1) can be considered in terms of the depth of processing involved. For instance, Jonassen (1984) suggests that taking patterned notes is more effective than conventional notetaking or underlining, and I have already suggested above that reorganizing information is a more effective learning strategy than is rote rehearsal.

Another set of quite different studies has examined how students read instructional text. These studies have distinguished between students who adopt what is called a 'surface-approach' to their studies and those who adopt a 'deep-approach' (Marton, Hounsell and Entwistle, 1984).

Table 12:1 *Information-processing strategies for learning.*

● Strategies concerned with *rehearsing* material – e.g. copying, underlining, reviewing.

● Strategies concerned with *organizing* material – e.g. generating headings, grouping, outlining, mapping.

● Strategies concerned with *integrating* material – e.g. re-telling, summarizing, making diagrammatic displays, constructing integrative summary tables.

● Strategies concerned with *elaborating* information – e.g. using mental imagery, creating analogies, paraphrasing, relating new to old information.

Note: Many strategies (e.g. reviewing) can be classified in different ways. Some strategies which are less familiar (e.g. mapping, networking) are discussed by Jonassen, 1984.

Students who adopt a surface–approach to learning are likely to learn material parrot–fashion in order to regurgitate it in examinations, and to concentrate on remembering examples rather than organizational principles. With this chapter, for example, such a person might remember thay had to do an experiment involving processing of words, but fail to grasp that what I am trying to do is *to get the reader to consider the contributions of cognitive psychology to the study of learning*. Students who adopt a deep–approach, on the other hand, would try to look for organizing principles in the text and to relate any new ideas to previous knowledge given in earlier chapters. The surface–learner approaches the task with the intention to memorize and complete task requirements: the deep-learner approaches the text with the intention to understand.

There is some evidence to support the notion that deep–learners do better in examinations, but it is somewhat contradictory. This may in part be due to the fact (a) that some learners seem to be able to switch strategies (according to whether or not the material is new, and why it is being learned), and (b) that many examinations encourage memorizing and thus students can get by with a surface–approach. Marton *et al.* (1984) provide a useful discussion of these issues.

How does our knowledge about our own learning skills affect our learning?

The knowledge that we have about our own learning skills is called our *metacognition*. In Chapter 6, Angus Gellatly discussed the concept of *metamemory* in terms of what children knew about their memorial capabilities. Metacognition is a similar but broader term. Children's metacognition (or adults' for that matter) can be discussed in terms of what they know or appreciate about their own cognitive processes (and this would include their memory).

The concept of metacognition is an important one for two reasons. First, it allows us to explore the knowledge that we have about our own skills of learning. Second, it allows us to consider how far the strategies that we have considered so far – organizing material, linking new material to old, and encouraging deeper processing – can become part of our own everyday activities when we are learning.

Let us first consider how much knowledge adults might have about their own learning processes. In a study carried out in 1979, Linda Baker presented fourteen students with six passages, each approximately 250 words long. Each passage contained three paragraphs, and the middle paragraph had one of three kinds of confusion. These confusions were either (a) inconsistencies, (b) inappropriate or unclear references back, or (c) inappropriate logical connectives (e.g. using 'however' instead of 'in addition'). The students were first asked to read all six passages. They were then asked to recall the middle paragraph in each passage. Finally they were told about the three kinds of confusion, and asked if they had noticed them.

The results indicated that the confusions did not markedly affect the free recall of the middle paragraphs – although the students did tend to recall less than control students who read the paragraphs without any of the confusions. The students in the experimental group either ignored the confusions, corrected for them, or made appropriate or inappropriate inferences in making sense of these paragraphs.

Baker reported that less than one-quarter of the confusions (23 per cent) were noticed by the students when they were reading and that only 38 per cent of the confusions were detected when the students were asked to search for them. She concluded that some students can and do monitor their comprehension whilst they are reading (at least in an experimental situation) and that some can be persuaded to do so (e.g. when asked to search for confusions) but that many do not do so.

Subsequent research by Baker and Anderson (1982), using the same texts presented sentence by sentence on computer terminals, showed more precisely that students did spend longer reading sentences which contained confusions and that they looked back at them more frequently. But even in this study only 62 per cent of the students detected one or more of the confusions.

Studies such as these (with children and adults) have encouraged research workers to see whether or not they can help learners to evaluate their comprehension as they are reading, that is to enhance their metacognitive processing. Brown *et al.* (1983), for instance, develop the concept of self-controlled learning. Here the idea is that learners monitor, check, and evaluate their progress as they are learning. In terms of studying text, for instance, they suggest that readers should be taught five critical abilities: summarizing (self-review), questioning, clarifying, predicting, and monitoring their comprehension.

A typical example of one of many studies carried out by Brown and her colleagues is as follows. In this study the investigators were concerned with helping students to summarize texts. On the basis of several previous experiments, Brown and Day (1983) isolated the strategies shown in Table 12.2 – strategies used (with different degrees of success by students and experts) when summarizing text.

Brown, Campione and Day (1981) describe developmental trends in the appropriate use of these strategies: for example, 6 and 7 year olds concentrate on the delete strategies, and 15 year olds only use the 'invent a topic sentence' strategy appropriately about 30 per cent of the time – unlike experts who do it in almost every case. Brown *et al.* (1981) were interested in teaching students to learn to summarize better. Accordingly they devised a study which compared three teaching methods:

(a)   *'blind' instruction*: here the students were given general encouragement to produce a good summary, to capture the main ideas and to dispense with trivia and all unnecessary words, but they were not told any rules for achieving this;

(b)   *informed instruction*: this was the same as the above but rules for achieving these ends were provided and practice was given in their use;

(c)   *self-controlled learning*: this was the same as (b) but explicit training was given in how to control the rules: that is to say, students were shown how to check that all trivia and redundancies were deleted, how to check that lists of items were replaced with superordinates, how to check they had a topic sentence for each paragraph, and how to check whether they needed to invent topic sentences.

The results of this study showed that there were gains for all the students in their ability to select and to invent topic sentences with all three teaching methods but that the self-controlled techniques were particularly effective with less proficient students and with more difficult tasks.

The studies of self-controlled learning conducted by Brown *et al.* suggest that improvements in learning can be brought about (a) by making the task more structured and (b) by making knowledge about success more explicit. It appears that there are age and ability effects in all of this but that self-controlled learning – where the responsibility for evaluating the success of the learning shifts from the teacher to the learner – is a powerful learning technique.

Table 12.2 *Examples of experts' verbalisations of rules of summarizing.* (From Brown and Day, 1983, reproduced with permission)

Deletions	'The details are dropped for a summary of this type. You need the generalizations, not the details' (trivia) 'This essay wastes two sentences. Both state the simple fact that desert animals are nocturnal due to the heat. You can omit one.' (redundancy)
Superordination	'One thing I've done is drop the kinds of plants. Instead of writing daisies, poppies, marigolds and lilies, all I've written is "annual plants", again leaving out details and talking about generalization.'
Topic sentence selection	'This sentence contains the essential point of the paragraph, it states the process by which plant life is maintained. It has to be included in any summary.'
Topic sentence invention	'The paragraph is about the cycle of the annual plants, that produce seeds, wait until rainfall, bloom, produce seeds again, etc. Although it doesn't say so explicitly, all you need is to state this cycle then you can drop the rest.'
Combining across paragraphs	'In the first two paragraphs the only really essential information is the fact about the heat and the lack of water in the desert. I'll combine the first two paragraphs into only two sentences – that contains all the information that I need. One sentence is simple, the other is a compound sentence.'

Implications for Teaching Study-Skills

Traditional courses and texts on study-skills concentrate on giving students information about various skills such as notetaking, essay writing, and preparing for examinations regardless of the disciplines that the students are actually following (such as English, Mathematics, or Psychology). Such courses neglect problems raised by different subject matters and by individual differences in students' perceptions of what learning is about – and, indeed, how these may change over time (see Perry, 1981). They also neglect problems raised by notions of self–controlled learning.

Modern study-skills courses and texts tend to focus more on these latter issues. For example, one such course devised by Gibbs (1981) considers student activities within specific disciplines. In the context of notetaking, for example, Gibbs first asks individual students to take notes from a particular piece of text or lecture that is part of their current instruction. He then asks them to work in pairs, examining each other's notes and trying to understand why they are written in the way they are. Following this the pairs form groups of four, and each student has to explain his or her partner's notes to the three other students. After this, the four students are asked to consider the characteristics of their notes that make them either 'good', 'poor' or 'useless', and to indicate which strategies are useful and which should be avoided. These characteristics are written down so that they can be read out to the whole group of students in a final plenary session.

Gibbs takes a similar approach with writing skills. He suggests that students should be provided with two essays on the same subject, written by previous students with strikingly different perspectives. The students first work individually answering the questions: 'Which essay is better, and why? and 'In what ways do they differ?'. They then work in pairs to compare their comments and to work out a joint solution to the same questions. Next, in groups of four, the students are asked to pool their conclusions, and to describe what they think each of the two essay writers was trying to do. Finally, in a plenary session, each group tells the others their conclusions and a general discussion follows.

Other modern study-skills courses tend to concentrate on teaching learners both general and specific skills. The general skills are those of being able to select for the task in hand a set of appropriate specific sub-skills from a wide array of choice. Students are taught sets of strategies: strategies that can be deployed differently in different learning circumstances.

Earlier, in Table 12:1, I listed sets of information-processing strategies when I was discussing how such different strategies might involve learners in deeper processing. To these information-processing strategies we can now add two more kinds: metacognitive strategies and support strategies. Metacognitive strategies, as discussed above, are concerned with techniques for monitoring one's comprehension – such as reviewing, paraphrasing, imagining, predicting and asking questions to test one's understanding. Support strategies are concerned with ways of coping with distractions and anxieties and with organizing one's environment for effective study. Such strategies include keeping a particular place for regular study, setting and keeping to deadlines, working out study timetables, and carrying out relaxation exercises in order to reduce anxiety. Weinstein and Mayer (1985) describe study-skills courses at all levels of education – from primary to tertiary – which have focused on particular information-processing, metacognitive and support strategies. Studies which combine training in several strategies from all three groups are rare, but Weinstein and Mayer do discuss four examples. Here, for the purpose of illustration I shall describe two such integrative approaches.

Study 1. Dansereau *et al.* criticised much of the early work on study-skills courses because they felt that these courses were too broad and did not pay sufficient attention to current cognitive psychology. Since the mid–1970s, Dansereau and his colleagues have devised a number of learning-strategy training programmes which have sought to remedy these deficiencies (e.g. Dansereau *et al.* 1979; Diekhoff, Brown, and Dansereau, 1982; Dansereau *et al.* 1983; Dansereau, 1985).

The best known Dansereau programme goes by the acronym MURDER where:

M = setting the *mood* for study;
U = reading for *understanding* important and difficult ideas;
R = *recalling* material without reference to the text;
D = *digesting* the material by correcting mistakes in the recall and by amplifying and reprocessing the material;
E = *expanding* the knowledge by asking questions; and
R = *reviewing* mistakes and learning from tests.

The acronym MURDER describes a set of six main executive strategies (i.e. what to do). Each executive strategy is accompanied by several more detailed operative sub-strategies (i.e. how to do it). Thus setting the *mood* for instruction involves utilizing relaxation techniques and constructive self-talk, (e.g. 'Now . . . what have I got to do . . . I see . . . Done it . . . Good'). *Recalling* involves utilizing sub-strategies such as paraphrasing, using imagery, mapping and the analysis of key ideas. In addition, the continual monitoring of one's comprehension is an operative sub-strategy of *all* of the executive ones.

To assess the effectiveness of this scheme, Dansereau *et al.* (1979) trained thirty-eight psychology students in the use of these executive and operative sub-strategies for two hours per week for a period of fifteen weeks. In comparisons with control groups, the experimental group showed significantly greater gains on subsequent tests of comprehension and recall and on self-report measures of learning-skills.

Study 2. Paris, Cross and Lipson (1984) devised a training programme called Informed Strategies for Learning (ISL) to help junior-school children improve their reading skills. This particular training programme lasted for fourteen weeks, and it included several features of direct instruction, such as (a) focusing the children's attention on the material to be learned, (b) generating high levels of involvement, and (c) providing frequent practice and immediate feedback. In addition, the teaching modules in the programme contained a 'rich variety' of activities designed to aid comprehension: these included lessons on understanding the purposes of reading, activating relevant background knowledge, allocating attention to the main idea in each paragraph, detecting inferences, and monitoring one's comprehension.

The ISL programme was tested with two groups of 8–9 year olds and two groups of 10–11 year olds (with matched control groups). The pupils in the ISL groups made larger gains than did the control groups on subsequent cloze tests (which involve filling in missing words in passages of text) and in error-detection tasks, but they did not do any better on two standardized tests of reading comprehension. Nonetheless, Paris *et al.* claimed that the ISL groups showed greater knowledge about reading strategies.

These two studies highlight the main concerns of workers in the field of learning strategies. The research involves (a) a fine grain cognitive analysis of what is involved in doing particular tasks, (b) the development of sets of strategies within a total system for coping with different aspects of different tasks, and (c) an evaluation of the success of the outcome. The results of the evaluation studies are then used to modify and improve the original training programme.

Conclusions

In this chapter, I have given a brief account of some of the areas of cognitive psychology that relate to learning. The focus has been more on laboratory experiments than on outcome studies of coaching in study skills, largely because there are more of the former than of the latter, and the former are more precise. Two major criticisms, however, of laboratory studies in this context are (a) their heavy reliance on simplified experimental materials and conditions, and (b) their concentration on verbal learning (at the expense of practical, social and affective issues). These deficiencies have not, of course, gone unnoticed, and undoubtedly future research will seek to remedy them.

FURTHER READING

BRANSFORD, J.D. (1979) *Human Cognition: Learning, Remembering and Understanding*. Belmont: Wadsworth.

A good, broad overview of cognitive psychology and learning.

NISBET, J. and SHUCKSMITH, J. (1986) *Learning Strategies*, London: Routledge and Kegan Paul.

A text that translates work on metacognition into practical concerns for teachers.

SECTION IV

THOUGHT AND SKILL

CHAPTER 13

SKILL AT REASONING

Angus Gellatly

Some readers may be familiar with the following riddle. 'Three Indians are walking single file along a path in the forest. The first Indian is the second Indian's father, and the second Indian is the third Indian's son. How can this be?' Many people, if they have not encountered a riddle of the same class before, find this one quite puzzling, at least for a time. The difficulty springs from the kind of interpretation people are inclined to give to the sentences comprising the riddle, the tendency to go beyond the information actually provided. Of course, the solution is that the third Indian is the second Indian's mother, but if you have unconsciously assumed that all the Indians are male the solution may be hard to spot.

At least two factors might encourage an assumption, or inference, as to the gender of the three Indians. First, the masculine references of the terms 'son' and 'father' may create a set, or expectation, towards masculinity. Second, a tendency may be operating to assign masculine default values when gender is unspecified, as in the common use of masculine pronouns in cases of indefinite gender. Whatever the relative importance of these two factors, the riddle works by trading upon the fact, discussed by John Sloboda in Chapter 4 and by Don Rogers in Chapter 10, that communication through language is only possible on the basis of a host of shared presumptions between speakers/writers and listeners/readers. To understand speech or text the listener/reader must supply all manner of inferences that go beyond what is actually stated, and the importance of the riddle of the Indians is that it demonstrates how unwarranted such inferences can prove to be.

In this chapter we will be examining people's propensity to draw inferences when reasoning about everyday matters or about logical problems, so it is necessary to be clear as to what is meant by the term 'inference'. An inference is said to be made, or drawn, when on the basis of particular assertions (the premises) we move to a conclusion not explicitly contained within the original assertions. To take an example from Chapter 4, if we read 'John was on his way to school. He was not looking forward to the maths lesson', we may infer that

John is a school pupil who is not very good at maths. Rightly or wrongly, we have moved beyond the premisses to a conclusion. Inferences have been made.

Philosophers distinguish between two kinds of inference, inductive inference and deductive inference. Since the part played in human reasoning by these two kinds of inference is the principal concern of the present chapter, we need to look more closely at the distinction between them.

Inductive Inference

It turns out that, in addition to language understanding, nearly all behaviour and thought rest upon assumptions and inferences that cannot be conclusively justified, a point originally emphasized by the eighteenth century philosopher, David Hume. An inference for which it is claimed only that the conclusion is *probably* true is an *inductive inference*. For example, from my observation of dark clouds in the sky today and my knowledge that it usually rains when there are dark clouds in the sky, I inductively infer that it will rain today; taking this conclusion as probable only. My conclusion may be stated verbally or it may be expressed in action as when, having looked at the sky, I take up my raincoat and leave the house. Life, and language, would be impossible if we did not allow ourselves inferences that are only likely to be correct. Many of our best endeavours rest on inferences to probable conclusions, and one part of expertise resides in accurately judging degrees of probability. Nevertheless, ever since Aristotle discovered – or, depending upon your point of view, invented – deductive reasoning, a special reverence has been accorded by the Western mind to inferences whose warrant has been taken to be conclusive rather than only probable.

Deductive Inference

An inference in which the premisses guarantee the conclusion is a deductive inference, and may appear in the guise of what is called a syllogism. A famous example of a valid syllogism is this:

(1)   All men are mortal.
       Socrates is a man.
       Therefore Socrates is mortal.

Reading this syllogism you just know that the conclusion follows from the premisses. If it were to transpire that Socrates were not mortal, we could confidently assert that one or both of the two premisses must have been false. This confidence stems from our intuitive sense that the syllogism has a *valid* form, where a valid argument form is one for which true premisses must always lead to a true conclusion.

Ever since Aristotle, people have been very impressed by deduction. Knowledge which is arrived at deductively, as in mathematics, seems peculiarly satisfying. For example, Euclid was able to state a small number of premisses – or postulates, as he called them – and from them deduce the whole of Euclidean geometry. In so doing, he set a mathematico-deductive ideal against which the methods of all other branches of knowledge tend to be measured.

Deduction and Reasoning

One consequence of the esteem in which deduction came to be held was that questions were raised about its relationship to rationality and human reasoning. Is rationality the ability to reason in accord with deductive logic? If so, do all, some, or any humans qualify as rational? One position that can be taken on this matter, and has been taken by, amongst others, the philosophers Kant and Boole, is that the rules of deductive logic are descriptive of human thinking. The claim is that in some sense logic exists in the mind; there is a 'mental logic' and thinking complies with its rules. The rules referred to are such as the following pair:

Modus Ponens	*Modus Tollens*
If p then q	If p then q
p	Not q
Therefore q	Therefore not p

An alternative to the conception of reasoning as guided by a mental logic is to consider it as a skill, like all the other forms of cognition dealt with in this book. Skilled performances have to be understood in their own terms. We do not look to underlying logics to explain them but for evidence of characteristic features of skill like input and output chunking, improvement with practice, fluency and rapidity of responses, automaticity, and so on (Chapter 2). So if reasoning is a skill we should be able to analyse it without invoking a mental logic. In fact, the debate as to whether reasoning is best conceived in terms of skill or of mental logic, or in terms compatible with either approach, is a complex one (Johnson-Laird, 1982, 1983; Gellatly, 1988). In the remainder of this chapter we will examine some of the evidence for and against both points of view but without trying to settle the dispute one way or the other. To begin our investigation of reasoning we can turn to a problem devised by Peter Wason (1966).

Wason's Problem

Wason's problem refers to four cards, depicted in Figure 13:1. Naturally, only the facing sides of the cards are visible and these show the symbols D, E, 4, and

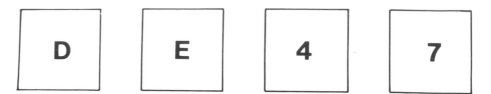

Figure 13:1   The Wason four-card selection task.

7 respectively. We are told that every card has a letter on one side and a digit on the other, and the truth of this is not in doubt. The following rule is, then given: 'If a card has a D on one side then it has a 4 on the other side'. The problem is to name those cards, and only those cards, which must be turned over in order to decide whether the rule is true or false.

There is no trickery in this problem, although it may help to emphasize that the rule is not a reversible one, so the converse of the rule does not apply. You should try to work out the solution for yourself before reading any further.

D'Andrade's Problem

Before the correct solution to Wason's problem is revealed, here is a second problem originally devised by Roy D'Andrade (see Rumelhart and Norman, 1981). Imagine that you are employed in a department store with responsibility for checking sales receipts. The store has a rule that 'If a purchase exceeds £30, then the sales slip must be signed on the back by the manager'. You are shown four sales slips, depicted in Figure 13:2. They show, respectively, receipt of £45, receipt of £15, a signed back, and an unsigned back. The problem is to name those slips, and only those slips, that must be turned over to check whether or not the rule has been followed. Once again, try this problem out for yourself.

Figure 13:2   The D'Andrade version of the selection task.

Experiments have shown that most people give the correct solution to D'Andrade's problem. They choose to turn over the slip showing receipt of £45 and the slip with an unsigned back. It is fairly obvious that the rule has been broken only if either the slip for the receipt of over £30 has not been signed (contravening modus ponens), or if the unsigned slip is found to have been for receipt of over £30 (contravening modus tollens). Easy, isn't it?

Now let us return to Wason's problem. Far fewer people – often ten per cent or less of University students – get the right answer to this one. The solution is to turn the card showing D and the card showing 7. The problem is to decide whether the given rule is true or false. If the combination of symbols on any of the four cards breaks the rule, the rule is false. Otherwise it is true. The rule states that 'If a card has a D on one side then it has a 4 on the other side'. It follows that the rule has been broken only if the card showing D does not have a 4 on the back, or if the card not showing 4 (and so showing 7) *does* have a D on the back. Yet the most common response people give is to choose to turn over the D card and the 4 card rather than the D card and the 7 card. That is, they turn over the cards showing the symbols mentioned in the rule. Instead of solving the problem, they simply 'match' their responses to the named symbols. The matching is not usually a conscious process and sometimes subjects in an experiment will argue heatedly that the correct solution really is D and 4, not D and 7 (Wason, 1983).

Reasoning and Memory

The interesting thing about this difference in performance with the two problems is that they are really two versions of the same problem; they have exactly the same logical structure. Indeed, D'Andrade's aim in devising his problem was precisely to come up with an easier version of Wason's problem, and anyone who has trouble accepting the correct solution to the latter can gain insight into its form by working it through in parallel with the D'Andrade version. Problems with the same logical structure can be difficult or easy depending upon the content with which they are fleshed out. Nor is this simply a matter of abstract content being harder than concrete or realistic content, since some concrete and realistic versions of Wason's problem are just as difficult as the abstract version.

Why, then, do people perform well on the D'Andrade version of the problem? Griggs (1983) argues that the facilitation observed with this – and some other versions of the problem – comes about because the content cues in long-term memory information about the solution. You need not have been a department store employee; experience or understanding of analogous kinds of relationship will suffice. Grigg's argument is that people do not so much solve D'Andrade's version as remember an analogous problem they have encountered before, and to which they know the solution. What this suggests is that people will tend to solve a novel problem only if they spot its resemblance to a familiar problem for which they have either a solution or a solution procedure at their disposal.

A slightly different way of putting this, but which again emphasizes the role of memory, is as follows, From Chapter 5 we know that problems which place a heavy load on STM, or working memory, are difficult to solve. One way of reducing STM load is by chunking input in accordance with patterns stored in LTM. So a problem that is stated in a way that matches one or more LTM patterns will be easier to interpret, to 'hold in mind', than one that is not. Now one sort of LTM pattern is what was already referred to in Chapter 5 as a 'script'. The D'Andrade version calls up from LTM the script for how managers and sales persons behave in department stores, and the problem can therefore be sensibly interpreted. Wason's original version, however, does not match any such familiar pattern. It has to be interpreted more or less word by word in working memory. This overloads working memory with the result that the problem is never properly understood by most people.

According to the above view, the role of reasoning is rarely, if ever, that of taking the information given about a problem and straightforwardly deducing a conclusion from it. More likely, reasoning will be deployed retrospectively to justify a solution that has been arrived at by other means. Such a view of how problems get solved is consistent with the notion of *if – then* production rules introduced in Chapter 2. The *action* of running through a solution procedure occurs only if the problem is configured in such a way as to meet the *conditions* for that *action*. The *action* sequence can be triggered automatically and will yield a solution that can subsequently be justified through the use of reasoning. Learning to configure new problems so that they resemble familiar ones is the process by which generalization, or transfer, is mediated (see Chapter 8).

Support for the idea that deductive problem solving depends upon the activation of productions stored in long-term memory and that generalization is a matter of learning to configure problems appropriately, comes from studies of the differences between novices and experts working on textbook physics problems. Professional physicists recognize (configure) types of problems more readily and respond to them with larger and more automatic solution procedures. Their solutions are executed as a few – even single – computations, or productions, rather than in a series of smaller steps. Even when novices are able to execute the *action* of a solution procedure, they tend to be poor at recognizing the *conditions* under which it is appropriate. Larkin, McDermott, Simon and Simon (1980) suggest that mathematical intuition can be understood as consisting of this highly developed pattern recognition of *conditions* from which an associated *action* follows automatically.

Reasoning and Actions

We have seen that familiarity with the content of verbal problems influences the success with which they can be tackled. The same has been found to be true with non-verbal problems that must be solved in actions rather than in words.

Kendler and Kendler (1967) tested children on a piece of apparatus that comprised three panels A, B, and C. First, panel A was presented and the children were taught that pressing a button on it led to a marble being dispensed. Panel A was then put away and replaced by Panel B, in which pressing a button yielded a ball bearing. Next panel C was presented along with a pile of marbles and ball bearings, any of which could fit into a slot in panel C. The children learnt that inserting a marble into the slot produced a reward, such as a toy or a sweet, but that inserting a ball bearing produced nothing. Finally, the children were presented with all three panels and invited to obtain a reward. Kendler and Kendler found that until about the age of ten, children found difficulty in putting together the two actions of pushing the button on panel A to get a marble and then inserting the marble into panel C to obtain the reward. Combining the two acts into an 'action inference' was very hard for younger children.

Cole, Gay, Glick and Sharp (1971) repeated this experiment in Liberia and found that non-literate Kpelle adults performed poorly on it, with only about 8 per cent achieving a solution. Were the Kpelle incapable of making the inference? Cole *et al.* felt that the complex machinery of their apparatus – which incorporated the principles of a vending machine – might be inhibiting the Kpelle. They transformed the task into one involving keys and a lock, objects with which the Kpelle were familiar. Panels A and B were replaced by two identifiably different match boxes containing, respectively, a red and a black key. Panel C was replaced by a locked box which could be opened by one of the keys to obtain a reward. As before, subjects first learnt which key was in which box, then, separately, which key fitted the locked box. When presented with the whole task more than 70 per cent of the Kpelle successfully obtained the reward. The content of the problem, in this case the nature of the apparatus, influenced solution rates. Cole *et al.* thought this was because the unfamiliar apparatus inhibited subjects from getting started on the solution procedure. Their finding will perhaps come as no surprise to those who are themselves wary of mechanical equipment.

Reasoning and Logic

That success with a problem is a function of its content as well as of its logical form is, in fact, a far from novel finding. Aristotle was well aware that the ease with which the validity of a syllogism can be judged varies with its content. For example, consider the following syllogism:
(2)   Some members of the Labour Party are self-educated people.
       No Wallonians belong to the Labour Party.
       Therefore at least some Wallonians are not self-educated people.
Begg and Denny (1969) found that as many as 55 per cent of students erroneously judged a syllogism similar to (2) to be valid. Sometimes people will argue heatedly for the validity of such a syllogism even when told that it is

invalid. Yet a change of content can reveal immediately that the form of the syllogism is flawed. For instance, (3) has the same form as (2) but few people are likely to judge it as valid.

(3)   Some mammals are creatures that swim.
      No fish are mammals.
      Therefore at least some fish are not creatures that swim.

The fact that the content of problems has such a bearing on people's ability to reason correctly about them could be taken as disconfirming the doctrine of mental logic. For it could be argued that if there were a mental logic, the efficiency with which it operated ought to depend only on form and not on content. Furthermore, the alternative view, that reasoning is a skill, is supported by a great deal of evidence. We know that the more time people practice solving mathematical problems or chess problems the better they get at that class of problem. Similarly, people's ability to evaluate categorical syllogisms can be improved if they are taught the technique of Euler's circles. This technique employs circles to represent the categories of entities mentioned in the syllogism, as in Figure 13:3, which also demonstrates that a given premise may have more than one possible representation. Understandably, people are more likely to make errors where there are a number of ways of representing a pair of premises than when only a single representation is possible (Johnson-Laird, 1983). In the former case there is simply more to think about, and therefore more opportunity for mistakes. Nevertheless, the point remains that practice and the acquisition of strategies, or techniques, leads to improvements in performance, and these are amongst the hallmarks of skill.

Proponents of mental logic, however, do not accept that the existence of content dependent errors in human reasoning renders their position untenable. A common defence, recently stated by Henle (1962, 1978), is to claim that reason itself is never at fault but that it is sometimes applied to distorted, or misperceived, information. In the case of syllogisms one of the premises may be forgotten, or an extra premiss deriving from factual knowledge may be incorporated into the problem, or a premiss may be misinterpreted. For instance, 'All A are B' may be taken to imply that, also, 'All B are A'. Henle suggests that when the trouble is taken to reconstruct the actual reasoning applied to a problem it turns out that people always reason validly though they sometimes set themselves to solve the wrong problem. Alternatively, they may not attempt to reason out the problem at all but may instead settle for guessing an answer, or they may evaluate the truth of a conclusion rather than the validity of the argument by which it was derived. Either way it can be claimed that reasoning itself does not go astray.

A difficulty with Henle's proposal is that it does not appear to be open to refutation. Whatever the response made to a problem it will always be possible to give a reconstruction that makes it appear rational, provided only that a suitable misinterpretation of the premisses is assumed. On the other hand, there

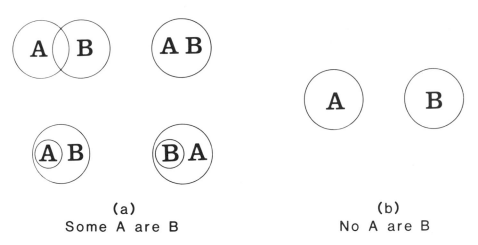

(a)   (b)
Some A are B   No A are B

Figure 13:3   Some examples of the use of Euler circles.

is no doubt that misinterpretations *do* offer a plausible explanation of many apparent errors on reasoning tasks. We can see this very clearly in connection with cross-cultural studies of cognition.

Logic, Culture, and Language

There is a long-established tradition in the West of wondering whether people from other cultures have the same or different mental processes as ourselves. Frequently, it has been claimed that so-called traditional peoples resemble Western children in their mental processes, and that both groups differ from Western adults (e.g. Piaget, 1974). Comparisons of this kind prove in practice to involve grave conceptual difficulties (Gellatly, 1988). Nevertheless, cross-cultural studies have yielded provocative findings.

A number of studies have been carried out in which non-literate, unschooled, and typically village-dwelling people from various parts of the world have been asked to reason with syllogisms. Scribner (1977) notes that when asked to repeat back premises that have just been read out, such people are often unable to do so. They omit premises altogether, or substitute them with personal knowledge. In a similar vein, when given the syllogism:

(4)   All women who live in Monrovia are married.
       Kemu is not married.
       Does she live in Monrovia?

a typical subject replied, 'Monrovia is not for one kind of people, so Kemu came to live there'. The hypothetical status of the syllogism is ignored in favour of practical information concerning the subject of conversation that has been introduced; in this case, residence in Monrovia. As a result of this habit, the kinds of distortion described by Henle are freely observed. And, like Henle, Scribner claims that non-literate people invariably reason logically about their own interpretations of a problem, if they will reason about it at all.

This last qualification is necessary because on occasion non-literate people entirely reject the reasoning tasks set by psychologists. In the 1930's Luria (1976) gave the following problem to Uzbek peasants in Central Asia:

(5)   In the far north all bears are white.
       Novaya Zemlya is in the far north.
       What colour are the bears there?

Among the responses he obtained were: 'You should ask the people who have been there and seen them' and 'We always speak of only what we see; we don't talk about what we haven't seen'. These respondents simply were not prepared to play Luria's question-and-answer game, and it is by their refusal that we are brought to the realization that there is a game to be played. Scribner (1977) says that the game rests upon an understanding of a particular type of discourse, and what becomes apparent is that a game (or a type of discourse) and its rules may be taken for granted in one culture yet be unfamiliar in another. The syllogism game, the type of discourse on which it is founded, proves to be unfamiliar in non-literate unschooled societies.

Rules and Discourse

We have already seen that understanding language involves the listener in making all kinds of linguistic inference relating to the topic of conversation. That is not all. As already described in Chapter 10, listeners also have to infer a speaker's intentions, what may be referred to as the 'conveyed meaning' of an utterance (Clarke, 1977). If somebody asks you, 'Do you know the way to the station?' and you reply, 'Yes thanks', then either you have not correctly inferred the person's intentions or else you have chosen to be hostile, humorous, or somesuch. Inferring a speaker's intentions, or conveyed meaning, requires an understanding of the type of discourse to which his utterance belongs. Different kinds of discourse have their own (overlapping) sets of rules for the guidance of listeners and speakers. The rules governing Anglo-American conversational discourse include that the utterance 'Do you know the way to the station?' be interpreted (a) as a request for information, not an enquiry as to the extent of the listener's knowledge of local geography, and (b) as calling for an answer in terms of directions only if the listener really does know the way to the station. In the conversational discourse of other cultures, rule (a) can continue to hold but in place of rule (b) good manners may dictate an answer in term of directions even when the listener has no idea at all as to the whereabouts of the station. This can prove disconcerting to the tourist who addresses a local resident without appreciating the divergence in their respective discourse rules.

The relevance of this analysis for performance on syllogisms should be apparent. In asking "does she (Kemu) live in Monrovia ' or 'What colour are the bears in Novaya Zemlya?", the psychologist is invoking a set of discourse rules including one rule that says listeners are to ignore their personal knowledge, or lack of it, and to answer in respect only of the information given in the premises, which may itself be factually false. Conversationally speaking, this is a very unusual demand (Gellatly, 1987). For, as we have seen, listeners are generally expected to contribute rather than to suppress their knowledge of a topic. Indeed, so odd is the demand that non-literate people do not recognize it. They stick by their habitual rules of conversation; answering the question with personal knowledge. Or, as in Luria's case, they may chide the psychologist for infringing their rules with a question that takes them beyond their personal knowledge.

Reasoning as a Skill

Abiding by discourse rules is itself a skill, as Don Rogers has discussed in chapter 10. This is forcefully brought home if you enter a social group in which an idiosyncratic form of humour is shared. You may well find yourself unable readily to interpret the conveyed meanings of speakers' utterances, to distinguish jokey insults from genuine insults, actual emotions from pretended emotions. If you spend long enough in the group, however, such problems resolve themselves. Through the application of your social skills (Chapter 11) you learn to decode the messages being transmitted. You fall in with the group's way of thinking and speaking. What this tells us, amongst other things, is that there is more than one level of skill in deductive reasoning. We have already seen that solving deductive problems is a skilful activity which may, like other skills, be represented in terms of production systems. Success with deductive problems is improved by practice, which leads to problems being configured in larger chunks that automatically activate bigger units of solution procedure. Now we see that a prior form of skill is also involved. To engage in deductive problem solving you have first to have mastered the discourse rules by which that kind of cognition is constrained. This consists, of course, in making linguistic/discourse inferences which are not themselves deductively secure; they may be proved wrong. Thus deduction, that ideal of secure knowledge, turns out to be built upon foundations of inductive inference. Far from transcending the inductive, deduction proves to be dependent upon skills of inductive inference making.

This does not mean that any of the above should be read as a disparagement of deduction. The casting of arguments in deductive form is, where applicable, an immensely important method for ensuring the soundness and rigour of our thinking. In science, and in many areas of daily life, we proceed by positing a theory then checking to see what consequences can be validly deduced from it, and then testing these. In mathematics, too, the Euclidean model of stating postulates followed by deductions from them remains a powerful one. What this chapter has attempted to show is that success on deductive problems is a matter of cultural learning, of cognitive skill. The solving of deductive problems does not differ in principle from general problem solving, which is the topic of the next chapter.

FURTHER READING

Readable introductions to the topic of deduction can be found in:
GILHOOLY K, J. (1981) *Thinking: Directed, Undirected and Creative*. London: Academic Press.

ANDERSON J. R. (1984) *Cognitive Psychology and its implications* (2nd edition). San Francisco: Freeman.

A comprehensive but more difficult treatment of deduction is given in:
JOHNSON-LAIRD P. N. (1983) *Mental Models*. Cambridge: Cambridge University Press.

CHAPTER 14

SOLVING PROBLEMS

Angus Gellatly

To begin this chapter here are two problems for you to attempt.

(a) One morning, at sunrise, a Buddhist monk began to climb a mountain, on
     a narrow path that wound around it. He climbed at a steady three miles an
     hour.
        After twelve hours, he reached the top, where there was a temple, and
     remained there to meditate for several days. Then, at sunrise, he started
     down, on the same path. He walked at a steady five miles an hour.
        Prove that there must be a spot along the path which he occupied on
     both trips at exactly the same time of day. (Based on a problem devised by
     Duncker.)
(b) You are organizing a singles knock-out tennis tournament, for which there
     are 111 entrants. For each match there must be a new set of balls. How
     many sets of balls do you need to order? (Based on a problem devised by de
     Bono.)

Solutions to the two problems will be revealed a few pages further on. For the
present they will have served their purpose if they started you thinking about
what is involved in problem-solving, why it is sometimes difficult, and how it
might be improved. These are the issues with which this chapter is concerned.
We will be examining both the processes that go to make up problem-solving
and the question of whether people can be trained to improve their problem
solving efficiency.
    To start with, however, some general remarks are required about the nature
of problems and their solutions.

The Nature of Problem Solving

It may seem strange that this book should contain a chapter devoted specifically
to problem solving. After all, previous chapters have also been concerned with

solutions to problems of remembering, communicating, and studying. In what way, then, is the present chapter more to do with problem solving than any of the others?

That depends on what we mean by a problem. Newell and Simon (1972) define a problem in the following way: 'A person is confronted with a problem when he wants something and does not know immediately what series of actions he can perform to get it.' On this definition, a problem is relative to the capabilities of the individual. For a four–year old child, remembering a word list of two animal names, two fruits, and two colours might be a problem. For the literate adult, it is no longer a problem because the appropriate steps – engaging in categorized rehearsal – are taken automatically. In a similar manner, reading or driving a car presents the novice with all manner of problems that simply do not exist for the expert. Many, though not all, of the problems mentioned in earlier chapters have been of this sort. That is, they are problems for which solution procedures are acquired in the course of normal social and cognitive development, or as a result of special training, and which therefore – on Newell and Simon's definition – cease to be problems at all.

Clearly, people can and do learn skills for eliminating all kinds of culturally identified problems; from mastering the grammar of English, to navigating without instruments or judging the validity of syllogisms. Some of these skills, such as comprehension monitoring, have a wide range of application, while others are of use only in very specific circumstances. Nevertheless, despite all these acquired skills, everyday life continually presents us with new problems for which we have no prepared solution. This, then, leads to the question of whether or not it is possible to learn a very general set of skills, or principles, for solving all kinds of problem. In other words, as well as becoming skilled in the use of solution procedures for particular problem domains, as in the example of the physicists discussed in Chapter 13, is it possible to become a skilled general problem solver? The remainder of the chapter will address this question. We will examine the processes, such as representation, that are involved in problem-solving, and then offer an assessment of attempts to improve the efficiency with which they are executed.

Problem Representation

We have already seen with Wason's selection task (Chapter 13) that the same logical problem may be more or less easily dealt with depending on the content with which the logical form is decked out. This is one example of the influence of representation. But in what ways beside content may representations differ? Well, one way is the mode of representation.

Verbal and Visual Image Representations

A good example of a difference in mode of problem representation is that between verbal encoding and imagery encoding. In practice this is a matter of degree since a verbal formulation is liable to elicit at least some visual imagery and an image is likely to be associated with at least some words. All the same, a problem can be represented either predominantly in words or predominantly in images, and which is employed can have important consequences. Duncker's buddhist monk problem, described earlier in the chapter, is presented verbally and in such a way as to encourage attempts at a verbal-mathematical solution. However, this way of representing the problem is not at all helpful. By contrast, the solution becomes trivial when the problem is represented in visual images. To do this, imagine a monk climbing a mountain in the course of a day. Imagine also a second monk descending the same mountain in the course of a day. Now superimpose the two images as if the two journeys were undertaken on the same day. Clearly at some time during that day the two monks must meet, and therefore be at the same point at the same time. This holds equally for the case of the single monk making the two journeys on separate days.

In the monk problem, a visual representation is superior to a verbal one. This is not always the case. De Bono's tennis tournament problem is much harder if you begin with the image of a sheet of paper with the draw for a knock-out tournament on it; a shape like a pyramid fallen on its side. This leads you to start adding one final match to two semi-finals, to four quarter-finals, and so on back to the first round, where allowances have to be made for byes since 111 is not a power of 2 like 64 or 128. A much simpler solution is available if the problem is represented verbally, like this. The number of entrants is 111, all of them lose once except for the winner of the tournament, so there must be 110 matches and that is the number of boxes of balls that is required.

These two examples demonstrate the importance of trying out different representations of a problem and assessing their relative potential for yielding a solution. Unfortunately, a number of factors combine to make flexible representation difficult to achieve in practice, and we now turn to an examination of some of these factors.

Mental Set

Past experience influences present behaviour in numerous ways, and without the ability to learn from experience we should be in a bad state indeed. All the same, old habits are not always adequate to the demands of new situations. We can become too set in our ways. Thomas Kuhn, the influential historian of science, argues that habits of thought are an important determinant of theoretical commitments in science. When a new theory is proposed to challenge an established theory, there is rarely conclusive evidence for deciding between them. The reason the older theory is gradually abandoned is because the generation that believed in it, and had learnt to think in its terms, dies out. Older scientists find a novel theory, that introduces unfamiliar concepts and postulates the existence of new entities, hard to come to grips with. Having learnt to construe the world in terms of an older theory, they do not readily make the transformation to a new world view. Kuhn (1970) illustrates the point with a discussion of the 'discovery' of oxygen. In 1774, Priestley isolated a sample of what we now call oxygen but which he thought to be either nitrous oxide or 'dephlogisticated' air. It was Lavoisier who, in 1777, proposed that the gas was one of two major constituents of air, and who developed a basis for the modern conception of the element, oxygen. Priestley was never able to accept Lavoisier's theory and continued to conceptualize the new gas in terms of the older, phlogiston theory with which he was familiar. Thus although Priestley was the first of the two to isolate the gas now called oxygen, he cannot really be credited with its discovery. In fact, 'discovery' turns out to be a difficult concept.

Kuhn's example deals with the long-term effects of experience, with mental habits accumulated over years of learning. Mental set can also be induced in the short term, however. This has been most famously demonstrated by Luchins and Luchins (1950) with their water-jars experiment, which is illustrated in Table 14:1. Given three jars of varying sizes and an unlimited water supply, the task is

Table 14:1 *An illustration of Luchin's water-jar problems.*

Problems	Capacity of Jug A	Capacity of Jug B	Capacity of Jug C	Desired Quantity
1	10	40	18	28
2	21	127	3	100
3	14	163	25	99
4	9	42	6	21
5	20	59	4	31
6	18	43	10	5
7	15	39	3	18

to obtain specified amounts of water. A series of problems is presented, the first problem being an easy one for practice. Problems two to six can all be solved in the same way (b − a − 2c). Problem seven, too, can be solved in the same manner but it also has a simpler solution. Luchins and Luchins found that people who had worked through numbers two to six tended to miss the simpler solution. Because a mental set had been created, problem seven got represented as one more in a series of identical problems.

Short-term mental sets are readily broken if one only becomes aware of them.

Long-term mental sets may be totally inescapable, or else have to be constantly guarded against. Long-term sets are part of a person's style of thinking.

Functional Fixedness

It is not only the overall representation of a problem that is important. The representation of individual problem elements may also influence the likelihood of success. We tend to represent objects to ourselves in terms of their functions, and while this may often be appropriate it can also prove unduly limiting. Functional fixedness, as this habit is termed, was investigated by Maier (1931). He set a problem in which the task was to tie together two strings hanging down from the ceiling of a room. The strings were far enough apart that it was not possible to hold one and simultaneously reach out and take the other. On the floor of the room were various objects, including a pair of pliers. One solution to the problem is to tie the pliers to the first of the strings, set it swinging, take hold of the second string, and catch the first string as it swings near. Maier found that people tended to think of the pliers only in terms of their usual function. Unless hints were given, it was difficult to perceive their potential as a pendulum bob.

The history of technology is a rich source of examples of functional fixedness, and of sudden escapes from it. Technical innovation frequently consists of an appreciation of how an existing machine can be adapted to solve problems quite outside its currently accepted range of application. Weizenbaum (1984) recounts how the steam engine had been in use for a hundred years to pump water out of mines before Trevithik became the first person to perceive its potential as a source of locomotive power. Trevithik put a steam engine on a carriage and the carriage on an already existent tramway, and thus provided a novel solution to the perennial problem of transportation. Weizenbaum points out that a similar functional fixedness also dominated the early use of computers, which were often treated as nothing more than very fast calculating or tabulating machines. Their versatility as general symbol manipulators was some time in being recognized (see Chapter 16).

Smuggled Assumptions

Both mental set and functional fixedness are special cases of a general factor that can inhibit flexible problem representation. This factor is the smuggled assumption. We saw in Chapter 13 that all thinking rests on implicit assumptions and inferences and that these are not always appropriate. A well known example of smuggled assumptions occurs in the 9–dot problem, in which the 9 dots in Figure 14:1 have to be joined up using four or fewer straight lines and without lifting the pencil from the page. Adams (1979) discusses the problem at length and provides a number of possible solutions. Most people

Figure 14:1   The nine-dot problem.

find any solution at all hard to come by, and Adams says this is because they smuggle into their representations of the problem various delimiting assumptions. For example, most people assume that the straight lines cannot be extended outside the square made by the dots. This blinds them to the possibility of the solution shown in Figure 14:2. Many people also discount the possibility of drawing a single very thick line that takes in all the dots in one go.

Another example of difficulty caused by a smuggled assumption occurs with the 6-match problem (Catona, 1940). The task is to form four identical equilateral triangles, all with sides one match long, using only 6 matches. People tend to assume that the problem calls for a solution in two dimensions. This blinds them to the solution of constructing a triangular pyramid.

In both the above examples, a smuggled assumption imposes an unnecessary limitation on what Newell and Simon (1972) have called the 'problem space'; a pleasingly literal metaphor for these two cases! What should be clear by now is that the way in which a problem is represented can greatly influence the likelihood of solution. Mode of representation and the omnipresent danger of mental set and functional fixedness must all be taken into consideration. Sometimes, as with the Buddhist monk example, a correct representation of a problem is equivalent to its solution. More often, however, representation is only the first stage, and must be followed by the search for a solution. It is to the solution stage of problem solving that we now turn our attention.

The Use of Heuristics

For some problems there is a known solution procedure which, if properly executed, guarantees a correct answer. Such procedures are known as *algorithms* (see Chapter 16). Most problems, however, cannot be cracked algorithmically, or if there is an algorithm it may be lengthy and difficult to operate. In such cases we usually grope our way towards a solution by calling upon various rules of thumb which go under the name of *heuristics*. Heuristics are guides to action that have been acquired through experience. Their advantages include simplicity and familiarity, their weakness is that we can never know in advance whether they will lead us in the right direction.

Means–Ends Analysis

An example of *Means–Ends Analysis* was given by John Sloboda in Chapter 2 when introducing the notion of a goal stack. The problem was one of getting from the country to London. A means–ends analysis leads to the question: What is the difference between your present state and the desired goal state? One of distance. What reduces distance? A train. Where do you find a train? At the station. How do you find the station? Find a map. Or ask a local inhabitant the way. (Hoping that local discourse conventions match your own – see Chapter 13.) And so on.

In this kind of analysis the problem solver oscillates between various ends – goals and sub-goals – on the one hand, and different means of achieving them on the other. The predominant tactic is to work backwards from the final solution and to eliminate perceived differences between the present state and some level of goal state, repeating the process at each level.

Means–ends analysis forms the basis of the widely applicable computer programme, General Problem Solver (Newell and Simon, 1972). It is a common sense method yet the systematic application of it is a powerful means of solving problems, from very simple ones to those involved in playing top level chess.

Human use of means–ends analysis was explicit in the 'think aloud' protocols of subjects in Duncker's (1945) study with the 'radiation problem'. This refers to a patient with an inoperable stomach tumour, and to rays which destroy tissue at sufficient intensity. The problem is to arrive at a procedure by which the tumour can be destroyed without damaging the healthy tissue surrounding it, as would occur with the simple approach of directing a beam of rays through to the tumour. Subjects tended to work backwards from the overall goal to sub-goals, such as irradiating the tumour while avoiding the healthy tissue. A solution was most likely to follow the setting of a sub-goal to lower the intensity of the rays as they travel through the healthy tissue. This sub-goal led to the notions of focusing, or converging, weak rays at the site of the tumour.

Means–ends analysis includes a number of component processes such as problem reduction, working backwards, and evaluating similarity between the present state and the goal state. All these would require chapters of their own to treat in detail (see Gilhooly, 1982).

Availability

When making judgements about a problem, we have to rely upon the information available to us. The information that is available may not, however, accurately portray the relevant state of affairs. This is especially true in cases where our exposure to information is determined by criteria not relevant to the problem with which we are concerned. For example, if you want to decide the safest means of long distance travel the information provided by the news media

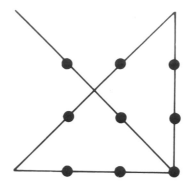

Figure 14:2   One elegant solution to the nine-dot problem.

will not help. Media coverage is determined largely by the criterion of 'newsworthiness', and emphasizes disaster rather than safe travel.

An experimental illustration of the influence of information availability was reported by Tversky and Kahneman (1973). They asked people whether each of the letters K, L, N, R, V appears more often in the first or third position in English words. All five letters were judged to occur more frequently in the first position, whereas in fact all are more common in the third position. Presumably people make this error because it is much easier to generate words starting with a particular letter than those with a given letter in the third position, and allowance is not made for the distorting effects of this bias.

Availability is a useful heuristic in problem solving only when the objective frequency of a class of events correlates with subjective availability of examples of the class. But this is often not the case. Besides the uneven exposure of information in the media, we all tend to seek out information that confirms our own prejudices. Flavell (1985) suggests that the reason it is so hard not to see things from our own point of view is that our own point of view is very available. Our own interpretations are those we practise the most, they have become automatic. A great deal of conscientious effort is necessary to acquire any proficiency at adopting another's point of view

Representativeness

Read the following description:
> Linda is 31 years old, single, outspoken and very bright. She majored in philosophy. As a student she was deeply concerned with issues of discrimination and social justice, and also participated in anti-nuclear demonstrations.

Now decide which of these two statements about Linda is the more probable:
1   Linda is a bank teller.
2   Linda is a bank teller and is active in the feminist movement.

Tversky and Kahneman (1982) found that the 87 per cent of subjects chose statement 2 as being more probable than statement 1. Yet a moment's reflection will indicate that this cannot be the case. The probability of a conjunction of two events, or features, cannot be greater than the probability of one of the events, or features, on its own. For instance, if it is unlikely that you will win a Nobel prize and unlikely that you will win an Olympic gold medal it can hardly be *more* likely that you will do both of these things than just one of them. Nevertheless, even subjects who have been trained in statistics and probability theory make the mistake of rating statement 2 as the more probable. It seems that people respond on the basis of what Tversky and Kahneman call 'representativeness'. The description of Linda was constructed to be representative of an active feminist but not of a bank teller, and people appear to base their judgements on this representativeness, or similarity, rather than on objective probabilities.

In problems for which there is little information available concerning objective probabilities, which is quite often, representativeness may be a sensible heuristic to employ. In certain circumstances, however, it can badly mislead our thinking. For example, a few well publicized cases of abuse of the welfare system may, if assumed to be representative, bias estimates of the degree of abuse amongst the whole population of welfare beneficiaries.

Anchoring

Tversky and Kahneman (1974) discuss a further source of error in human thinking, which is the influence that a starting point may have on performance in estimation tasks. This was strikingly demonstrated by having two groups of subjects estimate, within five seconds, the value of a numerical expression written on a blackboard. One group saw the expression 8 x 7 x 6 x 5 x 4 x 3 x 2 x 1, they gave a median estimate of 2,250. The other group saw the expression 1 x 2 x 3 x 4 x 5 x 6 x 7 x 8, they gave a median estimate of 512. Since the correct answer is 40,320 both groups were well below the mark but the underestimation was greater for those who had, presumably, had time to multiply a few of the smaller rather than a few of the larger digits. The starting point acted as an anchor.

Fiske and Taylor (1984) point out that anchoring effects are liable to occur whenever someone has to estimate the frequency of some characteristic in the population at large, or the probability of a particular form of behaviour. In most cases, people will start their deliberations with their own attitude to the matter in hand, and this provides an anchor. A very honest person is liable to overestimate the prevalence of honesty in the population (How could they . . .?), a very dishonest one the prevalence of dishonesty (I'll bet you would really . . .). In a similar manner, although we may doubt the claims that an advertiser forwards on behalf of a product, mere exposure to favourable advertisements could well provide the anchor from which our estimates of actual worth will be made; resulting in an estimate advantageous to the manufacturer of the product.

The Coaching of Problem Solving Skills

In the preceding two sections we have examined a number of processes involved in problem representation and the search for and execution of solution procedures. In the normal course of events, these important processes operate largely unconsciously. Ordinary behaviour would be impossible if we did not automatically detect similarities between the past and the present, if we did not simplify complex problems and extrapolate from inadequate data. None of what has gone before should be taken as criticism of the utility of these various cognitive habits. It is only when difficulties are encountered, when behaviour becomes inefficient or problems refuse to yield to habitual approaches, that our unthinking procedures must become subject to scrutiny. Somehow they have to be hauled into awareness.

Habits and Awareness

In recent years, concerted efforts have been made, especially in the United States, to develop training schemes for general problem-solving skills (Hunt, 1982; Mayer, 1983). Common to all of these schemes is an emphasis on 'increased awareness'.

Since everyday life bristles with problems that everyone learns to cope with, it follows that all of us must, in the very nature of things, be experienced problem-solvers. Now experience, no doubt, is a good thing but it can lead to the formation of bad habits, and it certainly results in various kinds of inattention to the processes of problem-solving. Training aims to bring those processes into awareness, to make people conscious of their own habits of thought and thereby to enable them to exercise greater control over their problem-solving activities. As with encounter groups and other forms of sensitivity training, the origins of this approach derive from the *gestalt* psychology that emerged in Germany in the early part of the century (Chapter 11).

Whereas the behaviourist tradition has always emphasized the importance of trial and error learning for problem-solving, with successful solutions becoming habitual, gestalt psychologists laid heavy stress on the role in problem-solving of what they called *insight*. This term refers to the understanding of the relationships involved in a problem. Gestalt psychologists argued that the way in which a problem is perceived, or configured, is vitally important to devising a solution. It was said that solutions are often preceded by insights in which the problem is suddenly seen as organized in a new way. An example would be the

6-match problem, cited above. The realization that the solution can be in three dimensions, the triangular pyramid, may be experienced as an insight into the nature of the problem. The notion of insight and the cognitive processes of problem *representation* are thought of as analogous to those of visual perception. Abrupt reorganization of the problem is likened to the perceptual restructuring of an ambiguous figure, as when Figure 5:2 (in Chapter 5) is perceived as two parallelograms rather than as a pair of egg-timer shapes. Problem-solving training that is derived from gestalt principles focuses on making people aware of the importance of representation, of the need to try out different ways of conceptualizing a problem and of the constraints that act against reconceptualization. By raising people's awareness of the factors involved in the representation of problems, it is hoped that they will become more flexible in their thinking.

The question is, then, does the training work?

The Assessment of Coaching

That general problem solving skills can be improved by coaching is certainly widely claimed. Books are written on the topic, university courses are run for students, and commercial courses are offered for which participants – or their sponsoring companies – pay large fees. If you were to judge purely from subjective reports of whether people felt that they had personally benefited from a particular course, you would have to conclude that at least some individuals do improve their problem solving skills as a result of coaching. There is a considerable degree of consumer satisfaction.

Subjective reports, however, are not necessarily to be relied upon. Mayer (1983) surveys a number of attempts at objective evaluation of training courses and comes to a less optimistic conclusion. He suggests that although training can be shown to improve problem-solving ability in specific areas such as mathematics or engineering, the evidence for the acquisition of general skills that transfer to other types of subject matter remains equivocal. Smaller studies, in which both coaches and students may be aware of taking part in an evaluation study and in which motivation may be correspondingly high, tend to demonstrate positive results. Large-scale studies, on the other hand, frequently yield small, if any, effects of training.

Conclusive demonstration of positive outcomes is a difficulty common to all enterprises which seek to coach high-level cognitive skills (see Chapters 8, 11, 12, and 15). Firm evidence for the successful coaching of general problem solving skills is undeniably hard to come by but part of the difficulty may lie in the nature of assessment itself. Are laboratory type tests the best indicators of improved skill? It might be that people make more effort, and better use of their training, in real-life settings. But perhaps the major obstacle to a proper evaluation of the coaching of these skills relates to the matter of practice. It has been said over and again that the development of skill requires large amounts of practice. Certainly more than can be provided during a course on problem solving lasting a few weeks. Techniques and systematic approaches can be taught but ultimately it is up to the individual to engage in practice. It may be for this reason that it is only in smaller scale evaluation studies, with their concomitantly higher levels of motivation, that consistently positive results are observed for the training of problem-solving skills. However, the question of coaching problem solving skills will arise again in the following chapter, this time in the context of creativity training.

FURTHER READING

R. E. MAYER (1983) *Thinking, Problem Solving, Cognition*. New York: Freeman.

A thorough and highly readable review of the problem solving literature.

J. L. ADAMS (1979) *Conceptual Blockbusting* (2nd Edition). New York: Norton.

An enjoyable and non-technical coverage of the topic.

CHAPTER 15

CREATIVITY AND COGNITIVE SKILLS

Alan Branthwaite

In Chapters 13 and 14, it was proposed that problem-solving procedures can become routinized within specialized domains and that certain skills and approaches can be acquired to assist in problem-solving across a wide range of problems. Brilliant thoughts, however, cannot be produced to order. Some problems go unsolved for many years, and some ideas are so innovative that they bring only posthumous acclaim to their originators. These are instances of creative thinking, some of which will be described in this chapter as we explore the role that cognitive skills can play in creativity.

The Nature of Creative Thought

It is not always easy to recognize creative ideas, and there is no clear standard or yardstick by which to measure them. Creativity, like genius, is elusive and an idea becomes labelled as creative and innovatory only through social consensus. This is particularly true in the Arts but also in Science and Technology, where some ideas or discoveries have lain dormant for generations because their creative value was not recognized at the time (for example, Mendel's explanation of inheritance).

History offers a number of celebrated examples of solutions to difficult and important problems that gained public acknowledgement and acceptance as creative innovations. In looking at some examples, we will pay particular attention to the way the solutions came about to see what light this casts on the creative process.

Archimedes

Archimedes' dramatic exclamation 'Eureka!' when he found the solution to his problem, is well known. The story goes like this. He had been given the problem of detecting whether some silver had been substituted for gold in a new crown that craftsmen had made. The crown weighed the same as the gold the craftsmen had been given. Archimedes reasoned that since silver has more volume than gold for the same weight, an adulterated crown would be larger than one of pure gold. Archimedes' problem was how to measure the volume of the crown which had an irregular shape. As we all know, the solution occurred to him in quite a different context, for coincidently Archimedes happened to notice while visiting the public baths that the further he immersed himself, the more the water overflowed. Archimedes' creativity was in grasping the implications of this mundane observation for the problem of measuring the volume of the crown. All at once he had the solution: by immersing the crown in water, he could measure its volume by the amount of water that was displaced. The tale ends with Archimedes excitedly running naked through the streets of Syracuse shouting 'Eureka' which means 'I have found it'. A coincidental, unrelated activity provided the clue to solving the problem which had preoccupied him, though he was probably not thinking about it at precisely the time when the solution occurred. By the way, the crown had been partly made with silver.

Darwin

Darwin kept notebooks in which he recorded his thinking and ideas and these provide a more accurate and detailed account of his creativity than does the story of Archimedes. These notebooks indicate how Darwin created his explanation for the process of evolution (Gruber, 1974). It took Darwin 15 months, in which time he tried a number of explanations that proved unsatisfactory and from which he had largely to free his mind. Slowly he accumulated a set of ideas which seemed to him relevant and around which he painstakingly amassed considerable supporting evidence. A particular break-through came with the idea of natural selection. Darwin wrote at the time: 'In October 1838, that is, fifteen months after I began my systematic enquiry, I happened to read for *amusement* 'Malthus on Population', and being well prepared to appreciate the struggle for existence which everywhere goes on from long-continued observation of the habits of animals and plants, *it at once struck me* that under these circumstances favourable variations would tend to be preserved, and unfavourable ones to be destroyed.' (Darwin, 1911, p. 68; emphasis added). While Darwin was immediately impressed by the new idea, he continued working on other thoughts, and he may not have realized at the time that this process of natural selection was to be the cornerstone in his explanation for evolution. One should bear in mind in examining other accounts of creativity, that it is all too easy after the event, when the whole solution has been completely grasped, to overemphasize a particular point as the moment of inspiration, without taking into account much work that went on before and after. In fact, Darwin spent another 20 years considering the theory and collecting supporting evidence.

Kekule

The 'discovery' that benzene molecules have atoms arranged in a closed ring, rather than in a chain, occurred to Kekule in the following way according to his own description (quoted in Koestler, 1964): 'I turned my chair to the fire and dozed. Again the atoms were gambolling before my eyes. This time the smaller groups kept modestly in the background. My mental eye, rendered more acute by repeated visions of this kind, could now distinguish larger structures, of manifold conformation; long rows, sometimes more closely fitted together; all twining and twisting in a snake like motion. But look! What was that? One of the snakes had seized hold of its own tail, and the form whirled mockingly before my eyes. As if by a flash of lightening I awoke . . . Let us learn to dream, gentlemen'.

Babbage

Another, similar example of creativity which arose partly by systematic, step-by-step logic and partly by imaginative dreaming, was Babbage's invention of an Analytical Machine, precursor of modern computers (quoted in Cohen, 1970, p. 65). 'The earliest idea that I can trace in my own mind of calculating arithmetical Tables by machinery arose in this manner: One evening I was sitting in the rooms of the Analytical Society in Cambridge, my head leaning forward on the table in a kind of dreamy mood, with a table of logarithms lying open before me. Another member, coming into the room and seeing me half asleep, called out "Well, Babbage, what are you dreaming about?" to which I replied, "I am thinking that all these Tables (pointing to the logarithms) might be calculated by machinery".'

Many other descriptions of how major creative ideas came about can be found in Koestler, 1964. But it is important to realize that creativeness is not confined to such classical instances which transformed understanding. These examples of creativity are celebrated because of the seriousness of the problems they solved and the usefulness of the solutions, rather than because they involved outstandingly imaginative or inventive ideas. But creativity is also found in inventive and imaginative solutions to an individual's everyday problems or even in the schoolboy who 'discovers' Archimedes' principle for himself, though history is unlikely to record such achievements. After all, Darwin only made his ideas public when someone else (Alfred Wallace) independently conceived the same idea, giving Darwin the support and encouragement to overcome his doubts and caution. That does not make Darwin's, or Wallace's, idea any less creative, though Wallace's creativity is much less well known. In assessing what is creative we should take into account not only the social significance of the outcome, but the resistance of the problem to solution and the difficulty which an individual overcomes in reaching a satisfactory resolution.

The Creative Process

What do these accounts of creative ideas tell us about the cognitive processes involved? The examples given provide something in the way of introspective reports as to how those creative ideas came about. We have seen in other chapters something of the limitations of introspective reports as a means for elucidating mental processes. This is especially true when a report is written after, rather than at the time of, the events it describes since reconstructive memory is selective and partial (see Chapter 5). Some researchers (e.g. Perkins, 1981) have combined biographical reports of naturally occurring creativity with observations of creativity in the laboratory when individuals are asked to talk aloud as they solve problems or compose poetry (a procedure which has its own limitations). On the basis of this evidence, there appear to be four processes involved. These were originally labelled some sixty years ago by Wallas (1926) as Preparation, Incubation, Illumination and Verification. This description of creativity has been endorsed by subsequent writers although these processes are not now seen as discrete stages but as being in dynamic interplay with each other during creativity.

(i) Preparation

Preparation involves defining and exploring the characteristics of the task or problem, and it is akin to the matter of problem representation discussed in Chapter 14. The processes involved in preparation are illustrated in some of the examples of creativity described above: Archimedes' deductions that silver has more volume than the same weight of gold; Darwin's observations of the manifestations of evolution and the ingredients on which the process might operate, such as variability within species and adaptation to habitats. During preparation, possible solutions are considered and tested logically to see if they work. With many problems a solution is arrived at in this way (see Chapter 14). It is only with more difficult and intransigent problems that further creativity is required. However this preparatory process of exploring the problem is an essential precursor to more creative and imaginative solutions. During this process, an awareness of the properties of a satisfactory solution emerges, which is important later in recognizing the solution when it occurs. Preparation also increases involvement with the problem, which is probably beneficial in increasing motivation and attentiveness to possible solutions when they emerge.

But heightened involvement can also be disadvantageous in that it produces mental sets and rigid thinking about the same possible solutions which are turned over and over.

Some psychologists have described the process of preparation in terms of a closed system of thinking, which focuses on logical possibilities and runs systematically along familiar lines using approaches that have been learnt from past experience with what seem like similar kinds of problem. But, during preparation, creative thinkers are 'feeling out' a problem, as if exploring a jigsaw to acquaint themselves with the shape of the missing piece, like Kekule who knew very well what criteria must be satisfied by the solution to the arrangement of atoms in a benzene ring. Similarly, for a very long time, Darwin had a clear notion of what had to be achieved by the mechanism of evolution that he was searching for.

(ii) Incubation

Incubation refers to the apparently unconscious processes that take place when a problem is not under active consideration, but out of which arises an imaginative and successful solution. This occurred most clearly in Kekule's and Babbage's daydreaming. The essence of incubation is that during relaxed (or sometimes restless) rumination upon the problem, new possibilities and combinations of ideas are generated. These result from free play of the imagination, from intuition, open and fluid thinking that brings new perspectives to bear on the problem. Bruner (1962) argues that intuition 'produces interesting combinations of ideas before their worth is known. It precedes proof; indeed it is what the techniques of analysis and verification are designed to test and check' (p. 102). These characteristics are clearly evident in Poincaré's description of how he established a mathematical proof after a period of preparation:

> Every day I seated myself at my work table, stayed an hour or two, tried a great number of combinations and reached no results. One evening, contrary to my custom, I drank black coffee and could not sleep. Ideas rose in crowds; I felt them collide until pairs interlocked, so to speak, making a stable combination. By the next morning I had established the existence of a class of Fuchsian functions, those which come from the hypergeometric series; I had only to write out the results, which took but a few hours.   (Ghiselin, 1952, p. 37)

During incubation, the mind appears to revert to more primitive modes of operation (as in dreaming) using fantasy, association, analogies and metaphors. Piaget (1926) called this autistic thought (as opposed to logical intelligent thinking). It is not adapted to reality but creates for itself a dream world of imagination; which is strictly individual and uncommunicable by language; and which works by images and symbols.

An alternative view of incubation has been suggested by Perkins (1981), who has questioned whether incubation involves a special kind of unconscious thinking to generate new alternatives as possible solutions for a problem. He has emphasized the role of more ordinary cognitive processes such as: fruitful *forgetting* of cherished but unsuccessful possibilities; physical and mental *refreshment*; *noticing* new clues in unrelated experiences (like Archimedes) which demands a high level of interest, alertness and unfocused attention; *contrary recognition* which involves recognizing things not only for what they are, but for what they might symbolize (such as seeing animals in the shapes of potatoes). The last process of contrary recognition has, however, strong similarities to autistic thinking and dreaming as described above.

I see no reason why the ordinary cognitive processes suggested by Perkins, as well as more primitive modes of thinking, should not be involved in incubation (see below). The main function of incubation is to increase the range of possible solutions and it is a characteristic of creative people that they are skilled in generating alternative ideas easily and effortlessly. Cohen (1970) notes that Norbert Weiner, the creator of cybernetics, 'treasured in himself what he felt to be a free-flowing kaleidoscopic imagination which by itself revealed for him the potentialities of a complicated situation' (p. 57), and Picasso crisply remarked 'I do not seek, I find', by which he meant that ideas came without deliberate or laborious searching. It may be that practice can lead to increased skill at generating ideas, and this is certainly an assumption underlying the creativity training techniques to be discussed below. But in addition, we must not underestimate the role of chance occurrances in stimulating alternative solutions, and of alertness to such serendipitous findings.

(iii) Illumination

Illumination is the moment of insight or sudden realization that an idea fits the problem and offers a solution. It is clearly illustrated when Archimedes grasped the significance of the water rising in the bath, or Darwin's experience when the idea of natural selection suddenly struck him (although he continued to work on other ideas while seeking verification of this illumination). The important feature here is the 'mental leap' whereby something seemingly irrelevant is related to the characteristics of the problem. This requires alertness and vigilance while not consciously attending to the problem, which comes from deep involvement with the task. It is for this reason that a clear understanding of the nature and characteristics (the 'shape') of a solution is important in the process of preparation.

In artistic creation, illumination comes when a possible idea gives the artist a feeling that a more satisfying, worthwhile expression has been achieved which enriches the meaning of the work. Illumination has a strong emotional quality, as experienced by Archimedes, which comes with the belief that the new idea will complete the problem. With illumination comes excitement and exhilaration that the pieces of the problem will fall into place and connect up in an understandable manner. This is a similar experience to seeing a joke or understanding double meanings in a riddle: sense emerges out of ambiguity.

(iv) Verification

Verification is similar to preparation, in that systematic and logical thought are used to check potential solutions for their goodness of fit to the characteristics of the problem. The creative inspiration is worked through and elaborated. This process was well illustrated by Darwin, but also by Babbage and Poincaré. Supporting evidence and arguments are adduced so that the solution can be communicated to others rationally and coherently. Knowledge and previously acquired skills are used to test the illuminating idea for its sensibleness and consistency. Unfortunately, some illuminating ideas which appeared to meet the requirements of the problem prove to be unsound on further examination, so the process of verification becomes only a further process of preparation!

Creative Processes and the Workings of the Two Hemispheres

The four processes that have been described involve two contrasting types of mental skill:

(a) conscious, rational, logical, systematic analysis (important in preparation and verification);

(b) unconscious intuition, symbolic analogies, metaphors and associations which create new perspectives and different possibilities for solutions (in incubation and illumination).

The existence of two contrasting modes of thinking has been recognised in many aspects of psychology (Bogen, 1977). For example:

rational	versus	metaphoric	(Bruner)
realistic	versus	impulsive	(Hilgard)
differential	versus	existential	(William James)
positive	versus	mystic	(Lévi–Strauss)
rational	versus	intuitive	(Maslow)
sequential	versus	multiple	(Neisser)
directed	versus	autistic	(Piaget)

Recently, a possible basis for these different modes of thinking has been identified in the different functions of the two hemispheres of the brain. (For a summary of the evidence, see Trueman, 1985; Springer and Deutsch, 1989.) It is suggested that the two hemispheres specialize in different forms of mental activity.

Left Hemisphere	*Right Hemisphere*
• analytical, sequential thinking	• holistic, simultaneous, integrative
• verbal	• spacial manipulation, body image and orientation in space
• logical	• intuitive
• serial processing	• parallel processing
• linear mode of operation, temporal	• processes information diffusely
• intellectual (conscious)	• relational, associative
• convergent	• divergent

The evidence that the two hemispheres are differentially related to aspects of the creative process is not conclusive, but certainly suggestive (Katz, 1978; Torrence, 1982). The right hemisphere appears to be involved in those aspects of creativity which depend on imagination, analogy, cognitive flexibility, and divergent thinking which were characteristic of incubation and illumination. It is almost certainly too simple to say that the right hemisphere is specialized for creativity. Almost all sophisticated thinking involves aspects of the activity of both hemispheres and the interplay between them, and this is equally true in creativity. In particular, there is a continual interplay between verbal and nonverbal imagery in our thinking. However, this comparison between processes which have long been held to be important in creativity and the specialized modes of working in the two hemispheres helps in clarifying the nature of the processes involved. It extends our understanding of the mysterious, primitive and nonverbal aspects of incubation and illumination. This explanation puts the description of creativity into a broader context of what is currently known about cognitive functions and explains why creative people often feel or sense the solution before they can precisely articulate it. Furthermore, it suggests that creativity might be improved by harnessing the skills of each hemisphere at different phases of the creative process. This, however, is not a new idea as can be seen in Schiller's reply to a friend who complained of his lack of creative power:

> The reason for your complaint lies, it seems to me, in the constraint which your intellect imposes upon your imagination. . . . Apparently it is not good – and indeed it hinders the creative work of the mind – if the intellect examines too closely the ideas already pouring in, as it were, at the gates. Regarded in isolation, an idea may be quite insignificant, and venturesome in the extreme, but it may acquire importance from an idea which follows it;

perhaps, in a certain collocation with other ideas, which may seem equally absurd, it may be capable of furnishing a very serviceable link. . . . In the case of a creative mind, it seems to me, the intellect has withdrawn its watchers from the gates, and the ideas rush in pell–mell, and only then does it review and inspect the multitude. You worthy critics, or whatever you may call yourselves, are ashamed or afraid of the momentary and passing madness which is found in all creators. . . . Hence your complaints of unfruitfulness, for you reject too soon and discriminate too severely.   (Brill, 1938, p. 193).

Schiller's argument is given new force and support when seen in terms of the operation of two modes of consciousness in the hemispheres of the brain.

The knowledge that two complementary kinds of mental skill are involved in creativity suggests two broad strategies for improving creativeness. Correspondingly, when we review the many diverse methods that have been put forward for increasing creativity, we find that they do fall into two broad categories which seek to improve what we might refer to for convenience as 'left' or 'right' hemisphere modes of thinking. Developing creative skills involves finding better strategies for producing candidate solutions, and in the rest of this chapter we shall look at some techniques that have been suggested. These techniques share two properties with many of the cognitive skills we have examined in the rest of the book. First, they are *heuristics* (see Chapter 16) in that none of them *guarantee* a solution to a particular problem, but they may assist in the search by stimulating ideas. Second, their application improves with practice (see Chapter 3). At first, many of the techniques will seem strange and hard to carry out. They only become really efficient after persistent application. They will not offer instant creativity on a first attempt.

Developing 'Left Hemisphere' Skills

These techniques promote more thorough, systematic, logical and rational analysis of the problem. Some of the tactics used to achieve this, are:

- restate the problem in your own words

- formulate questions about the problem

- get all the facts of the problem clearly in mind

- write things down

- list all the important objects/aspects in the problem and think carefully about each one

- look out for odd or puzzling facts in a problem, and concentrate on trying to explain them

- when there are several puzzling things in a problem try to explain them with a single idea that will connect them all together.

Some techniques aim to create new ideas by identifying omissions and creating new permutations out of existing characteristics. The techniques often involve checklists to encourage more thorough and exhaustive analysis of the problem. The following illustrations come mainly from the field of new product development (Whiting, 1958):

(i) Systematic review

Review all aspects of an existing product and its markets systematically, using the following checklist of prompts. Write down all possibilities that come to mind. Don't be negative; convince yourself there can be better solutions.

PRODUCTS	Consider changing	– physical characteristics
		– packaging
		– method of manufacture
	Examine	– ratings versus competitors
		– technical possibilities
CONSUMER	Consider changing	– method of use
		– purpose of use
		– perceived position
		– attitudes
	Examine	– alternative buyers
		– buying patterns and trends
PROMOTION	Consider changing	– advertising, promotion
	Examine	– pricing
		– competitive activity

(ii) Morphological analysis

This technique involves dividing a problem into its constituent dimensions. Each dimension is then subdivided into its possible values or forms, and the various combinations that result are examined for the usefulness of the solutions they offer. Consider, for example, the problem of developing a new type of packaging for selling milk. Packaging has three dimensions: size, shape and material. The dimension of size is subdivided into various units (half-pint, pint, two pint). Shape is subdivided into possible shapes (cube, cylinder, tetrahedron, etc.) and similarly for materials (glass, paper, metal etc.). The combinations of these categories are systematically examined for their potential usefulness as solutions. This is a very mechanical procedure and one could imagine using computers to simplify the labour involved.

(iii) Attribute listing.

The major attributes of a product or service (or other problem) are listed. Consideration is then given to ways of changing or improving each of them in every conceivable way, without judgement or evaluation. It has been found productive in new product development to concentrate on the more unique attributes of a product because these are the most significant features. You might like to try designing a new toothbrush using this approach.

Developing 'Right Hemisphere' Skills

These techniques improve creativity by stimulating novel, even bizarre, associations around the problem. They do not seek direct solutions but encourage lateral thinking to generate analogies and metaphors, which may almost seem to add confusion but which can produce completely new approaches to a problem.

The essence of these techniques lies in the use of metaphors whereby perspectives are carried over from one domain of reference to another. Schon (1979) has emphasized that the concepts and language in which we represent a problem guide our thinking to certain kinds of solution. Under the spell of the implicit, spontaneous metaphor in which we pose a problem, we are bound to certain types of solution rather than others. By using different metaphors, we can change the connotations of the problem and the frame of reference for a solution. This is known as 'frame restructuring'. Frame restructuring is an important and widespread mental phenomenon which is involved in perception, illusions, memory and even in appreciating jokes. This process is illustrated in the following example given by Schon.

A group of product development researchers were trying to improve the performance of a paintbrush made with synthetic bristles. They had tried a number of solutions to make the synthetic bristles more like real bristles, including changing their diameter and even giving them split ends. Their thinking however tended to be constrained by the term 'brush' to seek a solution by changes in the bristles. A breakthrough came when one of the team observed that a paintbrush was a kind of *pump*, in which the paint is forced through the space between the bristles. This analogy changed the perspective of the problem and became a new metaphor which altered the context so a solution was sought by changing the flow of the paint *between* the bristles.

The following techniques aim to develop skills in generating metaphors, analogies and associations. (Further details of the techniques described below can be found in Stein, 1975.)

(i) Synectics

Synectics relies on joining together different and apparently irrelevant elements (Gordon, 1961). The purpose is to make the familiar strange, and vice-versa, in order to change perspective. There are a number of devices for doing this by generating analogies and metaphors:

- *Personal analogies*   An individual tries to imagine himself to be the object he is working with, firstly, by describing the properties and characteristics of the object, then by imagining the feelings and emotions of the object and finally by identifying with the object to experience what it might feel like to be that thing. One can easily imagine the paintbrush-as-pump analogy, described above, emerging from this kind of intimate analysis of what it would be like to be a working paintbrush

- *Direct analogies*   Metaphors for the problem are sought from another field. Often analogies are sought for inorganic problems by reference to how living creatures work. For example, Brunel solved the problem of constructing tunnels underwater by direct analogy with the way a shipworm tunnelled into wood, and in inventing the telephone, Bell found a way of converting the voice into mechanical and electrical energy by making comparisons with the mechanism of the human ear.

- *Symbolic analogies*   Symbolic or poetic metaphors are sought to character- ize the essence of the problem. Nonverbal associations are explored by trying to find shapes, colours, textures, smells etc. which will characterize the concepts in the problems. The aim is to make abstract problems more concrete and vice versa.

- *Fantasy analogies*   The problem is stated in terms of how one wishes the problem could be easily and simply solved in an ideal world where anything is possible. In devising an air-tight closure for space suits, a group using this technique dreamed of a line of insects that would clasp claws on command to draw the suit closed. This led on to other ideas which yielded a viable solution (Gordon, 1961).

The technique of using analogies takes thinking away from the problem by various devious routes. The procedure is then to come back to the problem from wherever has been reached.

(ii) Brainstorming.

Brainstorming is usually carried out with a group of people but that is not essential. Ideas related to the problem are listed as a chain of associations, often in the manner of a stream of consciousness. There are four rules for brainstorming:

- criticism is ruled out. Ideas should be generated without concern for their value, feasibility or significance;

- in generating ideas, 'free-wheeling' is encouraged so that any idea, however apparently wild or unconnected can be put forward. The intention is again to rule out selection and censorship and to promote freedom in offering suggestions;

- quantity is wanted: the pressure is to try to generate very large numbers of ideas. There is an assumption that emphasizing quantity results in better quality, but that has not always been found to be true in research studies. Nevertheless, the emphasis on quantity assists in suspending criticism and evaluation;

- combination and improvement of ideas is sought, and priority is given to those which constructively build on previous suggestions. As well as encouraging the development of ideas, this rule seeks to remove embarrassment at borrowing and using other people's ideas.

Overcoming Blocks to Creative Thinking

The techniques described to facilitate creativity are only successful with the right mental attitude. Blocks occur for cognitive and social reasons – though the two are by no means separate. The social climate in which creative work is to be done can help or hinder. When rewards and bonuses are contingent on creativity, and there is external surveillance and extrinsic controls, creativity is reduced (Amabile, 1983). Such conditions constrain people from taking chances in their search for imaginative alternatives by emphasizing the social worth that might be put on their creative excursions. People are more likely to be successful when intrinsically motivated, deeply involved and enthusiastically committed to a problem. Creativity requires a positive, confident outlook and the security to be non-conforming and to question the status-quo. The creative process requires individuality and uniqueness which are best achieved in an environment that is socially unthreatening, relaxed and secure.

Blocks to creativity usually involve difficulties in transferring from systematic and rational analysis of the problem ('left' hemisphere thinking) to using imagination and free association to generate new perspectives ('right' hemisphere thinking). This is not surprising in that in many institutions (school, work) greater value and prestige are placed on logical and rational analysis, rather than 'childish' free-associations, and fanciful analogies. However, we should remember Schiller's advice not to let the intellect constrain imagination. In achieving this, there is some useful advice to bear in mind:

- choose conducive and appropriate conditions to work in, avoiding distracting stimulation, and encouraging contentedness, relaxed alertness and playfulness;

- have objects related to the problem available, move them around and play with them; pay attention to searching the objects and noticing their features; use visual imagination similarly to scrutinize the properties of things;

- don't try to hold ideas in mind; write down ideas, make lists and jottings; this helps to prevent overloading cognitive capacities and also frees thinking to let other ideas come forward;

- deliberately try to be original, creative and adventurous.

Conclusion

Creativity such as that of Archimedes, Darwin or Picasso, begins with the search for a solution to a problem in which the creative individual is deeply involved. The search for a solution activates many cognitive skills including analyzing, reasoning, remembering, noticing, recognizing, associating, making analogies and changing metaphors. It has long been considered that creativity involves conscious and unconscious processes. It has been argued that the special mystique and power of creativity lies in unconscious incubation and insight into the problem. However, an alternative way of looking at the processes involved is that creativity harnesses complementary abilities in which the right and left hemispheres of the brain are specialized. The essence of creativity lies in the power to generate alternatives in the search for a solution, both through logical reasoning (left hemisphere) and through association and metaphor which creates new perspectives or frames of reference on the problem (right hemisphere). The more radical the range of alternatives considered, the more likely is a creative solution to arise to a novel and intransigent problem. In order to be creative, therefore, we should concentrate on skills for generating new, better, and a wider range of alternatives in our thinking. But in the final analysis one should remember the role of chance and luck in stumbling on the profound alternative, in noticing the relevant but unrelated incident, or having the right experience at the right time. Perhaps the most that individuals can do is to encourage such fortuitous occurences and to make themselves receptive to those that come their way.

FURTHER READING

BRANSFORD, J. D. and STEIN, B. S. (1984) *The Ideal Problem Solver* San Fransisco: Freeman.

This book aims to encourage better problem-solving by describing the processes involved and using exercises to encourage the skills needed.

PERKINS, D. N. (1981) *The Mind's Best Work*. Camb. Mass.: Harvard University Press.

Perkins gives a thoughtful re-evaluation of the nature of creativity in which he emphasizes the part played by normal, everyday cognitive skills.

WEISBERG, R. W. (1989) *Creativity: Genius and other myths*. San Francisco: Freeman.
A thorough treatment of the topic within a skills framework.

CHAPTER 16

COMPUTERS AND COGNITION

John Sloboda

This chapter is in the way of a coda to the rest of the book. As Angus Gellatly said in Chapter 1, we have tried to avoid excessive use of the computer metaphor in our discussion of the various aspects of cognition. A principal reason for this is that most people do not understand computers very well, and it makes little sense to try to explain the workings of the mind in terms which are not generally accessible. Nonetheless, to ignore totally the role of the computer in modern cognitive psychology would be a grave disservice.

This chapter is about two specific applications of computers which have become the hallmark of a discipline called Cognitive Science, which is a meeting ground for psychologists, philosophers, linguists, and computer scientists (Norman, 1981). The first of these is the deployment of the computer metaphor as a means of sharpening our understanding of what mind is, or is not. This is an enterprise which engages the more philosophically and conceptually minded exponents of cognitive science. Second, but closely related, is the writing of computer programs which mimic one or other aspect of human functioning. Such work is called *computer simulation*, and is a branch of the discipline of Artificial Intelligence. It requires a degree of expertise in programming and an understanding of the potentials and limitations of computers as practical tools. In a book of this sort it is easier to give some flavour of the first, conceptual, aspect than it is to write about the second, more practical, endeavour. Although I will write about both, I will spend proportionately more space on the former. Those who wish to go further into details of simulation work should consult the suggestions for further reading at the end of the chapter.

What is a Computer?

A computer is a machine. Machines perform specific and repeatable physical functions, given certain inputs. For instance, my typewriter is a machine.

Whenever I give it a particular input (e.g. pressing a particular key) it responds by moving a particular hammer. The same hammer moves every time I press a given key. Machines generally act to transform energy in some way. A typewriter transforms the downward push of my fingers into the horizontal stabs of hammers on to paper. A motor car transforms the explosive force of ignited petrol and the hand and foot movements of a driver into controlled but rapid movement; and so on. The forms of energy involved may be diverse: mechanical, electrical, electromagnetic, or atomic.

One of the principal characteristics of most machines is that their functions are severely limited. The physical configuration of their parts restricts them to doing one particular job. You can't turn a typewriter into something else without actually dismembering the parts and reconstructing them. We may call the fixed physical configuration of a machine its *hardware*. For most machines, the hardware therefore determines the function.

In a sense, all this is true of a computer too. A specific computer takes electrical impulses as inputs and moves the impulses around inside it in ways totally determined by its hardware configuration, and produces transformed electrical outputs. Feed the same computer with the same set of inputs and you will always get the same outputs (providing that the hardware does not malfunction). A huge difference comes, however, when we look at the *function* of a computer. We cannot define a specific function for a computer in the same way that we can for a typewriter. Rather, we may say that a computer's function is to manipulate symbols. If this doesn't seem very helpful, I can clarify this by saying that, in principle, a computer can be made to mimic any other machine you care to mention, *without altering its hardware*. This is done by partitioning the input into two sets. One set of inputs is called a *program* and this determines how a second set of inputs (the *data*) are going to be handled.

Let us go back to my typewriter for a moment. It works the way it does because there are a set of rods and levers which connect particular keys to particular hammers. It is quite easy to observe these levers working by lifting the lid. Suppose, however, that I were to seal the lid so that you couldn't look inside. Suppose further that I were to replace the mechanical connection between keys and hammers with electrical connections which were diverted via a computer. If I programmed the computer correctly, you would not be able to tell, just by typing on the typewriter, that the connections were not mechanical. But the computer, in fact, makes my typewriter very much more versatile. I could reprogram it so that any key-press you liked resulted in any hammer press you liked. I could even make a single key-press result in a complete word or sentence.

The computer program does this essentially by telling the computer what outputs to specify for given inputs or combinations of inputs. If each of the inputs from the different typewriter keys are identified by a unique, but arbitrary number, and the outputs to hammers by other numbers, then a part of the program might in effect say:

IF INPUT IS 27 THEN MAKE OUTPUT 36

or

IF INPUT IS 13 THEN MAKE OUTPUT 11 THEN 3 THEN 15 THEN 19

The crucial thing to note is that the computer has no idea what these inputs and outputs signify in the real world. It has no means of knowing that, in this particular case, input 27 corresponds to someone pressing the W key, or that output 36 is activating the W hammer. For the computer, there are just abstract symbols which it shunts around according to the program's rules. These symbols could be driving a car, calculating a wage packet, or starting World War III.

A computer program, therefore, can be thought of as a set of instructions to a computer to manipulate symbols in a certain way on the receipt of certain inputs. The computer is a *general-purpose machine* which a program converts, for the duration which it is loaded, into a *specific* machine to do a specific job.

It is not necessary for our purposes to know in detail how the hardware of a computer allows one to store programs and data. One can imagine it as a collection of many thousands of electrical cells, connected together in a specific way, each of which may be turned on or off by the application of electrical currents to a relatively small number of input cells. A program determines the sequence or the logic of the passages of impulses through the hardware. Computers have changed considerably in the design of their hardware over the last 30 years. Where there were once valves, you will now find microelectronic chips. Nonetheless, one can run programs written 30 years ago on today's computers and get exactly the same results. As well as computers mimicking other machines, they mimic one another. Hardware developments have not essentially changed the type of program one can run, rather, they have meant that computers have become cheaper, faster, more reliable, and capable of handling larger programs and more data.

The Computer Metaphor of Mind

As pointed out in Chapter 1, many people have been struck by certain apparent similarities between computers and human brains, and these have yielded some new possibilities for understanding mental processes. Here are some of the main similarities that have been proposed:

(a) Both computers and brains can be viewed as processors of information. That is, they take inputs from various sources, transform and manipulate them, and produce outputs.

(b) Both can be described as achieving their diverse results by the combination of many similar elements performing simple functions. In computers, electrical cells get switched on and off. In brains, nerve cells are excited or inhibited.

(c) Both computers and brains can be seen as general purpose devices. They can perform many different operations with the same hardware.

(d) Both can store and use large amounts of information.

(e) Both might be said to follow organized plans for action (programs).

These proposed similarities are connected with a number of uncontroversial and generally accepted conclusions. First is that some aspects of human behaviour can and have been successfully mimicked by computer. To take just one example, Siegler (1986) has written a computer programe which simulates the performance of children on subtraction problems (e.g. 'take 4 from 6'). That is, when run on a computer, it makes the same kind of mistakes as they do. It also takes the same sort of relative time to perform different problems as they do. It also improves as a result of experience in the same sort of way as they do. Because Siegler wrote the program, he is in a good position to describe its underlying logic, and can propose this logic as a hypothetical model for the way children actually go about the task of subtracting numbers. If children use this logic then they would produce exactly the pattern of errors and timing that they in fact do show. (One must remember, however, that there are possibly other systems which could produce the same results.)

Second, it is generally accepted by most scientists that the intellectual discipline required to produce a program which actually works is a valuable aid to better theorizing about human functioning. Because a computer needs to be told *exactly* what to do there is no room for woolly or vague thinking. The computer also demonstrates hidden inconsistencies in one's thinking in a very direct way. If there are internal contradictions the program will simply fail to work, or give bizarre results. Indeed, for this reason many educationalists (e.g. Papert, 1972) see the computer as a valuable 'intellectual gymnasium'. There are some aspects of controlling a computer which can be almost compulsively rewarding (see also Weizenbaum, 1984), and so children can acquire skill as an incidental by-product of 'getting the damn thing to work'.

Beyond such relatively uncontroversial points, however, rages a fierce debate over what is sometimes called the 'strong claim' of artificial intelligence. This is the claim that when certain kinds of programs are operating in a computer, the computer does more than mimic human behaviour. It can actually be said to be 'thinking', 'knowing', or 'understanding'.

Can Computers Think?

The advent of computers immediately raised in popular consciousness profound questions about the ultimate nature of consciousness and personality. Many of these questions have been obsessively worked over in the Science-fiction genre, particularly in respect of "androids", robots embedded in synthetic flesh that makes them appear human. Some of the questions have moral implications. Should androids be treated as persons with rights? Tales in which slave computers ran amok and turn on their masters express the deep apprehension (shared by the Frankenstein stories of an earlier age) that scientists may be opening a Pandora's Box.

The working-out of our fascination with computers in popular fiction should not detract from the profundity of the issues raised. Indeed, popular obsession may be taken as a measure *of* their profundity. These issues continue to haunt and polarize the intellectual community. I should like to outline the views of two articulate and persuasive protagonists of opposite views about computers, Alan Turing and John Searle. The protagonists have never met in the flesh. Turing died some years ago, and Searle conducts his debate with Turing's intellectual heirs. Turing's views are beautifully and wittily expressed in a paper published in 1950, and Searle's views are set out with equal aplomb in a 1980 paper. Relevant extracts of both are reprinted in Hofstadter and Dennett (1981).

Turing's Test

Turing begins by asking what might be a suitable test of whether a computer can think. He rightly rejects the notion that we should hang anything on the appearance of the computer (i.e. whether we can make it to look like a human being). Rather he asks us to imagine a situation in which an interrogator sits in a room facing two teletypes. These allow him to type messages to and receive messages from two other beings in a separate location. In this 'Turing Test', one of the beings is a human being and the other one is a computer. The job of the interrogator is to try to determine, by asking whatever questions he likes, which teletype communicates with the human and which with the computer. If the interrogator is unable to make a confident decision after extensive questioning we may say the computer has passed the Turing Test. Turing argues that if a computer can pass such a test then we have no option but to grant that it can think.

This is the classic formulation of the 'strong claim' of artificial intelligence. In the paper, Turing then goes on to counter a number of possible objections. Here are just two of the major objections, and his replies to them:

OBJECTION 1 Even though a computer behaves as if it were thinking, you cannot conclude that it has anything going on inside it akin to what we would call conscious experience.

REPLY The only being that you can know to have such experiences is yourself. You cannot know that other humans have consciousness either, yet you assume they do. Why not the computer?

OBJECTION 2 Although computers can simulate *some* aspects of human behaviour you will never be able to get them to fall in love, or do something really creative, etc.

REPLY I agree that no computer program in existence could yet pass the Turing Test. This is no reason to suppose that we cannot go on and on writing programmes for more and more aspects of human behaviour until one day we succeed. You must supply some principled reason for your belief that certain things are unprogrammable.

We now turn to Searle who, like Turing, asks us to play a thought game with him to make his point.

Searle's 'Chinese Room'

Searle's imaginary game has been called the 'Chinese Room Test'. It is based on a computer program described by Schank and Abelson (1977) which some people have claimed 'understands' stories. The program is intended to simulate the operation of the sort of world knowledge that we saw readers to use when interpreting stories or speech (Chapters 4 and 10). Searle's writing is so direct and compelling that I will leave him to speak for himself:

> Very briefly, and leaving out the various details, one can describe Schank's program as follows: The aim of the program is to simulate the human ability to understand stories. It is characteristic of human beings' story understanding capacity that they can answer questions about the story even though the information that they give was never explicitly stated in the story. Thus, for example, suppose you are given the following story: 'A man went into a restaurant and ordered a hamburger. When the hamburger arrived it was burned to a crisp, and the man stormed out of the restaurant angrily, without paying for the hamburger or leaving a tip.' Now, if you are asked 'Did the man eat the hamburger?' you will presumably answer, 'No, he did not.' Similarly, if you are given the following story: 'A man went into a restaurant and ordered a hamburger; when the hamburger came he was very pleased with it; and as he left the restaurant he gave the waitress a large tip before paying his bill,' and you are asked the question, 'Did the man eat the

hamburger?' you will presumably answer, 'Yes, he ate the hamburger.' Now Schank's machines can similarly answer questions about restaurants in this fashion. To do this, they have a 'representaiton' of the sort of information that human beings have about restaurants, which enables them to answer such questions as those above, given these sorts of stories. When the machine is given the story and then asked the question, the machine will print out answers of the sort that we would expect human beings to give if told similar stories. Partisans of strong AI claim that in this question and answer sequence the machine is not only simulating a human ability but also (1) that the machine can literally be said to *understand* the story and provide the answers to questions, and (2) that what the machine and its program do *explains* the human ability to understand the story and answer questions about it.

Both claims seem to me to be totally unsupported by Schank's work, as I will attempt to show in what follows. I am not, of course, saying that Schank himself is committed to these claims.

One way to test any theory of the mind is to ask oneself what it would be like if my mind actually worked on the principles that the theory says all minds work on. Let us apply this test to the Schank program with the following *Gedankenexperiment* [thought experiment]. Suppose that I'm locked in a room and given a large batch of Chinese writing. Suppose furthermore (as is indeed the case) that I know no Chinese, either written or spoken, and that I'm not confident that I could recognize Chinese writing as Chinese writing distinct from, say Japanese writing or meaningless squiggles. To me, Chinese writing is just so many meaningless squiggles. Now suppose further that after this first batch of Chinese writing I am given a second batch of Chinese script together with a set of rules for correlating the second batch with the first batch. The rules are in English, and I understand these rules as well as any other native speaker of English. They enable me to correlate one set of formal symbols with another set of formal symbols, and all that 'formal' means here is that I can identify the symbols entirely by their shapes. Now suppose also that I am given a third batch of Chinese symbols together with some instructions, again in English, that enable me to correlate elements of this third batch with the first two batches, and these rules instruct me how to give back certain Chinese symbols with certain sorts of shapes in response to certain sorts of shapes given me in the third batch. Unknown to me, the people who are giving me all of these symbols call the first batch a 'script', they call the second batch a 'story', and they call the third batch 'questions'. Furthermore, they call the symbols I give them back in response to the third batch 'answers to the question,' and the set of rules in English that they gave me, they call the 'program'. Now just to complicate the story a little, imagine that these people also give me stories in English, which I understand, and they then ask me questions in English about these stories, and I give them back answers in English. Suppose also that after a while I get so good at following the instructions for manipulating the Chinese symbols and the programmers get so good at writing the programs that from the external point of view – that is, from the point of view of somebody outside the room in which I am locked – my answers to the questions are absolutely indistinguishable from those of native Chinese speakers. Nobody just looking at my answers can tell that I don't speak a word of Chinese. Let us also suppose that my answers to the English questions are, as they no doubt would be, indistinguishable from those of other native English speakers, for the simple reason that I am a native English speaker. From the external point of view – from the point of view of someone reading my 'answers' – the answers to the Chinese questions and the English questions are equally good. But in the Chinese case, unlike the English case, I produce the answers by manipulating uninterpreted formal symbols. As far as the Chinese is concerned, I simply behave like a computer; I perform computational operations on formally specified elements. For the purposes of the Chinese, I am simply an instantiation of the computer program.

Now the claims made by strong AI are that the programmed computer understands the stories and that the program in some sense explains human understanding. But we are now in a position to examine these claims in light of our thought experiment.

1 As regards the first claim, it seems to me quite obvious in the example that I do not understand a word of the Chinese stories. I have inputs and outputs that are indistinguishable from those of the native Chinese speaker, and I can have any formal program you like, but I still understand nothing. For the same reasons, Schank's computer understands nothing of any stories, whether in Chinese, English, or whatever, since in the Chinese case the computer is me, and in cases where the computer is not me, the computer has nothing more than I have in the case where I understand nothing.

2 As regards the second claim, that the program explains human understanding, we can see that the computer and its program do not provide sufficient conditions of understanding since the computer and the program are functioning, and there is no understanding.

If we accept Searle's arguments (and many have tried to demolish them) then we must ask what it is about humans which makes them special. Here Searle is not quite so compelling. Briefly, he believes that intentional attributes such as thinking, knowing, understanding, are tied up with the fact that the human computer is made manifest in nerves, flesh and blood.

What matters about brain operations is not the formal shadow cast by the sequence of synapses but rather the actual properties of the sequences. All the arguments for the strong version of artificial intelligence that I have seen insist on drawing an outline around the shadows cast by cognition and then claiming that the shadows are the real thing.

Here we must let the debate rest. If and when it is resolved it will bring us closer to the core of what it is to be human. For now, we must live with uncertainty.

Programs and Simulations

For many years now, computer experts have been writing chess-playing programs with the aim of producing something which no human could beat. Chess is a tantalizing challenge for programmers because its basic rules are so simple and well-defined and yet there is almost no limit to the refinement of chess skill. In 1957 Herbert Simon predicted that in ten years time there would exist a computer program that no–one would beat. Almost 30 years later, his prediction has still not come true, although there are a couple of American systems (notably 'Belle' at Bell Laboratories, New Jersey) that can beat over 99.5 per cent of all competition players.

Algorithms

As already mentioned in Chapter 14, there are basically two approaches to cracking a computing problem. One is to try to discover an efficient *algorithm* for the task, the other is to develop a workable *heuristic* system. An algorithm is a procedure which guarantees a solution for members of some problem class. For instance, most of us learned algorithms for solving long multiplication when we were at school. If one follows all the steps in the right order and makes no calculation errors then one always ends up with the right answer.

Is there an algorithm for chess? Well, in theory there is. It involves considering each alternative move, then each possible reply by your opponent, then each possible reply you could make, and so on, until you had explored the consequences of every possible move right through to the point where one or other player won. You would then choose the move associated with the largest number of winning outcomes.

Unfortunately, such an algorithm is unworkable. Someone has calculated that there are more possible chess games than there are atoms in the universe. Even if one only looked five moves ahead one would have to consider up to 50,000,000 different combinations of moves. It would probably take even the fastest existing computer with unlimited storage space, several million years to play a game of chess using such an algorithm.

Heuristics

In order to 'reduce the search space' in problems of this sort, what one usually needs are heuristics. These are like rules of thumb which have a reasonable probability of producing acceptable results. It is pretty clear that human problem-solving normally proceeds with a large helping of heuristics (see Chapters 13 and 14), and such heuristics are the usual stock in trade of coaches. Thus, most chess primers will advise a player to prefer moves which gain control over the middle four squares of the board. Another heuristic is to take one's opponent's pieces whenever the opportunity arises. Every heuristic has its limitations. In chess your opponent can set up a 'sacrifice' whereby he gains a larger advantage if you can be tempted by the smaller reward of taking one of his pieces.

In general, however, the advantages of heuristics far outweigh their limitations. Many human problems are too ill-defined for algorithms to apply. Often we are unaware of all the possibilities available to us and so cannot evaluate all the alternative courses of action. Even when we can do this, it may take far too long or take up too many mental resources. Heuristics offer the prospect of rapid response to a situation. In the real world one rarely has unlimited time to decide. Simple heuristics have also been shown to have very wide computing application. Pioneering work by Simon and associates (Newell and Simon, 1972) resulted in a program called General Problem Solver (GPS), based on a set of heuristics. One of these has been called the means-ends heuristic (see Chapter 14). Simply put it says that if you want to go from some initial state A to some final state Z, and there is some intermediate state M that is nearer Z on some dimension than is A, then try getting to M. This approach underlies the way that the 'getting to London' problem was tackled in Chapter 2.

Newell and Simon showed that heuristics such as this can be rigorously formulated and implemented in a computer program that is capable of making coherent attacks on a large variety of problems (such as finding proofs of mathematical assertions). The production rules described in Chapter 2 may also be seen as embodiments of heuristics (related to, but of a rather more specific nature than, the means-ends heuristic). A system such as GPS can easily be implemented as a computer-based production system, and there now exist programs that are capable of learning by moving from rather general heuristics, which are supplied as givens, towards specific rules tailored to individual situations (Anderson, 1982).

Chess programmers are driven to heuristics because it is the only way they are ever going to get computers playing good and speedy chess. They are not, on the whole, particularly concerned to simulate human performance. Their goal is to exceed it, to do the best possible job. Like them, many workers in artificial intelligence are primarily concerned with providing good solutions to problems. Whenever algorithms are available, they will tend towards using them, because they increase reliability. They also cash in on the incredible speed with which computers can perform repetitive operations. Speed and reliability are the main reason why computers have replaced humans in many of the more mechanical areas of the work-place. A properly programmed computer can keep track of wages much more efficiently than a wages-clerk.

For those, however, who are primarily interested in using computers to simulate, and thus better understand, human functioning, it is not important to get the *best* programme. It is precisely the program which makes "human" errors and shows the human capacity for going beyond the data given (as in Schank's 'story understanding' program) which is of most psychological interest.

It is possible that at rather peripheral levels of sensory and motor functioning (see for example Marr, 1983) the brain operates on algorithmic principles. The computation of visual depth from a stereoscopic image seems to be algorithmically based. As soon, however, as we get into prime cognitive territory, the heuristic seems to abound. From the perception of visual form through to the creation of a work of art, the human characteristic of imperfection seems to confer a peculiar advantage on us. Although computers are slowly coming to be able to mimic some of these qualities of flexibility and open-endedness that characterise the human mind, it is not at all clear that the computer approach has cracked or is going to crack every unsolved mystery. Like all metaphors, it highlights similarities and clarifies understanding, but the understanding it provides is only partial.

FURTHER READING

HOFSTADTER, D. R. and DENNETT, D. C. (1981) *The Mind's I*. New York: Basic Books.

Provide an imaginative collection of articles on the conceptual and philosophical issues, linked together by their own commentary.

BODEN, M. A. (1987). *Artificial Intelligence and Natural Man*. Hassocks: Harvester.

This is the indispensable source book for accessible descriptions of the major classes of computer simulations, written by a committed 'Turing' follower.

WEIZENBAUM, J. (1984) *Computer Power and Human Reason* (2nd Edition). San Francisco: Freeman.

A thought provoking and critical appraisal of computer simulations which takes a position similar to Searle.

NEWELL, A. and SIMON, H. (1972) *Human Problem Solving*. Englewood Cliffs, N.J.: Prentice Hall.

The classic account of their own seminal work. Sometimes hard going.

REFERENCES

ADAMS, J. L. (1979) *Conceptual Blockbusting* (2nd edition). San Francisco: Freeman.

AITCHISON, J. (1989) *The Articulate Mammal*. London: Hutchinson (3rd edition).

ALLPORT, D. A., ANTONIS, B., and REYNOLDS, P. (1972) 'On the division of attention: a disproof of the single channel hypothesis'. *Quarterly Journal of Experimental Psychology*, 24, 225–35.

AMABILE, T.M. (1983) *The Social Psychology of Creativity*. New York: Springer Verlag.

ANDERSON, J. R. (1982) 'Acquisition of cognitive skills'. *Psychological Review*, 89, 369–406.

ARGYLE, M. (1969) *Social Interaction*. London: Tavistock publications in association with Methuen & Co.

ARGYLE, M. (1983) *The Psychology of Interpersonal Behaviour*. Harmondsworth: Penguin.

ARGYLE, M. (1984) 'Some new developments in social skills training'. *Bulletin of the British Psychological Society*, 37, 405–10.

ARGYLE, M. and COOK, M. (1976) *Gaze and Mutual Gaze*. Cambridge: Cambridge University Press.

AUSTIN, J.L. (1962) *How to do things with words*. (Ed. J.O. Urmson). London: Oxford University Press.

BADDELEY, A.D. (1979) 'Working memory and reading'. In P. A. Kolers, M. E. Wrolstad, and H. Bouma (Eds) *Processing of Visible Language. Volume 1*. New York: Plenum.

BADDELEY, A. D. (1984) 'Neuropsychological evidence and the semantic/episodic distinction'. *The Behavioural and Brain Sciences*, 7, 238–39.

BADDELEY, A.D. and HITCH, G.J. (1974) 'Working Memory'. In G. H. Bower (Ed.) *The Psychology of Learning and Motivation (Vol. 8)*. New York: Academic Press.

BAKER, L. (1979) 'Comprehension monitoring : identifying and coping with text confusions'. *Journal of Reading Behavior*, 11, 366–74.

BAKER, L. and ANDERSON, R. I. (1982) 'Effects of inconsistent information on text processing : evidence for comprehension monitoring'. *Reading Research Quarterly*, 17, 281–94.

BARTLETT, F. C. (1958) *Thinking*. London: Allen & Unwin.

BATESON, G. (1982) 'Totemic knowledge in New Guinea'. In U. Neisser (Ed.) *Memory Observed*. San Francisco: Freeman.

BEARD, R. M. and HARTLEY, J. (1984) *Teaching and Learning in Higher Education*. (4th edition). London: Harper & Row.

BEATTIE, G. W. (1981) 'Interruption in conversational interaction, and its relation to the sex and status of the interactants'. *Linguistics, 19*, 15–35.

BEATTIE, G. W. (1982) 'Turntaking and interruption in political interviews – Margaret Thatcher and Jim Callaghan compared and contrasted'. *Semiotica, 39*, 93–114.

BEATTIE, G. W. (1983) *Talk: An analysis of speech and non-verbal behaviour in conversation.* Milton Keynes: Open University Press.

BEGG, I. and DENNY, J. P. (1969) Empirical reconciliation of atmosphere and conversion interpretations of syllogistic reasoning errors. *Journal of Experimental Psychology, 81*, 351–54.

BELMONT, J. M. and BUTTERFIELD, E. C. (1971) 'Learning strategies as determinants of mental deficiencies'. *Cognitive Psychology, 2*, 411–20

BIRDWHISTELL, R. L. (1968) 'Kinesics' *International Encyclopaedia of the Social Sciences, Vol 8*, 379–385. New York: MacMillian.

BLURTON-JONES, N. (1972) *Ethological Studies of Child Behaviour.* London: Cambridge University Press.

BOGEN, J. E. (1977) 'Some educational implications of hemispheric specialization'. In M.C. Wittrock (Ed.) *The Human Brain.* New York: Prentice Hall.

de BOISBAUDRAN, H. L. (1911) *The Training of the Memory in Art.* London: Macmillan.

BOWER, G. H. (1972) 'A selective review of organizational factors in memory'. In E. Tulving and W. Donaldson (Eds.) *Organization of Memory.* New York: Academic Press.

BOWER, G. H. (1976) 'Comprehending and recalling stories'. Paper given at the Washington meeting of the American Psychological Association.

BOWER, G. H. and KARLIN, M. B. (1974) 'Depth of processing pictures of faces and recognition memory'. *Journal of Experimental Psychology, 103*, 751–57.

BRANSFORD, J. D. (1979) *Human Cognition : Learning, Remembering and Understanding.* Belmont: Wadsworth.

BRILL, A. A. (1938) *The basic writings of Sigmund Freud.* New York: Random House.

BROADBENT, D. E. (1982) 'Task Combination and selective intake of information'. *Acta Psychologica, 50*, 253–90.

BROWN, A. L., BRANSFORD, J. D., FERRARA, R. A. and CAMPIONE, J. C. (1983) 'Learning, remembering and understanding'. In P.H. Mussen (Ed.) *Handbook of Child Psychology, Vol. 3.* New York: Wiley.

BROWN, A. L., CAMPIONE, J. C. and DAY, J. D. (1981) 'Learning to learn: on training students to learn from texts'. *Education Researcher, 10*, 14–21.

BROWN, A. L., CAMPIONE, J. C. and MURPHY, M. D. (1974) 'Keeping track of changing variables: Long-term retention of a trained rehearsal strategy by retarded adolescents'. *American Journal of Mental Deficiency, 78*, 446–53.

BROWN, A. L. and DAY, J. D. (1983) 'Macro-rules for summarizing texts : The development of expertise'. *Journal of Verbal Learning and Verbal Behavior, 22*, 1–14.

BROWN, G. (1978) *Lecturing and Explaining.* London: Methuen.

BRUNER, J. S. (1962) *On Knowing – Essays for the left hand.* Cambridge, Mass.: Belknop Press.

BRYAN, W. L. and HARTER, N. (1899) 'Studies on the telegraphic language: The acquisition of a hierarchy of habits'. *Psychological Review, 6*, 345–75.

BUTTERWORTH, B. (1980) 'Evidence from pauses in speech'. In Butterworth, B. (Ed.) *Language Production, Vol. 1: Speech and Talk.* London: Academic Press.

CERMAK, K. S. BUTTERS, N. and MOREINES, J. (1974) 'Some analyses of the verbal encoding deficit of alcoholic Korsakoff patients'. *Brain and Language, 1*, 141–150.

CHASE, W. G. (1983) 'Spatial representations of taxi-drivers'. In D. R. Rogers and J.A. Sloboda (Eds.) *Acquisition of Symbolic Skills*. New York: Plenum.

CHASE, W. G.and ERICSSON, K. A. (1981) 'Skilled memory'. In *Cognitive Skills and their Acquisition*. Edited by J.R. Anderson. Hillsdale, New Jersey: Lawrence Erlbaum. Pp. 141–89.

CHASE, W. G. and ERICSSON, K. A. (1982) 'Skill and working memory'. In *The Psychology of Learning and Motivation, vol. 16*. Edited by G.H. Bower. New York: Academic Press. Pp. 1–58.

CHASE, W. G. and SIMON, H. A. (1973) 'The mind's eye in chess'. In W. G. Chase (Ed.) *Visual Information Processing*. New York: Academic Press.

CHI, M. T. H. (1978) 'Knowledge structures and memory development'. In R. Seigler (Ed.) *Children's Thinking: What Develops?* Hillsdale: Lawrence Erlbaum.

CHI, M. T. H. (1983) *Trends in Memory Development Research*. New York: Karger.

CHI, M. T. H. (1985) Changing conceptions of sources of memory development. *Human Development, 28*, 50–6.

CLARKE, A. M. and CLARKE, A. D. B. (1976) *Early Experience: Myth and Evidence*. London: Open Books.

CLARKE, H. H. (1977) 'Bridging'. In P.N. Johnson-Laird and P.C. Wason (Eds) *Thinking: Readings in Cognitive Science*. Cambridge: Cambridge University Press.

COHEN, J. (1970) *Homo Psychologicus*. London: Allen & Unwin.

COLE, M., GAY, J., GLICK, J. and SHARP, D. (1971) *The Cultural Context of Learning and Thinking*. New York: Basic Books.

COLE, M. and SCRIBNER, S. (1974) *Culture and Thought*. New York: Wiley.

CONDON, W. S. and OGSTON, W. D. (1966) 'Sound film analysis of normal and pathological behaviour patterns'. *Journal of Nervous and Mental Disease, 143*, 338–47.

CONDON, W. S. and OGSTON, W. D. (1967) 'A segmentation of behaviour'. *Journal of Psychiatric Research, 5*, 221–35.

CRAIK, F. I. M. and LOCKHART, R. S. (1972) 'Levels of processing: A framework for memory research'. *Journal of Verbal Learning and Verbal Behaviour, 11*, 671–84.

CRAIK, F. I. M. and TULVING, E. (1975) Depth of processing and retention of words in episodic memory. *Journal of Experimental Psychology: General, 104*, 268–94.

CROWDER, R. G. (1982) *The Psychology of Reading: an Introduction*. New York: Oxford University Press.

CUCELOGLU, D. M. (1972) 'Facial code in affective communication'. In B.C. Speer (Ed.) *Non-Verbal communication: Contemporary Science Issues, 10*. Beverly Hills: Sage Publications.

DANNER, F. W. (1976) 'Children's understanding of intersentence organization in the recall of short descriptive passages'. *Journal of Educational Psychology, 68*, 2, 174–83.

DANSEREAU, F. W. (1985) Learning strategy reserach. In J. W. Segal, S. F. Chifman and R. Glaser *(Eds.) Thinking and Leraning Skills, Vol 1, Relating Instruction to Reserach*. Hillsdale, N.J.: Erlbaum.

DANSEREAU, D. F., BROOKS, L. W., HOLLEY, C. D. and COLLINS, K. W. (1983) 'Learning strategies training : effects of sequencing'. *Journal of Experimental Education, 51*, 3, 102–08.

DANSEREAU, D. F., COLLINS, K. W., MCDONALD, B. A., GARLAND, J., DIEKHOFF, G. M. and EVANS, S. H. (1979) 'Development and evaluation of a learning strategy program'. *Journal of Education Psychology, 71*, 64–73.

DARWIN, C. (1872) *The Expression of Emotion in Man and Animals*. London: J. Murray.

DARWIN, C. (1911) *The life and letters of Charles Darwin*. Vol.I. New York: Appleton.

DAVIES, F. and GREENE, T. (1984) *Reading for Learning in the Sciences*. Edinburgh: Oliver and Boyd.

DAVIES, G. (1981) 'Face-recall systems'. In G. Davies, H. Ellis, and J. Shepherd (Eds) *Perceiving and Remembering Faces*. London: Academic Press.

DAVITZ, J. R. (1964) *The Communication of Emotional Meaning*. New York: McGraw Hill.

DEFFENBACHER, K. A., BROWN, E. K. and STURGILL, W. (1978) 'Some predictors of eyewitness memory accuracy'. In M.M. Gruneberg, P.E. Morris, and R.N. Sykes (Eds) *Practical Aspects of memory*. London: Academic Press.

DEFFENBACHER, K. A. and HORNEY, J. (1981) 'Psycho-legal aspects of face identification'. In G. Davies, H. Ellis, and J. Shepherd (Eds) *Perceiving and Remembering Faces*. London: Academic Press.

DIEKHOFF, G. M., BROWN, P. J. and DANSEREAU, D. F. (1982) 'A prose-learning strategies training program based upon networking and depth-of-processing models'. *Journal of Experimental Education, 50*, 4, 180–84.

DOOLING, D. J. and LACHMAN, R. (1971) 'Effects of comprehension on retention of prose'. *Journal of Experimental Psychology, 88*, 216–22.

DOWNES, W. (1984) *Language and Society*. London: Fontana.

DRIVER, R. (1983) *The Pupil as Scientist?* Milton Keynes: Open University Press.

DUNCAN, S. (1972) 'Some signals and rules for taking speaking turns in conversation'. *Journal of Personality and Social Psychology, 23*, 283–92.

DUNCKER, K. (1945) 'On problem solving'. *Psychological Monographs, 58:5,*Whole No. 270.

EIBL-EIBESFELDT, I. (1972) 'Similarities and differences between cultures in expressive movements'. In Hinde, R.A. (Ed.) *Non–verbal Communication*. Cambridge: Cambridge University Press.

EICH, J. E. (1980) 'The cue-dependent nature of state-dependent retrieval'. *Memory and Cognition, 8*, 157–73.

EKMAN, P. (1972) 'Universal and cultural differences in facial expressions of emotion'. In J. Cole (Ed.) *Nebraska Symposium on Motivation*. Lincoln, Nebraska: University of Nebraska Press.

EKMAN, P.and FRIESEN, W. V. (1969) Non–verbal leakage and cues to deception. *Psychiatry, 32*, 88–105.

EKMAN, P. and FRIESEN, W. V. (1976) 'Communicative Body Movement: American Emblems'. *Semiotica, 15*, 4, 335–53.

EKMAN, P. and FRIESEN, W. V. (1978) *Facial Action Coding System: investigator's guide*. Palo Alto, California: Consulting Psychologists' Press.

EKMAN, P., FRIESEN, W. V. and TOMKINS, S. S. (1971) 'Facial Affect Scoring Technique: a first validity study'. *Semiotica, 3*, 37–58.

ERICSSON, K. A. (1985) 'Memory skill'. *Canadian Journal of Psychology, 39*, 188–231.

ERICSSON, K. A. and CHASE, W. G. (1982) 'Exceptional memory'. *American Scientist, 70*, 607–15.

ESPOSITO, A. (1979) 'Sex differences in children's conversations'. *Language and Speech, 22*, 213–21.

EVANS, J. ST B. T. (1982) *The Psychology of Deductive Reasoning*. London: Routledge & Kegan Paul.

EYSENCK, H. J. versus KAMIN, L. (1981) *Intelligence Controversy*. New York: John Wiley.

FAST, J. (1972) *Body Language*. London: Pan Books.

FISKE, S. T. and TAYLOR, S. E. (1984) *Social Cognition*. Reading, Mass.: Addison–Wesley.

FITTS, P. M. and POSNER, M. I. (1967) *Human Performance* Belmont, California: Brooks/Cole.

FLAVELL, J. H. (1971) 'What is memory development the development of?' *Human Development, 14*, 272–86.

FLAVELL, J. H. (1985) *Cognitive Development* (2nd edition) Englewood Cliffs: Prentice Hall (first published 1977).

FLAVELL, J. H., BEACH, D. R. and CHINSKY, J. M. (1966) 'Spontaneous verbal rehearsal in a memory task as a function of age'. *Child Development, 37*, 283–99.

FODOR, J. A., BEVER, T. G. and GARRET, H.M.F. (1974) *The Psychology of Language*. New York: McGraw Hill.

FOWLER, R., HART, J. and SHEEHAN, M. (1972) 'A prosthetic memory: an application of the prosthetic environment concept'. *Rehabilitation Counselling Bulletin, 15*, 80–85.

FREUD, S. (1905) 'Fragment of an analysis of a case of hysteria'. *Collected Papers, vol. 3*. N.Y. Basic books, 1959.

FROMKIN, V. A. (1973) *Speech errors as linguistic evidence*. The Hague: Mouton.

GARDNER, H. (1982) *Developmental Psychology*. New York: Little, Brown and Company.

GARDNER, H. (1983) *Frames of Mind*. London: Heinemann.

GARRETT, G. A., BAXTER, J. C. and ROZELLE, R. M. (1981) 'Training University Police in Black-American nonverbal behaviours: An application to police-community relations'. *Journal of Social Psychology, 113*, 217–29.

GARRETT, M. F. (1980) 'Levels of planning in sentence production'. In Butterworth, B. (Ed.) *Language Production, vol. 1: Speech and Talk*. London: Academic Press.

GELLATLY, A. R. H. (1987) 'The acquisition of a concept of logical necessity'. *Human Development*. (Forthcoming).

GELLATLY, A. R. H. (1988) 'Influences on conceptions of logic and mind'. In I. Hronszky, M. Feher, and B. Dajka (Eds) *Scientific Knowledge Socialized*. Dordrecht: Reidel.

GELLATLY, A. R. H., JONES, S. and BEST, A. (1988) 'How good are young children at concentration?' *Australian Journal of Psychology, 40*, 1–10.

GHISELIN, B. (1952) *The Creative Process*. Berkeley: University of California Press.

GIBBS, G. (1981) *Teaching Students to Learn*. Milton Keynes: Open University Press.

GIBSON, E. J. and LEVIN, H. (1975) *The Psychology of Reading*. Cambridge, Mass.: MIT Press.

GIBSON, E. J., PICK, A., OSSER, H., and HAMMOND, M. (1962) 'The role of grapheme-phoneme correspondence in the preception of words'. *American Journal of Psychology. 75*, 554–70.

GILHOOLY, K. J. (1982) *Thinking: Directed, Undirected, and Creative*. London: Academic Press.

GLADWIN, T. (1970) *East is a Big Bird*. Cambridge, Mass.: Harvard University Press.

GOFFMAN, E. (1956) *The Presentation of Self in Everyday Life*. Edinburgh: University of Edinburgh Press.

GOODGLASS, H. and KAPLAN, E. (1979) 'Assessment of cognitive deficiency in the brain-injured patient'. In M. Gazzaniga (Ed.) *Handbook of Behavioral Neurobiology, 2.* New York: Plenum.

GORDON, W. J. J. (1961) *Synectics: the development of creative capacity.* New York: Harper and Row.

GRANT, E. (1969) 'Human Facial Expression'. *Man, 4,* No. 4.

GREEN, D. W. and SHALLICE, T. (1976) 'Direct visual access in reading for meaning'. *Memory and Cognition, 4,* 753–58.

GRICE, H. (1975) Logic and Conversation. In P. Cole and J. L. Morgan (Eds.) *Syntax and Semantics, Vol. 3: Speech Acts.* New York: Academic Press.

GRIGGS, R. A. (1983) 'The role of problem content in the selection task and in the THOG problem'. In J. St B.T. Evans (Ed.) *Thinking and Reasoning.* London: Routledge & Kegan Paul.

GRUBER, H. E. (1974) *Darwin on Man: A psychological study of Scientific Creativity.* New York: E.P. Dutton.

GRUNEBERG, M. M. (1985) 'The Gruneberg–Linkword Language System for Teaching Foreign Languages'. *Training and Development,* February, 1985.

GRUNEBERG, M. M., MORRIS, P. E., and SYKES, R. N. (1978) (Eds) *Practical Aspects of Memory.* London: Academic Press.

HABER, R. N. (1979) 'Twenty years of haunting eidetic imagery: where's the ghost?'. *The Behavioural and Brain Sciences, 2,* 583–629.

HARDYCK, C. D. and PETRINOVICH, I. F. (1970) 'Subvocal speech and comprehension level as a function of the difficulty level of the reading material'. *Journal of Verbal Learning and Verbal Behaviour, 9,* 647–52.

HARRE, R. and SECORD, P. W. (1972) *The Explanation of Social Behaviour.* Oxford: Blackwell.

HARRIS, J. E. (1980a) 'Memory aids people use: two interview studies'. *Memory and Cognition, 8,* 31–38.

HARRIS, J. E. (1980b) 'We have ways of helping you remember'. *Concord: Journal of the British Association for Service to the Elderly, 17,* (May), 21–27.

HARRIS, J. E. (1984) 'Remembering to do things'. In J.E. Harris and P.E. Morris (Eds) *Everyday Memory, Actions and Absent-mindedness.* London: Academic Press.

HARTLEY, J. (1985) *Designing Instructional Text* (2nd edition). London: Kogan Page.

HASHER, L. and ZACKS, R. T. (1979) 'Automatic and effortful processes in memory'. *Journal of Experimental Psychology: General, 108,* 356–88.

HATANO, G. and OSAWA, K. (1983) 'Digit memory of grand experts in abacus–derived mental calculation'. *Cognition, 15,* 95–110.

HENLE, M. (1962) 'On the relation between logic and thinking'. *Psychological Review, 69,* 366–78.

HENLE, M. (1978) Foreword to R. Revlin and R.E. Mayer (Eds) *Human Reasoning.* Washington, DC: Winston.

HERMANN, K. (1959) *Reading Disability.* Copenhagen: Munksgaard.

HINDE, R. A. (1966) *Animal Behaviour.* New York: McGraw Hill.

HINDE, R. A. (1972) *Non-verbal communication.* London: Cambridge University Press.

HIRST, W. and VOLPE, B. T. (1984) 'Automatic and effortful encoding in amnesia'. In M.S. Gazzaniga (Ed.) *Handbook of Cognitive Neuroscience,* New York: Plenum Press.

HITCH, G. J. (1980) 'Developing the concept of working memory'. In G. Claxton, (Ed.) *Cognitive Psychology: New Directions.* London: Routledge and Kegan Paul.

HOCHBERG, J. (1970) 'Components of literacy: speculations and exploratory research'. In H. Levin and J. P. Williams (Eds) *Basic Studies on Reading*. New York: Basic Books.

HOFSTADTER, D. R. and DENNETT, D. C. (1981) *The Mind's I*. New York: Basic books.

HOWE, N. J. A. (1984) 'Questions of memory'. In J. Nicholson and M. Lucas (Eds) *All in the Mind: Psychology in Action*. London: Thames Methuen.

HOWE, M. L., BRAINERD, C. J. and JINGSMA, H. (1985) 'Development of organization in recall: a stage of learning analysis'. *Journal of Experimental Child Psychology, 39*, 230–51.

HULME, C., THOMSON, N., MUIR, C. and LAWRENCE, A. (1984) 'Speech rate and the development of short-term memory span'. *Journal of Experimental Child Psychology, 38*, 241–53.

HUNT, M. (1982) *The Universe Within*. Hassocks, Sussex: Harvester.

HUNTER, I. M. L. (1964) *Memory*. Baltimore: Penguin.

HUNTER, I. M. L. (1985) 'Memory development: the cultural background'. In J.A. Branthwaite and D.R. Rogers (Eds) *Children Growing Up*. Milton Keynes: Open University Press.

ILLICH, I. D. (1973) *Deschooling Society*. London: Penguin.

INGHAM, R. J. (1972) 'Cross cultural differences in social behaviour'. D. Phil. Thesis, Oxford University.

ISTOMINA, Z. M. (1982) 'The development of memory in children of pre-school age'. In U. Neisser (Ed.) *Memory Observed*. San Francisco: Freeman.

JAMES, D. E. (1967) *A Student's Guide to Efficient Study*. London: Pergamon.

JOHNSON, C. N. and WELLMAN, H. M. (1980) 'Children's developing understanding of mental verbs: remember, know and guess'. *Child Development, 51*, 1095–1102.

JOHNSON-LAIRD, P. N. (1982) 'Thinking as a skill'. *Quarterly Journal of Experimental Psychology, 34A*, 1–30.

JOHNSON–LAIRD, P. N. (1983) *Mental Models*. Cambridge: Cambridge University Press.

JONASSEN, D. H. (1984) 'Developing a learning strategy using pattern notes: a new technology'. *Programmed Learning and Educational Technology, 21*, 3, 163–75.

JONES, G. and ADAM, J. (1979) 'Towards a prosthetic memory'. *Bulletin of the British Psychological Society, 32*, 165–67.

JORM, A. F. (1983) *The Psychology of Reading and Spelling Difficulties*. London: Routledge and Kegan Paul.

JOYNSON, R. B. (1974) *Psychology and Common Sense*. London: Routledge & Kegan Paul.

KAGAN, J., LAPIDUS, D. R., and MOORE, N. (1978) 'Infant antecedents of cognitive functioning: a longitudinal study'. *Child Development, 49*, 1005–23.

KAIL, R. (1984) *The Development of Memory in Children* (2nd edition). New York: Freeman.

KANDEL, E. R. (1976) *Cellular Basis of Behavior*. New York: Freeman.

KATONA, G. (1940) *Organizing and Memorizing*. New York: Columbia University Press.

KATZ, A. N. (1978) 'Creativity and the right cerebral hemisphere'. *Journal of Creative Behaviour, 12*, 253–64.

KEARINS, J. (1981) 'Visual spatial memory in Australian Aboriginal Children of desert regions'. *Cognitive Psychology, 13*, 435–60.

KENDLER, H. H. and KENDLER, T. S. (1967) 'Experimental analysis of inferential behavior in children'. In L.P. Lipsitt and C.C. Spiker (Eds) *Advances in Child Development and Behavior*, Vol.3. New York: Academic Press.

KENDON, A. (1967) 'Some functions of gaze patterns in social interactions'. *Acta Psychologica, 26,* 24–47.

KLEIMAN, G. M. (1975) 'Speech recoding in reading'. *Journal of Verbal Learning and Verbal Behaviour. 14,* 323–29.

KOESTLER, A. (1964) *The Act of Creation.* New York: Dell.

KOBASIGAWA (1974) 'Utilization of retrieval-cues by children in recall'. *Child Development, 45,* 127–34.

KOLB, B. and WHISHAW, I. Q. (1985) *The Fundamentals of Human Neuropsychology* (2nd Edition). New York: W. H. Freeman and Company.

KREUTZER, M. A., LEONARD, C. and FLAVELL, J. H. (1975) 'An interview study of children's knowledge about memory'. *Monographs of the Society for Research in Child Development, 40,* (1, Serial No. 159), 1–58.

KUHN, T. S. (1970) *The Structure of Scientific Revolutions* (2nd edition). Chicago: University of Chicago Press.

LABERGE, D. (1973) 'Attention and the measurement of perceptual learning'. *Memory and Cognition, 1,* 268–76.

LANZETTA, J. T. and KLECK, R. (1970) 'Encoding and decoding facial affect in humans'. *Journal Personality and Social Psychology, 16,* 12–19.

LARKIN, J. H., MCDERMOTT, J., SIMON, D. P. and SIMON, H. A. (1980) 'Expert and novice performance in solving physics problems'. *Science, 208,* 1335–42.

LEVELT, W. J. M. (1981) 'The speaker's linearization problem'. In *The Psychological Mechanisms of Language.* London: Royal Society and British Academy.

LINDE, C. and LABOV, W. (1975) 'Spatial networks as a site for the study of language and thought'. *Language, 51,* 924–39.

LINDSAY, P. H. and NORMAN, D. A. (1977) *Human Information Processing* (2nd edition). New York: Academic Press.

LOFTUS, E. F. and PALMER, J. C. (1974) 'Reconstruction of automobile destruction: an example of the interaction between language and memory'. *Journal of Verbal Learning and Verbal Behaviour, 13,* 585–89.

LORAYNE, H. and LUCAS, J. (1974) *The Memory Book.* New York: Stein and Day.

LORD, A. B. (1982) 'Oral poetry in Yugoslavia'. In U. Neisser (Ed.) *Memory Observed.* San Francisco: Freeman.

LUCHINS, A. S. and LUCHINS, E. H. (1950) 'New experimental attempts at preventing mechanization in problem solving'. *Journal of General Psychology, 42,* 279–97.

LUNN, J. H. (1948) 'Chicken Sexing'. *American Scientist, 36,* 280–87.

LURIA, A. R. (1969) *The Mind of the Mnemonist.* London: Cape.

LURIA, A. R. (1973) *The Working Brain.* Harmondsworth: Penguin.

LURIA, A. R. (1976) *Cognitive Development: Its Cultural and Social Foundations.* Cambridge, Mass.: Harvard University Press.

MAIER, N. R. F. (1931) 'Reasoning in Humans II: The solution of a problem and its appearance in consciousness'. *Journal of Comparative Psychology, 12,* 181–94.

MARR, D. (1983) *Vision.* San Francisco: Freeman.

MARSLEN-WILSON, W. D. and TYLER, L. J. (1981) 'Central processes in speech understanding'. In *Psychological Mechanisms of Language.* London: Royal Society and British Academy.

MARTON, F., HOUNSELL, D. and ENTWISTLE, N. (E) (1984) *The Experience of Learning.* Edinburgh: Scottish Academic Press.

MAYER, R. E. (1983) *Thinking, Problem Solving, Cognition*. San Francisco: Freeman.

MAYES, A. R. and MEUDELL, P. R. (1983) 'Amnesia in man and other animals'. In A. R. Mayes (Ed.) *Memory in Animals and Humans*. Wokingham: Van Nostrand Reinhold.

MCGREW, W. C. (1972) *An Ethological Study of Child Behaviour*. Cambridge: Cambridge University Press.

MEACHAM, J. (1972) 'The development of memory abilities in the individual and society'. *Human Development, 15*, 205–28.

MEHRABIAN, A. (1970) 'Non-verbal communication'. Chicago: Aldine Atherton.

MEYER, B. H. F. (1985) 'Signaling the structure of text'. In D.H. Jonassen (Ed.) *The Technology of Text, Vol. 2*. Englewood Cliffs, N.J.: Educational Technology Publications.

MILLER, G. A. (1956) 'The magical number seven, plus or minus two: some limits on our capacity for processing information'. *Psychological Review, 63*, 81–96.

MOELY, B. E., OLSON, F. A., HALWES, T. G. and FLAVELL, J. H. (1969) 'Production deficiency in young children's clustered recall'. *Developmental Psychology, 1*, 26–34.

MORRIS, C. D., BRANSFORD, J. D. and FRANKS, J. J. (1977) 'Levels of processing versus transfer appropriate processing'. *Journal of Verbal Learning and Verbal Behaviour, 16*, 519–33.

MORRIS, D. (1977) *Manwatching: A field guide to human behaviour*. London: Book Club Associates.

MORRIS, P. E., GRUNEBERG, M. M., SYKES, R. N. and MERRICK, A. (1981) 'Football knowledge and the acquisition of new results'. *British Journal of Psychology, 72*, 479–84.

MORTON, H. (1964) 'The effects of context on the visual duration threshold for words'. *British Journal of Psychology, 55*, 165–80.

NAIDOO, S. (1970) 'Remedial re-education'. In A.W. Franklin and S. Naidoo (Eds) *Assessment and teaching of dyslexic children*. London: Invalid Childrens' Aid Association.

NEISSER, U. (1976) *Cognition and Reality*. San Francisco: Freeman.

NEWELL, A. and ROSENBLOOM, P. S. (1981) 'Mechansims of skill acquisitioin and the law of practise'. In J.R. Anderson (Ed.) *Cognitive Skills and their Acquisition*. Hillsdale NJ: Erlbaum.

NEWELL, A. and SIMON, H. (1972) *Human Problem Solving*. Englewood Cliffs, N.J.: Prentice Hall.

NEWSON, J. (1978) *Dialogue and Development Action, Symbol and Gesture, the emergence of language*. J. Newson (Ed.) London: Academic Press.

NORMAN, D. A. (1976) *Memory and Attention* (2nd Edition). New York: Wiley.

NORMAN, D. A. (Ed.) (1981) *Perspectives on Cognitive Science*. New York: Ablex.

O'REGAN, K. (1979) 'Moment to moment control of eye saccades as a function of textual parameters in reading'. In P. A. Kolers, M. E. Wrolstad, and H. Bouma (Eds) *Processing of Visible Language, Volume 1*. New York: Plenum.

OPIE, I. and OPIE, P. (1959) *The Lore and Language of Schoolchildren*. London: Oxford University Press.

ORNSTEIN, P. A., NAUS, M. J. and STONE, B. P. (1977) 'Rehearsal training and developmental differences in memory'. *Developmental Psychology, 13*, 15–24.

PAPERT, S. (1972) 'Teaching children thinking'. *Mathematical Teaching, 58,* Spring, 1972.

PARIS, S. G., CROSS, D. R. and LIPSON, M. Y. (1984) 'Informed strategies for learning: a program to improve children's reading awareness and comprehension'. *Journal of Educational Psychology,* 76, 6, 1239–52.

PERFETTI, C. A., GOLDMAN, S. A., and HOGABOAM, T. W. (1979). 'Reading skill and the identification of words in connected discourse'. *Memory and Cognition,* 7, 273–82.

PERKINS, D. N. (1981) *The Minds's Best Work.* Cambridge, Mass.: Harvard University Press.

PERRY, W. G. (1981) 'Cognitive and ethical growth: the making of meaning'. In A. Chickering (Ed.) *The Modern American College.* San Francisco: Jossey Bass.

PIAGET, J. (1926) *The Language and Thought of the Child.* London: Routledge and Kegan Paul.

PIAGET, J. (1974) 'Need and significance of cross-cultural studies in genetic psychology'. In J. W. Berry & R. R. Dasen (Eds) *Culture and Cognition: Readings in Cross-Cultural Psychology.* London: Methuen.

PIAGET, J. and INHELDER, B. (1973) *Memory and Intelligence.* New York: Basic Books.

POWELL, G. E. (1981) *Brain Function Therapy.* Aldershot: Gower Press.

REASON, J. and MYCIELSKA, K. (1982) *Absent Minded? The Psychology of Mental Lapses and Everyday Errors.* New York: Prentice Hall.

REVESZ, G. (1925) *The Psychology of a Musical Prodigy.* London: Kegan Paul, Trench and Trubner.

ROGERS, D. R. (1985) 'Infants, mothers and intentional communication'. In J. A. Branthwaite and D.R. Rogers (Eds) *Children Growing Up.* Milton Keynes: Open University Press.

ROSENTHAL, R. (Ed.) (1979) *Skill in Nonverbal Communication: Individual Differences.* Cambridge, Mass.: Oelgeschlager, Gunn and Main.

ROVEE-COLLIER, C. K. and LIPSITT, L. P. (1982) 'Learning, adaptation and memory in the newborn'. In P. Stratton (Ed.) *Psychobiology of the Human Newborn.* Chichester: Wiley.

RUESCH, J. and KEES, W. (1956) *Nonverbal Communication: Notes on the visual perception of human relations.* Berkeley: University of California Press.

RUMELHART, D. E. and NORMAN, D. A. (1981) 'Analogical processes in learning'. In J.R. Anderson (Ed.) *Cognitive Skills and their Acquisition.* Hillsdale, N.J.: Erlbaum.

SANFORD, A. J. and GARROD, S. C. (1981) *Understanding Written Language: Explorations in Comprehension Beyond the Sentence.* Chichester: Wiley.

SCHANK, R. C. and ABELSON, R. (1977) *Scripts, Plans, Goals and Understanding.* Hillsdale N.J.: Erlbaum.

SCHEFREN, A. E. (1964) 'The significance of posture in communication systems'. *Psychiatry,* 27, 316–31.

SCHON, D. A. (1979) 'Generative metaphor: a perspective on problem-setting in social policy'. In A. Ortony (Ed.) *Metaphor and Thought.* Cambridge: Cambridge University Press.

SCRIBNER, S. (1977) 'Modes of thinking and ways of speaking: culture and logic reconsidered'. In P. N. Johnson-Laird and P. C. Wason (Eds) *Thinking: Readings in Cognitive Science.* London: Cambridge University Press.

SEARLE, J. R. (1975) 'Indirect Speech Acts'. In Cole, P. and Morgan, J. L. (Eds) *Syntax and Semantics, Vol. 3: Speech Acts.* New York: Academic Press.

SEARLE, J. R. (1980) 'Minds, brains, and programs'. *The Behavioural and Brain Sciences,* *3*, 417–457.

SHAFFER, L. H. (1976) 'Intention and performance'. *Psychological Review, 83*, 375–93.

SHEPHERD, G. (1983) 'Social-skills training with adults'. In S. Spence and G. Sheperd, (Eds) *Development in Social Skills Training*. London: Academic Press.

SIEBEL, R. (1963) 'Discrimination reaction time for a 1023 alternative task'. *Journal of Experimental Psychology, 66*, 1005–23.

SIEGLER, R. S. (1986) 'Strategy choices in substraction'. In J. A. Sloboda and D. R. Rogers (Eds) *Cognitive Processes in Mathematics*. London: Oxford University Press.

SIQUELAND, E. R. and LIPSITT, L. P. (1966) 'Conditioned head-turning in human newborns'. *Journal of Experimental Child Psychology, 3*, 357–76.

SLOBODA, J. A., HERMELIN, B., and O'CONNOR, N. (1985) 'An exceptional musical memory'. *Music Perception*, in press.

SMITH, H. K. (1967) 'The responses of good and poor readers when asked to read for different purposes'. *Reading Research Quarterly, 3*, 53–83.

SMITH, S. M. (1979) 'Remembering in and out of context'. *Journal of Experimental psychology: Human Learning and Memory, 5*, 460–71.

SMODE, A. (1958) 'Learning and performance in a tracking task under two levels of achievement information feedback'. *Journal of Experimental Psychology, 56,* 297–304.

SPITZ, H. H. (1966) 'The role of input information in the learning and memory of mental retardates'. In N.R. Ellis (Ed.) *International Review of Research in Mental Retardation, Vol. 2*. New York: Academic Press.

SPRINGER, S. P. and DEUTSCH, G. (1989) *Left Brain, Right Brain (3rd Edition)*. San Francisco: Freeman.

SQUIRE, L. R. and COHEN, H. J. (1984) 'Human memory and amnesia'. In G. Lynch, J. L. McGaugh and N. M. Weinberger, (Eds) *Neurobiology of Learning and Memory*. New York: The Guildford Press.

STEIN, M. I. (1975) *Stimulating Creativity*. Vol.II. New York: Academic Press.

STOPPARD, T. (1967) *Rosencrantz and Guildenstern Are Dead*. London: Faber. Reprinted 1978.

STUBBS, M. (1983) *Discourse Analysis*. Oxford: Blackwell.

TERRACE, H. S., PETTITO, L. A., SANDERS, R. J. and BEVER, T. G. (1980) 'On the grammatical capacity of apes'. In Nelson, K. (Ed.) *Children's Language, Vol. 2*. New York: Gardner.

THOMAS, A. and CHESS, S. (1977) *Temperament and Development*. New York: Brunner.

TINBERGEN, N. (1974) 'Ethology and stress disease'. *Science, 185*, 20–27.

TINKER, M. A. (1965) *Bases for Effective Reading*. Minneapolis: University of Minnesota Press.

TORRENCE, E. P. (1982) 'Hemisphericity and creative functioning'. *Journal of Research and Development in Education, 15*, 29–37.

TRUEMAN, M. (1985) 'The different abilities of the two halves of the brain'. In J. A. Branthwaite and D. R. Rogers (Eds) *Children Growing Up*. Milton Keynes: Open University Press.

TULVING, E. (1962) 'Subjective organization in free recall of "unrelated" words'. *Psychological Bulletin, 69*, 344–54.

TULVING, E. (1972) 'Episodic and semantic memory'. In E. Tulving and W. Donaldson (Eds) *Organisatuion of memory*. London: Academic Press.

TULVING, E. (1984) Precis of 'Elements of episodic memory'. *The Behavioural and Brain Sciences, 7*, 223–268.

TURING, A. M. (1950) 'Computing machinery and intelligence'. *Mind, 59*, 433–60.

TVERSKY, A. and KAHNEMAN, D. (1973) 'A heuristic for judging frequency and probability'. *Cognitive Psychology, 5*, 207–32.

TVERSKY, A. and KAHNEMAN, D. (1974) 'Judgement under uncertainty: Heuristics and biases'. *Science, 185*, 1124–31.

TVERSKY, A. and KAHNEMAN, D. (1982) 'Judgements of and by representativeness'. In D. Kahneman, P. Slovic, and A. Tversky (Eds) *Judgement under uncertainty: Heuristics and biases*. New York: Cambridge University Press.

WALLAS, G. (1926) *The Art of Thought*. New York: Harcourt Brace.

WASON, P. C. (1966) 'Reasoning'. In B. Foss (Ed.) *New Horizons in Psychology, 1*. Harmondsworth: Penguin.

WASON, P. C. (1983) 'Realism and rationality in the selection task'. In J. St B. T. Evans (Ed.) *Thinking and Reasoning*. London: Routledge and Kegan Paul.

WEINSTEIN, C. E. AND MAYER, R. E. (1985) 'The teaching of learning strategies'. In M. C. Wittrock (Ed.) *Handbook of Research on Teaching*. New York: Macmillan.

WEISBURG, R. W. (1986) *Creativity: Genius and other myths*. San Francisco: Freeman.

WEIZENBAUM, J. (1984) *Computer Power and Human Reason* (2nd edition). Harmondsworth: Penguin.

WELFORD, A. T. (1968) *Fundamentals of Skill*. London: Methuen.

WHITING, C. S. (1958) *Creative thinking*. New York: Reinhold.

WILKINSON, A., STRATTON, L. and DUDLEY, P. (1974) *The Quality of Listening*. London: Macmillan.

WILLIAMS, J. P. (1970) 'From Basic Research on Reading to Educational Practice'. In H. Levin and J. P. Williams (Eds) *Basic Studies on Reading*. New York: Basic Books.

WILSON, B. and MOFFAT, N. (1984) 'Rehabilitation of Memory for Everyday Life'. In J. E. Harris and P. E. Morris (Eds) *Everyday Memory, Actions and Absent-Mindedness*. London: Academic Press

WINOCUR, G., KINSBOURNE, M and MOSCOVITCH, M. (1981) 'The effect of cuing on release from productive interference in Korsakoff amnesic patients'. *Journal of Experimental Psychology: Human Learning and Memory, 1*, 56–65.

WITTROCK, M. C., MARKS, C. and DOCTOROW, M. (1975) 'Reading as a generative process'. *Journal of Educational Psychology, 67*, 4, 484–89.

WOLF, T. (1976) 'A cognitive model of musical sight-reading'. *Journal of Psycholinguistic Research, 5*, 143–71

WONG, B. Y. Z. and JONES, W. (1982) 'Increasing metacomprehension in learning-disabled and normally-achieving students through self-questioning training'. *Learning Disability Quarterly, 5*, 228–40.

WOOD, G. (1983) *Cognitive Psychology: A Skills Approach*. Monterey: Brooks/Cole.

YATES, F. A. (1966) *The Art of Memory*. Chicago: University of Chicago Press.

ZIMMERMAN, D. H. and WEST, C. (1975) 'Sex roles, interruptions and silences in conversation'. In B. Thorne and N. Henley (Eds) *Language and Sex: Difference and Dominance*. Rowley, Mass.: Newbury House.

SUBJECT INDEX